GENDER, POWER AND THE

Gender, Power and the Household

Edited by

Linda McKie
Senior Lecturer in Health Education
University of Aberdeen

Sophia Bowlby
Senior Lecturer in Geography
University of Reading

and

Susan Gregory
doctoral student
University of Surrey

Consultant Editor: Jo Campling

First published in Great Britain 1999 by
MACMILLAN PRESS LTD
Houndmills, Basingstoke, Hampshire RG21 6XS and London
Companies and representatives throughout the world

A catalogue record for this book is available from the British Library.

ISBN 0–333–69573–9 hardcover
ISBN 0–333–69574–7 paperback

First published in the United States of America 1999 by
ST. MARTIN'S PRESS, INC.,
Scholarly and Reference Division,
175 Fifth Avenue, New York, N.Y. 10010

ISBN 0–312–22410–9

Library of Congress Cataloging-in-Publication Data
Gender, power and the household / edited by Linda McKie, Sophia
Bowlby, Susan Gregory.
p.   cm.
Includes bibliographical references.
ISBN 0–312–22410–9 (cloth)
1. Sex role.   2. Sexual division of labor.   3. Households.
4. Married women—Social conditions.   5. Work and family.
6. Equality.   7. Power (Social sciences)   I. McKie, Linda.
II. Bowlby, S. R. (Sophia R.)   III. Gregory, Susan, 1945–   .
HQ1075.G4648   1999
306.3'615—DC21   99–19797
                                                            CIP

10   9   8   7   6   5   4   3   2   1
08   07   06   05   04   03   02   01   00   99

Printed and bound in Great Britain by
Antony Rowe Ltd, Chippenham, Wiltshire

For our parents: Jim and Irene,
Doe and Tony, Lynne Peter and Rozia

Contents

List of Tables and Figures

CHAPTER 12

Acknowledgements

The editors would like to thank all those involved in the various stages of producing this book. We are grateful to the contributors for each of the chapters and in particular, to Jo Campling and Janey Fisher for their support, comments and guidance. Annabelle Buckley, Macmillan, also helped to keep us on track and Netta Clark and Dawn Leith provided invaluable secretarial support.

Chapter 4 is based upon research funded by the ESRC as part of the Nation's Diet Research Programme. The project was entitled 'The Effect on the Family of One Member's Change in Diet' (grant number L209 252018). The grant holders were Spencer Henson, Susan Gregory, Malcolm Hamilton and Anne Walker.

Chapter 5 is based upon research funded by the ESRC (grant number X20625002). The principal grant holder was Gillian Parker and interviews were conducted jointly by Gillian Parker and Julie Seymour, when both at the Social Policy Research Unit, University of York.

Chapter 8 was based upon research funded by the ESRC (grant number R000234663). Leonie Kapadia and John McKendrick were employed as researchers on the project and their input is gratefully acknowledged.

Chapter 10 is based upon a secondary analysis of General Household Survey data (1992–4). Permission to use data was received from the ESRC Data Archive, University of Essex, University of Manchester Computer Centre, and Office of National Statistics. The assistance of Tom Daly and Jay Ginn with the preparation of data and of the chapter is gratefully acknowledged.

Chapter 11 is based upon research funded by the Leverhulme Trust (grant number t/740) and the project team was assisted by Rachel Linacre. The authors acknowledge the support of the enterprises which participated in the research. The views expressed are those of the authors and not necessarily those of the funding body.

Chapter 12 is published by kind permission of the Controller of Her Majesty's Stationery Office. No part of this publication may be reproduced in any form without the permission of the Department of Social Security. The chapter draws upon work commissioned by the Department of Social Security. The views expressed are those of the authors and not necessarily those of the commissioning body.

At every stage we received tremendous support from our respective families and friends. We are indebted to everyone who provided practical and social support during the process of compiling and editing this book.

Notes on the Contributors

Sara Arber is Professor and Head of Department of Sociology, University of Surrey. She is co-author with Jay Ginn of *Gender and Later Life* (Sage, 1991) and *Connecting Gender and Ageing* (Open University, 1995), and with Nigel Gilbert *Women and Working Lives: Divisions and Change* (Macmillan, 1992).

Sophia Bowlby is Senior Lecturer in Geography, Department of Geography, at the University of Reading. Her research and publishing work has included the gendered organization of activities in urban spaces and the presentation of self in public spaces. She is currently working with Sally Lloyd Evans on racialized gendering in the experiences of young people entering the labour market. With Sue Gregory and Linda McKie she edited a special issue of the journal *Women's Studies International Forum* (1997) on 'Concepts of Home'.

Anne Corden is Research Fellow at the Social Policy Research Unit, University of York. Her main research interests are in social security and family policy. She has completed a programme of research on self-employed people. She is co-author with Rebecca Boden of *Measuring Low Incomes: Self-Employment and Family Credit* (HMSO, 1994).

Anna Dudleston is a research student in the Centre for Residential Development, the Nottingham Trent University. Her research is in the area of housing finance. She was formerly a Research Assistant on the Dual Careers project.

Vincent Duindam is a Lecturer at the Faculty of Social Sciences, University of Utrecht, the Netherlands. His research and publishing work has focused upon parenthood and gender and socialization. He has published widely on parenthood and caring fathers. Recent books include *Parenting Arrangements and Gender Identity* (Lemma, 1991) and *Caring Fathers* (Van Gennep, 1997).

Tony Eardley is Senior Research Follow, Social Policy Research Centre, University of New South Wales, Australia. Recent publications include *Low Income Self-Employment: Work, Benefits and Living Standards* (Avebury, 1996), with Anne Corden. He was also one of the authors of *Social Assistance in OECD Countries* (HMSO, 1996).

Sarah Gilroy lectures in the Sociology of Sport and Leisure at Chichester Institute of Higher Education where she is Dean of Undergraduate Studies. Her main research interests are the sociology of the body, the construction of gender power relations, and negotiations within households over work and leisure. Recent publications include 'Working on the Body and Researching the Links between Women's Involvement in Physical Activity and Social Power' in G. Clarke and B. Humberstone (eds), *Researching Women and Sport* (Macmillan, 1997); with Rosemary Deem, 'Physical Activity, Life-Long Learning and Empowerment – Situating Sport in Women's Leisure', *Sport, Education and Society*, Vol. 3, no. 1, 1998.

Anne Green is Principal Research Fellow at the Institute for Employment Research, University of Warwick. She has particular research interests in spatial dimensions of economic, social and demographic change, notably the geography of employment, unemployment and migration. Much of her research has been concerned with local labour market issues.

Susan Gregory is conducting research for a doctorate at the Department of Sociology, University of Surrey. Her main research interests are the sociology of food, the sociology of the family and the sociology of health and illness. Her most recent article, '"Doing Home": Patriarchy, Caring and Space', co-authored with Sophia Bowlby and Linda McKie, was published in *Women's Studies International Forum* (1997).

Irene Hardill is Reader in the Department of International Studies, the Nottingham Trent University. She has particular research interests in career and migration histories, and household decision making. She has also published papers on the economic performance of small firms in the textile and clothing industry.

Linda McKie is Senior Lecturer in Health Education, Department of General Practice and Primary Care, University of Aberdeen. Her research work includes the identification and management of domestic violence in primary health care, the anticipation of ageing, and lay and professional perceptions of health issues in rural localities. She is author of a number of articles and book chapters on gender, health and health promotion. Her most recent contribution to an edited book is 'Women's Public Toilets: a Serious Issue for the Body Politic', co-authored with Julia Edwards and published in *Embodied Practices: Feminist Perspectives on the Body* (Sage, 1997).

David H.J. Morgan is currently Professor of Sociology at the University of Manchester, where he has been, in one capacity or another, for over 30 years. He has published extensively in the areas of sociology of the family and sociology of gender. Recent publications include *Discovering Men* (Routledge, 1992) and *Family Connections* (Polity, 1996). He is currently President of the British Sociological Association.

David Owen is Senior Research Fellow at the Centre for Research in Ethnic Relations, University of Warwick. His research interests lie in the quantitative analysis of local labour markets and the socio-economic circumstances of minority ethnic groups in Great Britain.

Julie Seymour is Lecturer at the School of Comparative and Applied Social Sciences, University of Hull. Research interests include the distribution of resources in households and the associated negotiations between household members with a particular emphasis on gender, disability and social exclusion. She has contributed to the edited books *Men, Gender Divisions and Welfare* (Routledge, 1998) and *Welfare Research: a Critique of Theory and Method* (UCL Press, 1998).

Kay Standing is Lecturer in Women's Studies at Liverpool John Moores University. She has completed a PhD on 'Lone Mothers' Involvement in their Children's Schooling'. Her current research interests are in the area of family law and disputed contact cases. She has a young daughter.

Janet Stephens is a Lecturer in Women's Studies and Gender at the University of Wales, Cardiff. Her research interests include the sociology of the family and feminist theory. She was a founder member of the community-based action group for women, Women's Forum.

Gill Valentine is Lecturer in Geography at the University of Sheffield. She has published widely on the fear of crime, children and parenting, geographies of sexuality and most recently food. She is co-author of *Consuming Geographies* (Routledge, 1997) and co-editor of *Mapping Desire* (Routledge, 1997), both with David Bell; with Tracey Skelton she co-edited *Cool Places* (Routledge, 1997).

Part I
Theoretical Issues

1 Connecting Gender, Power and the Household

Linda McKie, Sophia Bowlby and Susan Gregory

INTRODUCTION

Theoretical and empirical research on gender, the family and the household has tended to focus upon work conducted within the home, and the negotiation and allocation of resources within households (Oakley, 1974a; Whitehead, 1981; Harris, 1984; Pahl, 1984; Berk, 1985; Morris, 1985; Brannen and Wilson, 1987; Mansfield and Collard, 1988; Van Every, 1995). The origins of many of these studies can be traced to Oakley's work in the early 1970s which heralded a new approach to research on women, the home, and (paid) work. Oakley's study of housework not only concerned an examination of the housewife role but also the division of labour in the household and ideologies of domesticity (Oakley, 1974a; Oakley, 1974b). She argued that 'the kitchen is the symbol of women's domesticity, and the lifelong activities and identities of women outside the kitchen are determined and defined by their domesticity' (Oakley, 1974a: 222). Change in women's role would only follow, Oakley argued, from the abolition of the housewife role, the family and gender roles. At the time this was considered a radical approach to the study of gender and the household and it was one which placed and re-emphasized conceptions of the household, power and hierarchy between men and women as central to the analysis of women in society.

More recently the household has been drawn upon as a strategic site in which to locate research, to conceptualize gender and power as processes, and to illuminate how the household and activities therein are implicated in the construction and reinforcement of gendered roles, family life and participation in paid employment (Charles and Kerr, 1985; Deem, 1986; Pahl, 1989; Lees, 1993; Charles, 1993; Sainsbury, 1994; Morgan, 1996). These largely empirical studies have had a lasting impact upon policy and academic debates. For example, consideration of the responsibility for housework rather than a limited concentration upon the allocation and conduct of tasks has shifted the dialogue to reflect the psychological and emotional, as well as the physical consequences, of family and household

3

work (Barrett and Philips, 1992; Van Every, 1995). Delphy and Leonard (1992) considered empirical studies of factory workers' families in Britain and farm families in France. They developed a theoretical framework of the family as an economic system which both reinforces and re-creates a system of labour relations. Within this context emotional and familial labour are interwoven with economic necessity and thus devalued; 'we see men and women as economic classes with one category/class subordinating the other and exploiting their work' (Delphy and Leonard, 1992: 258). Thus socio-economic class and gender can be seen to interact to create gender roles and divisions across differing economic systems, from factory work in the UK to farming in France. Adkins (1995) has also considered the interaction between sexuality, family and labour market in her study of 'gendered work'.

Interestingly, Walby (1997) has suggested that women's lives are increasingly shaped by their participation in education, employment and politics, and that the household is no longer the chief structure in determining public forms of patriarchy. However the contributions to this book demonstrate the significant influence that home, family and household have over the lives of women regardless of age, social class, and experiences of employment. Further, Morgan traces the influence of feminism and sociology upon the development of a sociology of the family to argue that 'family practices have a key place in the analysis of a complex and fluid society' (Morgan, 1996: 14). Debates continue regarding what we mean by the term 'the family' and increasingly researchers are considering the interaction between individual experiences over the life course and socio-economic and political change (Hutton, 1994). Issues concerning the family and gender roles are never far from political debates, and as employment patterns change so arguments concerning the role of women and men as workers and carers intensify (Barrett and Phillips, 1992; Hutton, 1994; Pilcher, 1995).

Women still tend to carry the main responsibility for the care of children, the ill and older people, together with other domestic tasks. Depending upon age and family structure women generally have less leisure time than men in the same household (Deem, 1986). Men have been slow to demand change in domestic labour (and many aspects of public life) as this requires their increased physical labour and psychological investment in responsibility for household and other tasks. Research has demonstrated the gap between, on the one hand, the aims and beliefs held by men and women about equality and the division of labour within the household and, on the other, what actually happens (Kieran, 1992). This has highlighted the need to develop a more dynamic approach to resource allocation and the relationship between domestic life, labour market activities and the generations (Hunt, 1978; Lewis and Meridith, 1988; Arber and Ginn, 1993). Thus the roles and responsibilities which both demonstrate and reflect family life provide a central feature of theoretical and empirical research on gender, power and the household.

This book brings together contemporary empirical research and theoretical work on the themes gender, power and the household. We are seeking to promote debates on the significance of gender in the understanding of household and family dynamics (Morgan, 1985; Finch, 1989; Yanagisako and Collier, 1987; Morris, 1990; Delphy and Leonard, 1992; Jackson and Moores, 1995; Van Every, 1997). To that end, the contributions in this book are derived from a number of disciplines – women's studies, sociology, social policy, geography – and demonstrate how a range of approaches may be employed to consider gender, and related concepts, in and around the site of the household (McKie, Bowlby and Gregory, 1996).

The aims of this introductory chapter are twofold: firstly to consider current key concepts, and secondly to set the context for the contributions which follow. This chapter comprises three further sections. In 'The Household in Social Context' we review concepts of the household, home, and notions of space and place and the household. The section 'Gendering the Family' considers the relationship between gender, power and the household noting that the inappropriate use and inadequate conceptualization of a number of key concepts continues to hamper theoretical and research developments. In the final section of the chapter, 'About the Book', the four sections of the book and contributions to each are introduced.

THE HOUSEHOLD IN SOCIAL CONTEXT

A 'household' requires a 'house' – or rather some dwelling within which members usually sleep and eat. In other words, part of our understanding of the term 'household' is that it involves the use of a particular type of space – 'domestic' space. This space is designated both by material structures – walls and roofs – but, perhaps more importantly also by the social activities that are held to be appropriate to it. The location, design and internal arrangement of this space is both a product of and an influence on these social activities. The activities seen as proper to the domestic space of a household vary over space and through time as do the social rules concerning who should carry out those activities and in what form.

The domestic dwelling exists and is defined in part in relation to a number of other types of spaces – such as, the spaces of leisure, work and education. Households also exist through time – they are constituted in part through the daily, weekly and yearly performance of particular tasks and behaviours. They have a life-course – members join and leave, die and are born. Households themselves are created and die. Expectations about this life-course are part and parcel of understandings of the meaning of belonging to a household and affect the behaviour of its members. Thus households exist within a number of different temporalities and spatialities which are mutually interacting characteristics of their organisation (Lawrence, 1983; Werner *et al.*, 1985).

The term 'household' partially overlaps the more culturally emotive terms of 'home' and 'family' so that any examination of the activities and power relations within households must be aware of the normative pressures exerted by social expectations concerning family relationships and the desires to create and live in a 'home' (Loyd, 1981; Allan and Crow, 1989; Bowlby, Gregory and McKie, 1997). These include expectations about appropriate day-to-day organization and co-ordination of activities of household members and in particular the significance of 'shared' events such as meals, leisure in the home and entertaining outsiders.

Social expectations about home and family extend to the need to have – own or rent – a socially acceptable material 'house' or dwelling and to present and care for it in acceptable ways (Pratt, 1981; Madigan, Munro and Smith, 1990; Munro and Madigan, 1996). There has been debate concerning the importance of home-ownership to 'ontological security' (Forrest, 1983; Dickens, 1989; Saunders, 1990; Gurney, 1996) and the significance of gender to attitudes to the 'home' and home-ownership (Madigan, Munro and Smith, 1990; Saunders, 1990; Darke, 1994; Gilroy, 1994). Until relatively recently much housing literature largely ignored the importance of relationships between household members in understanding such issues as the decision to move, the choice of house and the organization of finances to pay mortgage or rent. A variety of recent studies have begun to redress this imbalance (Bruegel, 1996; Christie, 1996; Green, 1997; Hardill *et al.* in Chapter 11 of this volume) and to emphasize that there are important differences between women's and men's ability to influence these significant decisions. This research has shown that women have been the less powerful parties to negotiations over these issues in part because of their lack of access to well-paid jobs and in part because of their acceptance of the social priority given to men's jobs or career moves. Women thus tend to have less influence than men over the shaping of the main features of the household's path through time and space.

The Internal Space of the Household

With the important exception of single-person households, domestic space is shared space. An obvious set of questions therefore centres on the basis on which this space is shared – how are decisions made about who uses which parts of the house for different tasks and at different times; who can exclude whom from different household spaces and when? In the West, expectations and realizations of individual privacy and temporal and spatial autonomy and flexibility within the domestic dwelling have generally increased during this century (Roberts, 1991; Bell and Valentine, 1997). Changing notions of the acceptability of the display of bodily functions and sexuality within domestic spaces as well as changing conceptions of privacy between ages, genders and classes have also been reflected in domestic architecture, as have changing ideas concerning gender and class relations (Hayden, 1981; Elias, 1982; Hayden, 1984; Matrix, 1984; Brown, 1986; Marsh, 1990; Lummis and Marsh, 1990; Roberts, 1991; Munro and Madigan, 1993; Veness, 1994).

Ethnographic and anthropological studies have suggested that the internal divisions of domestic space can be understood both in terms of the prevailing political economy with its divisions of gender, race and ethnicity and in terms of the cultural and metaphysical order which is used by participants as a self-evident explanation for social and economic relations (Ardener, 1993). Some of these studies present a somewhat static picture of the gendered spatial organization of domestic activities, however others emphasize the importance of processes of negotiation between household members in the context of broader secular changes in economies and cultures (Jackson and Moores, 1995).

Both space and time can be thought of as resources which can be used for various ends. Most obviously they can be used as inputs into the achievement of particular tasks. Cooking requires not only equipment for chopping and mixing and heating ingredients but also space and time to do so. Similarly washing, ironing, school homework and money-earning activities require both space and time. Childcare, in particular, is a task which is substantially eased by the availability of unconstrained time and plentiful space. Equally significant is the ability to regulate the activities of others within time and space which adds to their value as a resource. Although there are exceptions, such as the work of Van Every (1995), many studies which have addressed issues of negotiation and power relations between household members have tended to emphasize time and to ignore the significance of space as a resource to be struggled over (Brannen and Wilson, 1987).

An alternative way of thinking about the implications of the control of time and space as resources is to turn the relationship round and to focus on spatial and temporal divisions as a means of control or of evading control. Here boundaries become significant. Spatial boundaries impermeable to sight or sound allow evasion of surveillance and control by others. The existence of clearly demarcated women's quarters, in some cultures, may offer a space of opposition for women which is absent from contemporary western houses. Likewise the availability of 'a time of one's own' (possibly, but not necessarily, in a private space), the use of which is not controlled or limited by the demands of others, can offer opportunities for both pleasure and opposition. One of the positive aspects of housework as opposed to paid work for many women is the ability to organize the timing of particular tasks within the daily, weekly or yearly round (Oakley, 1974b).

An understanding of the complexity of the experience of being part of a household can also be sought through the notion of place. Particular houses come to have meaning for their inhabitants not only because they are or contain symbols of social status (their size, address, house type, cladding, furnishings) but because they encode in their design, decor and physical layout personal meanings linked to the partially shared history of the household's members. Gurney has argued, with the use of ethnographic data, that particular episodes in the life-course of the members of a household are often highly significant to those people's feelings about house, home and home ownership and are not infrequently attached to particular rooms or dwellings (Gurney, 1996; Gurney, 1997). Feelings about home, loss of home, and homelessness thus are strongly linked to the housing histories of individuals but also to the roles and activities that those histories involve (Somerville, 1992; Tomas and Dittmar, 1995; Doyle, 1997).

Thinking about a dwelling as a 'place' requires us to recognize that the meanings that the dwelling has are not fixed. These meanings are partly the product of discussions, negotiations and events taking place within the household but are also strongly influenced by evaluations and expectations derived from the wider social world in which household members are enmeshed.

The External Links of the Household

The daily activities of household members link its internal activities and social organization to external places and activities. The temporal and spatial organization of paid work, school, shopping, leisure and the maintenance of friendship networks all impinge on the ways in which household members interact and vice versa (Morris, 1987; Dyck, 1989; Dyck, 1990; Jordan *et al.*, 1992; Hanson and Pratt, 1995). These external activities are often undertaken *with* other members of the household, *for* other members of the household or in order to *escape* other members of the household. The dwelling becomes an important node in the daily, weekly, monthly and yearly time-space paths of its members. The temporality and spatiality of the dwelling are bound up with the temporality and spatiality of the 'outside' world. Its meanings as a place arise partly in contradistinction to the meanings of and activities in those other places in which household members are involved – as is implied by the public/private metaphor. However, as many feminist critiques of the public/private distinction have made plain, the apparent fixity and impermeability of the divide between the private world of the household and the public world is itself a (powerful) fiction (Mackenzie, 1989; Duncan, 1996).

An analysis of gendered differences in power and expectations concerning the world outside the household is clearly vital to an understanding of the spatial and temporal organisation of relationships within it. The importance of paid work is the most obvious example. But, as this example also reminds us, domestic relationships and the social networks and knowledge of other household members also may be central to an understanding of patterns of participation in paid work (Grieco, 1987; Morris, 1987; Jordan *et al.*, 1992; Morris and Irwin, 1992; Hanson and Pratt, 1995). The notion of social networks provides an excellent image of the connections of household members to the world outside. A household may also be a place of emotional and social significance to the members of some of those networks who are not part of that household: for example, the households of friends and neighbours or the significance of the mother's house to adult children as a place in which to meet their siblings.

GENDERING THE FAMILY

We now consider the relationship between gender, power, the family and the household. This relationship is complex and dynamic and informs and shapes all aspects of everyday life both within and outside the household. Changes in the form and patterns of the labour market generally, and women's participation specifically, together with both the identification of a range of inequalities in household structures and improvements in life expectations, have illuminated diversity and inequalities in power and resources in the family (Morgan, 1985; Brannen and Wilson, 1987; Morris, 1990; Pilcher, 1995).

Post-war social policies were premised upon the idea of full male employment. This premise has been fundamentally challenged by falling levels of employment and a changing composition of the labour force. More women work than ever before but much of their work is part-time and casual (Morris, 1990; Hutton, 1994). For lone parents with dependent children the tensions between caring for children and achieving an appropriate standard of living are examples of the impact of new family structures and gender relations upon economic and social policies. It is clear that women's daily lives continue to be fragmented around caring work, paid employment and the provision of domestic labour. Managing this fragmentation can restrict opportunities for women in and outside the household and family and result in their sheer physical and psychological exhaustion (Delphy and Leonard, 1992).

The nature of the paid employment undertaken by many women frequently mirrors a nurturing 'family' role with the majority of women employed in caring professions and providing emotional and physical labour similar to that of family work (Dale, 1991). There has been a shift from manufacturing work to employment in the service industry. Work in service industries, such as the caring professions of nursing and teaching, as well as catering and retail work, continue to be considered predominately jobs or careers for women. And the distinction between a job or career marks the social class differences between women, and women and men. In addition, most women also manage a range of responsibilities and access services in support of, for example, children or elderly relatives. Laura Balbo (1987) describes women's work as 'stitching together the patchwork quilt of welfare' and the time spent doing this means women have often been conceived of as carers and mothers rather than citizens in their own right.

Whilst it seems clear that changes in the domestic division of labour are slow and tend to rest in what might be hoped for rather than in what actually happens, Walby (1986) suggests that a continued spotlight upon women in the family and the creation and organization of gendered work can become 'the study of a deviant minority'. Such a focus can deny the study of men's power over women and the relationship of masculinity and femininity to structures of power and privilege (Maynard, 1990). To exclude men from research on the family and gender is to enshrine further a notion of both cultural and research 'norms' on gender and the family.

Conceptualizing Gender

The study of gender and the family has been hampered by inadequately defined or misleading terms such as sex and gender and the dualisms of mind and body, and the public and private. Whilst these reflect debates in many areas of social inquiry they continue to have particular resonance for theoretical work and empirical research on gender and the family (Walby, 1986; Sydie, 1987; Van Every, 1995).

Inappropriate use of concepts is evident in the manner in which some commentators and researchers continue to equate gender with sex difference and confuse the meanings of these two terms. Conceptualizing gender as sex creates a number of problems in considering, for example, the study of same-sex households (Oerton, 1997) and promotes a 'nature over culture' explanation for household roles (Harris, 1984; Charles, 1993). Limiting the term 'sex' to a description of primary biological differences related to sexual reproduction allows the term 'gender' to describe the social enactment of 'sex' differences. This may be made up not only of what women and men *do* in a social setting to demonstrate their sexual assignment, but also the social expectations of what women and men *should do*. The conflation of gender with sex can, and has, supported a reductionism or essentialism (Scott and Morgan, 1993) which does not do justice to the complex social process it hides. Further, the conceptualization of sexuality as predominately heterosexual is increasingly questioned and these challenges note that the terms male and female, sex and gender, femininity and masculinity, and heterosexual and homosexual, cannot be used in an unproblematic fashion (Connell, 1995).

Inadequate conceptualizations of gender and the family have also promoted dualisms of mind and body, which serve further to obscure issues of production and reproduction in and around the body, the family, and the household. Cartesian thought created a separation between 'mind' and 'body' which associated 'mind' with the notion of rationality and 'body' with that of emotionality. This division has paralleled and interacted with the duality of 'cultural' man and 'natural' woman (Sydie, 1987). The cultural, rational mind was placed central to science and academic research, and until recently, influenced who conducts that research and what the research is about.

Research on gender and the family, which has concentrated on household tasks and resource allocation, has often been conceptualized as research on what women do in the family. The perception of this research as the domain of women researchers, often employing feminist theories, and frequently utilizing qualitative methods, has resulted in something of a separation of research on gender from the mainstream of academic research and theory work. This could be seen as denying the need to connect such work with a consideration of power and the structures of privilege both in and out of the household. However, as Finch (1993) notes, there is now a growing debate on conceptualizing gender, one in which both women and men are involved as researchers and the researched. Thus the study of gender, power and the household, as evidenced by contributions to this book, is increasingly seeking to connect with debates on theory and empirical research on power, and privilege, as well as political and economic structures.

The connecting of theory and research on the household with political and economic structures has not been promoted by legislation or social and public policies, which are premised upon a dichotomy of the public and the private. This is illustrated by apparent divisions of the 'private' world of the home and the 'public' world outside, most commonly associated with work and employment. Such a division reflects a view of the female 'private' and male 'public' spheres of activity as separate, limited in interactive influence, and hierarchical. Evidence of this can be found in the British legislation for equal opportunities which accepts a private–public divide (Edwards and McKie, 1993). This presumes that how women or men behave in the labour market, as consumers, and how women and men relate to the family and employment, are not subject to domestic arrangements, conceptions of gender or the operation of power relations in the family and household. This legislation relies upon a 'liberal' notion of equality (Jewson and Mason, 1986) which denies the relationship between the social construction of roles, sexuality, and the family (Stacey and Thorne, 1985). As a result the impact upon women's lives of the need to stitch together the patchwork quilt of activities and services required to maintain home and work may not be fully conceptualized. There is a need to develop theories of femininity and masculinity, and of gender work, which emphasize the social and the structural and not solely the biological and individual (Maynard, 1990).

Researching Gender, the Family and the Household

Morgan, (1996: 11) considers that the term 'family' is best employed as an adjective rather than as a noun and, as such, uses the term to refer to kinship and marriage and 'the expectations and obligations which are associated with these practices'. Households more often than not tend to be comprised of people related by marriage, partnership and kinship and thus the notion of the household is likely to overlap with that of the family. The study of the household as an economic unit may illuminate process and differences in resource allocation, but exclude the examination of those who not only support the labour market and wider economy, but also do emotional and obligation work in support of each other and relatives (Finch, 1989).

Morgan (Chapter 2) recognizes tensions between studies of gender and studies of the household. Studies of the household such as those of Brannen and Wilson (1987) and Morris (1990) may have begun with social divisions and inequality as a more general concern than gender, but, Morgan concludes, such tensions are often resolved at the level of individual studies. He argues that gender must be conceived of as a process and households as dynamic. For example, in the area of the growth in single-person households and consideration of men in households: research on these topics promotes reflection on gender within the household but also recognizes the role of the family and kinship relationships in the process of determining and defining gendered work.

Much research to date has considered a number of aspects of the emotional, social and economic construction of the family. Material aspects of everyday life are often the focus of research, as with Whitehead's (1981) work on the politics of domestic budgeting. Whitehead considered relations between men and women within home economies with very different consumption and production patterns, namely direct production in rural Ghana and the purchase of wage goods in industrial Britain. Whilst the basis of production and household maintenance was very different, similar gendered inequalities in power and spending became evident in the allocation arrangements of goods, services and income. Conflicts of interest were rooted in relationships, and women in both cultures were found to be more concerned with the collective or family aspects of resources and resource allocation. In contrast men acted in a more individualized fashion towards resources and consumption. Research by Murcott (1983), Charles and Kerr (1988) and DeVault (1991) on food in families has illustrated the relationship between the provision of meals by wives for husbands as a symbolic of expression of love whilst also demonstrating the obligation of providing food for the family. And Deem's (1986) work demonstrates how marriage constrained women's leisure at various stages of the life-course.

The impact of changing labour markets upon work, income and employment has been considered by Morris (1985; 1990) who examined local labour markets in South Wales and the North-East of England. She has demonstrated how access to and control over household resources have been constrained by experiences in the local labour market and, in particular, how male unemployment affects resource allocation and patterns of power within households. Rather than male unemployment encouraging female partners to take up paid employment the impact of a gendered welfare system has presumed roles and obligations in the family combined with gendered social expectations which ensure a range of barriers to female employment. In many households male earning potential and career structures still ensure that male employment dominates family thinking and practice on income and paid work (Delphy and Leonard, 1992; Arber, Chapter 10 of this volume; Hardill *et al.*, Chapter 11 of this volume). Thus the conventional distinctions between gender roles and employment are more complex and dynamic than suggested by the private–public distinctions found in much policy and research.

The interaction between a range of factors outlined above presents a strong case for considering gender, family and the household in broader and more complex contexts (Sydie, 1987; Delphy and Leonard, 1992; Adkins, 1995; Morgan, 1996). Differences within the household and family, around for example, the allocation of resources (Brannen and Wilson, 1987), and the continuing allocation of power and tasks around the earning potential of family members (Gallie, March and Vogler, 1994) demonstrate the complexities of developing research and theory on gender and the family (Morgan, 1996). The contributions to this book address these issues in a manner which demonstrates the connections between gender, power and the household.

ABOUT THIS BOOK

The book is divided into four sections which group together contributions linked by dominant themes found in the debates around gender and the household. This chapter, together with the next chapter by David Morgan, sets the stage for these debates by highlighting the tension between notions of gender and those of the household. **Morgan** ('Gendering the Household: Some Theoretical Considerations') draws attention to the range of definitions of the household and the fluidity of boundaries around this social institution, created and re-created over time and in different settings. Morgan sees the household as both shaped by and shaping gender, which, in turn, he sees as 'a process rather than as a once-and-for-all achievement' (p. 28). This gendering process takes place within all of social life, but is perhaps most significantly represented within the household. 'Doing gender' is a male as well as a female activity and is a matter of difference as well as inequality, which is crosscut by all other social differences.

The next section, 'Gendered Care', offers three chapters which illustrate aspects of an activity strongly associated with home and family.

Duindam ('Men in the Household: Caring Fathers') focuses upon a group he acknowledges to be small and unusual, men within Dutch households who take a major role of caring in families. In doing so he at the same time points to the potential for gender role-reversal in families, and recognizes the starting points men and women come from: 'mothers may leave the gate open, but fathers have to wish to walk through' (p. 57). **Gregory** ('Gender Roles and Food in Families') shows how food and meals provide a focus and a practical channel through which family members (and particularly female home managers) can identify and perform gendered caring. **Seymour** ('Using Gendered Discourses in Negotiations: Couples and the Onset of Disablement in Marriage') uses the process of negotiation around disablement between couples to examine gender relations. As competitors for coping resources, men and women in families engage in a range of potential behaviours, many of which incorporate aspects of gender as a bargaining device.

The contributions in the third section of the book, 'Gendered Time and Space', draw attention to less concrete aspects of home life which, nevertheless, generate gendered assumptions about the activities and behaviour of both men and women within households. **Stephens** ('A Fight for Her Time: Challenges Facing Professional Mothers who work in Hospital Medicine') describes the multiple identities of the working mother, whose use of time both on a day-to-day and a life-long basis requires strategic decision making embodied in 'earned' time, 'bought' time and 'stolen' time. Women are particularly subject to the gendered nature of timing, caught between the ideology of work and the ideology of motherhood. **Standing** ('Negotiating the Home and the School: Low Income, Lone Mothering and Unpaid Schoolwork') echoes these dilemmas by outlining the unspoken gendered expectations around parental input to schooling. These are realized through gendered assumptions about practical maintenance, and emotional and educational support work which takes place within the home. **Valentine** ('"Oh Please Mum. Oh Please Dad": Negotiating Children's Spatial Boundaries') examines children's use of space and how it is negotiated with parents over time. Although parental judgement makes use of ideas of competence and performance to determine children's spatial boundaries, gender is found to be a strategic factor in expectations of children's performance, and also in contributions to parenting as well as parenting style. The last chapter in this section **Gilroy** ('Intra-household Power Relations and their Impact on Women's Leisure') shows how women's leisure time is identified and negotiated within discourses of femininity and motherhood. Again, the complex nature of household dynamics is demonstrated through evidence indicating that women's time for leisure is subject to concrete issues of finance and employment, but also to gender relations and the domestic division of labour.

The final section of the book, 'Gendered Work, Income and Power', brings together three chapters which illustrate how permeable are the boundaries between home and work, particularly within the context of gender. **Arber** ('Unequal Partners: Inequalities in Earnings and Independent Income within Marriage'), using General Household Survey data, demonstrates continued differentials between men's and women's income from paid employment. These are due to occupational segregation and frequently linked to gendered family priorities. Arber's analysis also illustrates significant differentials in unearned income. This has implications for gendered power relations in relation to decision making, the domestic division of labour and the potential for personal independence. Gendered decision making is a central theme of **Hardill** *et al.*'s contribution ('Decision Making in Dual-Career Households'). This chapter shows how, in families where both parents follow career paths, joint decision making may take place over infrequent lifestyle decisions, but not over career prioritisation. Within these families there emerge 'leader' careers and 'follower' careers, and the former tend to be male. The (in)visibility of gender in relation to work is revealed in the final chapter where **Corden and Eardley** ('Sexing the Enterprise: Gender, Work and Resource Allocation in Self-Employed Households') examine gender effects within small-scale self-employed enterprises. Where the business was in the hands of women, their spouse tended to be in non-related employment, whilst where it was run by the male spouse, these businesses were heavily dependent upon wives' participation which was not routinely or formally recognized.

The chapters in this book illustrate, from a number of perspectives, the ways in which power is located and articulated through gendered negotiations acted out within the changing and differing setting of the household. Whilst many of the scenarios provided by the authors support much of the literature which has shown gendered inequalities which favour the male experience over that of women, they also indicate that these divisions are never straightforward, frequently contested and constantly changing.

REFERENCES

Adkins, L. (1995) *Gendered Work: Sexuality, Family and the Labour Market.* Buckingham: Open University Press.

Allan, G. and Crow, G. (eds) (1989) *Home and Family: Creating the Relationships.* Basingstoke: Macmillan.

Altman, I. and Werner, C. (eds) (1985) *Home Environments, Human Behaviour and Environment Advances in Theory and Research 8*. New York: Plenum Press.

Arber, S. (1993) 'Inequalities in the Household', in L. Stanley and D. Morgan (eds) *Debates in Sociology, 1967–1992*. Manchester: Manchester University Press.

Arber, S. and Ginn, J. (eds) (1995) *Connecting Gender and Ageing: A Sociological Approach*. Buckingham: Open University Press.

Ardener, S. (1993) (revised edition) *Women and Space: Ground Rules and Social Maps*. Oxford: Berg.

Balbo, L. (1987) 'Crazy Quilts: Rethinking the Welfare State Debate from a Women's Point of View' in A. Showstack Sassoon (ed.) *Women and the State*. London: Hutchinson.

Barrett, M. and Phillips, A. (eds) (1992) *Destabilising Theory: Contemporary Feminist Debates*. Cambridge: Polity Press.

Bell, D. and Valentine, G. (1997) *Consuming Geographies: We Are Where We Eat*. London: Routledge.

Berk, S. (1985) *The Gender Factory: the Apportionment of Work in American Households*. London: Plenum.

Bowlby, S., Gregory, S. and McKie, L. (1997) *'Doing Home': Patriarchy, Caring and Space*. Women's Studies International Forum Special Issue on 'Concepts of Home', 20, 3, 343–50.

Brannen, J. and Wilson, G. (eds) (1987) *Give and Take in Families: Studies in Resource Allocation*. London: Allen and Unwin.

Brown, F. (1986) 'Continuity and Change in the Urban House: Developments in Domestic Space Organisation in 17th Century London'. *Comparative Studies in Society and History*, 28, 3, 558–90.

Bruegel, I. (1996) 'The Trailing Wife: a Declining Breed? Careers, Geographic Mobility and Household Conflict in Britain 1970–89' in R. Crompton, D. Gaillie, and K. Purcell (eds) *Changing Forms of Employment*. London: Routledge.

Charles, N. (1993) *Gender Divisions and Social Change*. Hemel Hempstead: Harvester Wheatsheaf.

Charles, N. and Kerr, M. (1988) *Women, Food and Families*. Manchester: Manchester University Press.

Christie, H. (1996) 'Gender and Mortgage Default in Swindon'. Unpublished PhD, Department of Geography, University of Cambridge.

Connell, R. (1985) *Masculinities*. Oxford: Polity Press.

Dale, A. (1991) 'Women and the Labour Market: Policy in Perspective' in N. Manning (ed.) *Social Policy Review 1990–91*. Harlow: Longman.

Darke, J. (1994) 'Women and the Meaning of Home' in R. Gilroy and R. Woods (eds) *Housing Women*. London: Routledge.

Deem, R. (1986) *All Work and No Play: the Sociology of Women's Leisure*. Milton Keynes: Open University.

Delphy, C. and Leonard, D. (1992) *Familiar Exploitation: a New Analysis of Marriage in Contemporary Western Societies*. Cambridge: Polity.

DeVault, M. (1991) *Feeding the Family*. Chicago: University of Chicago Press.

Dickens, P. (1989) 'Human Nature, Society and the Home'. *Housing Studies*, 4, 227–37.

Doyle, L. (1997) 'Another Day in Paradise? Conceptions of "Home" and Experiences of Domestic Violence'. Unpublished paper, available from the author, Department of Geography, University of Reading.

Duncan, N. (1996) 'Renegotiating Gender and Sexuality in Public and Private Spaces' in N. Duncan (ed.) *BodySpace: Destabilising Geographies of Gender and Sexuality*. London, Routledge.

Dyck, I. (1989) 'Integrating Home and Wage Workplace: Women's Daily Lives in a Canadian Suburb'. *Canadian Geographer*, 33, 4, 329–41.

Dyck, I. (1990) 'Space, Time and Renegotiating Motherhood: an Exploration of the Domestic Workplace'. *Environment and Planning D: Society and Space*, 8, 4, 459–83.

Edwards, J. and McKie, L. (1993) 'Public Policy and Equal Opportunities: an Agenda for Change'. *Public Policy and Administration*, 8, 54–67.

Elias, N. (1992) *The Civilising Process*. New York: Patheon.

Finch, J. (1989) *Family Obligations and Social Change*. Cambridge: Polity.

Finch, J. (1993) 'Conceptualising Gender' in D. Morgan and L. Stanley (eds) *Debates in Sociology*. Manchester: Manchester University Press.

Forrest, R. (1983) 'The Meaning of Home-Ownership'. *Society and Space*, 1, 205–16.

Frank, A. (1990) 'Bringing Bodies Back In: a Decade Review'. *Theory, Culture and Society*, 7, 131–62.

Gallie, D., Marsh, C. and Vogler, C. (eds) (1994) *Social Change and the Experience of Unemployment*. Oxford: Oxford University Press.

Gilroy, R. (1994) 'Women and Owner Occupation in Britain: First the Prince and then the Palace?' in Gilroy and Woods (1994) *Housing Women*. London: Routledge.

Gilroy, R. and Woods, R. (eds) (1994) *Housing Women*. London: Routledge.

Graham, H. (1984) *Women, Health and the Family*. Brighton: Wheatsheaf Books.

Green, A.E. (1997) 'A Question of Compromise? Case Study Evidence on the Location and Mobility Strategies of Dual Career Households'. *Regional Studies*, 31, 7, 641–57.

Grieco, M. (1987) 'Family Networks and the Closure of Employment', in G. Lee and R. Loveridge (eds) *The Manufacture of Disadvantage*. Milton Keynes, Open University Press.

Gurney, G. (1995) '… "Oh We Wouldn't Live in a Council House …". Contested Notions of Home and Tenure'. Paper presented at the Annual British Sociological Association Conference, University of Leicester.

Gurney, C. (1996) 'Meanings of Home and Home Ownership: Myths, Histories and Experiences'. Unpublished PhD, School of Advanced Urban Studies, University of Bristol.

Gurney, G. (1997) '"… Half of Me was Satisfied": Making Sense of Home Through Episodic Ethnographies'. *Women's Studies International Forum*, 20, 3, 373–86.

Hague, G. and Mallos, E. (1994) 'Domestic Violence, Social Policy and Housing'. *Critical Social Policy*, 42, 112–25.

Hanson, S. and Pratt, G. (1995) *Gender, Work and Space*. New York, Routledge.

Hardill, I., Dudleston, A.C., Green, A.E. and Owen, D.W. (1999) 'Decision Making in Dual-Career Households' in L. McKie, S. Bowlby and S. Gregory (eds) *Gender, Power and the Household*. Basingstoke: Macmillan.

Harris, O. (1984) 'Households as Natural Units' in K. Young, C. Wolkowitz and R. McCullagh (eds) *Of Marriage and the Market: Women's Subordination Internationally and its Lessons*. Second Edition. London: Routledge.

Hayden, D. (1981) *The Grand Domestic Revolution: a History of Feminist Designs for American Homes, Neighbourhoods, and Cities*. London: MIT Press.

Hayden, D. (1984) *Redesigning the American Dream: the Future of Housing, Work and Family*. London: W.W. Norton and Co.

Humm, M. (ed.) (1992) *Feminisms: a Reader*. Hemel Hempsted: Harvester Wheatsheaf.

Hunt, P. (1978) 'Cash Transactions and Household Tasks'. *Sociological Review*, 26, 555–74.

Hunt, P. (1989) 'Gender and the Construction of Home Life' in G. Allan and G. Crow (eds) *Home and Family: Creating the Domestic Sphere*. Basingstoke: Macmillan.

Hutton, W. (1994) *The State We're In*. London: Jonathan Cape.

Jackson, S. and Moores, S. (eds) (1995) *The Politics of Domestic Consumption: Critical Readings*. London: Prentice Hall and Harvester Wheatsheaf.

Jewson, N. and Mason, D. (1986) 'The Theory and Practice of Equal Opportunities Policies: Liberal and Radical Approaches'. *Sociological Review*, 34, 2, 307–34.

Jordan, B., James, S., Kay, H. and Redley, M. (1992) *Trapped in Poverty? Labour Market Decisions in Low Income Families*. London: Routledge.

Kieran, K. (1992) 'Men and Women at Work and Home' in R. Jowel, L. Brook, G. Prior and B. Taylor (eds) *British Social Attitudes, Ninth Report*. Aldershot: Dartmouth Press.

Land, H. (1980) 'The Family Wage'. *Feminist Review*, 6, 55–78.

Lawrence, R. (1983) 'Understanding the Home Environment: Spatial and Temporal Perspectives'. *International Journal for Housing Science and its Applications*, 7, 13–25.

Lees, S. (1993) *Sugar and Spice: Sexuality and Adolescent Girls*. London: Penguin Books.

Lewis, J. and Meredith, B. (1998) *Daughters Who Care*. London: Routledge.

Lovenduski, J. and Norris, P. (1993) *Gender in Politics*. Cambridge: Polity Press.

Loyd, B. (1981) 'Women, Home and Status' in J. Duncan (ed.) *Housing and Identity: Cross-Cultural Perspectives*. London: Croom Helm.

Lummis, T. and Marsh, M. (1990) *The Woman's Domain: Women and the English Country House*. London: Viking.

Mackenzie, S. (1989) *Visible Histories: Women and Environments in a Post-War British City*. Montreal: McGill-Queen's University Press.

McKie, L., Bowlby, S. and Gregory, S. (1996) 'Gender Perspectives on Household Issues. Conference Report'. *European Journal of Women's Studies*, 3, 79–81.

Madigan, R. and Munro, M. (1996) ' "House Beautiful": Style and Consumption in the Home'. *Sociology*, 30–1, 41–57.

Madigan, M., Munro, M. and Smith, S. (1990) 'Gender and the Meaning of Home'. *International Journal of Urban and Regional Research*, 14, 625–47.

Mallos, E. and Hague, G. (1997) 'Women, Housing, Homelessness and Domestic Violence'. *Women's Studies International Forum*, 20, 3, 397–409.

Mansfield, P. and Collard, J. (1988) *The Beginning of the Rest of Your Life: a Portrait of Newly-Wed Marriage*. London: Macmillan.

Marsh, C. (1991) *Hours of Work of Women and Men in Britain*. London: Equal Opportunities Commission/HMSO.

Martin, J. and Roberts, C. (1984) *The Women and Employment Survey: a Lifetime Perspective*. Department of Employment/OPCS. London: HMSO.

Matrix (1984) *Making Space: Women and the Man-Made Environment*. London: Pluto Press.

Maynard, M. (1990) 'The Re-Shaping of Sociology? Trends in the Study of Sociology'. *Sociology*, 24, 2, 269–90.

Morgan, D. (1985) *The Family, Politics and Social Theory*. London: Routledge and Kegan Paul.

Morgan, D. (1996) *Family Connections: an Introduction to Family Studies*. Cambridge: Polity Press.

Morris, L. (1985) 'Local Social Networks and Domestic Organisation'. *Sociological Review*, 33, 327–42.

Morris, L. (1987) 'Constraints on Gender'. *Work, Employment and Society*, 1, 85–106.

Morris, L. (1990) *The Workings of the Household*. Cambridge: Polity Press.

Morris, L. and Irwin, S. (1992) 'Unemployment and Informal Support'. *Work, Employment and Society*, 6, 186–202.

Munro, M. and Madigan, M. (1993) 'Privacy in the Private Sphere'. *Housing Studies*, 8, 29–45.

Munro, M. and Madigan, M. (1996) 'Style and Consumption in the Home'. *Sociology*, 30, 41–58.

Murcott, A. (1983) ' "It's A Pleasure to Cook for Him" ' in E. Gamarnikow (ed.) *The Public and the Private*. London: Heinemann.

Netting, R., Wilk, R. and Arnould, E. (eds) (1984) *Households: Comparative and Historical Studies of the Domestic Group*. Berkley: University of California Press.

Oakley, A. (1974a) *Housewife*. London: Pelican Books.

Oakley, A. (1974b) *The Sociology of Housework*. London: Penguin.

Oerton, S. (1997) ' "Queer Housewives?": Some Problems in Theorising the Division of Domestic Labour in Lesbian and Gay Households'. *Women's Studies International Forum*, 20, 3, 421–30.

Pahl, J. (1984) 'The Allocation of Money within the Household' in M. Freeman (ed.) *The State, the Law and the Family*. London: Tavistock.

Pahl, J. (1989) *Money and Marriage*. Basingstoke: Macmillan.

Parry, G., Moyser, G. and Day, N. (1992) *Political Participation and Democracy in Britain*. Cambridge: Cambridge University Press.

Pilcher, J. (1995) *Age and Generation in Modern Britain*. Oxford: Oxford University Press.

Pratt, G. (1981) 'The House as an Expression of Social Worlds' in J. Duncan (ed.) *Housing and Identity: Cross-Cultural Perspectives*. London: Croom Helm.

Putnam, T. (1990) 'Introduction: Design, Consumption and Domestic Ideals' in C. Newton and T. Putnam (eds) *Household Choices*. London: Furures Publication.

Roberts, M. (1991) *Living in a Man-Made World: Gendered Assumptions in Modern Housing Design*. London: Routledge.

Sainsbury, D. (ed.) (1994) *Gendering Welfare States*. London: Sage.

Saunders, P. (1990) *A Nation of Homeowners*. London: Unwin-Hyman.

Saunders, P. and Williams, P. (1988) 'The Constitution of the Home: Towards a Research Agenda'. *Housing Studies*, 3, 81–93.

Scott, S. and Morgan, D. (eds) (1993) *Body Matters: Essays on the Sociology of the Body*. London: The Falmer Press.

Sommerville, P. (1992) 'Homelessness and the Meaning of Home: Rooflessness or Rootlessness?' *International Journal of Urban and Regional Research*, 16, 4, 529–39.

Somerville, P. (1994) 'Tenure, Gender and Household Structure'. *Housing Studies*, 9, 329–49.

Stacey, J. and Thorne, B. (1985) 'The Missing Feminist Revolution in Sociology'. *Social Problems*, 32, 301–316.

Swift, J. (1997) 'Common Place, Common Sense'. *Women's Studies International Forum*, 20, 3, 351–60.

Sydie, R. (1987) *A Feminist Perspective on Sociological Theory*. Toronto: Methuen.

Thorogood, N. (1987) 'Race, Class and Gender: the Politics of Housework' in J. Brannen and G. Wilson (eds) *Give and Take in Families: Studies in Resource Distribution*. London: Allen and Unwin.

Tomas, A. and Dittmar, H. (1995) 'The Experience of Homeless Women: An Exploration of Housing Histories and the Meaning of "Home"'. *Housing Studies*, 10, 4, 493–515.

Van Every, J. (1995) *Heterosexual Women Changing the Family: Refusing to be a 'Wife'!* London: Taylor & Francis.

Van Every, J. (1997) 'Understanding Gendered Inequality: Reconceptualizing Housework'. *Women's Studies International Forum*, 20, 3, 411–20.

Veness, A. (1994) 'Designer Shelters as Models and Makers of Home – New Responses to Homelessness in Urban America'. *Urban Geography*, 15, 2, 150–67.

Walby, S. (1986) *Patriarchy at Work*. Cambridge: Polity Press.

Walby, S. (1997) *Gender Transformations*. London: Routledge.

Wallace, C. (1987) *For Richer, For Poorer*. London: Tavistock.

West, C. and Zimmerman, D. (1991) 'Doing Gender' in J. Lorber and S. Farrell (eds) *The Social Construction of Gender*. London: Sage.

Werner, C., Altman, I. and Oxley, D. (1985) 'Temporal Aspects of Homes: A Transactional Perspective' in I. Altman and C. Werner (eds) *Home Environments*. New York, Plenum Press.

Whitehead, A. (1981) '"I'm Hungry, Mum": The Politics of Domestic Budgeting' in K. Young, C. Wolkowitz and R. McCullagh (eds) *Of Marriage and the Market: Women's Subordination in International Perspective*. London: CSE Books.

Williams, P. (1987) 'Constituting Class and Gender: A Social History of the Home' in N. Thrift and P. Williams (eds) *Class and Space: The Making of Urban Society*. London, Routledge and Kegan Paul.

Yanagisako, S. and Collier, J. (1987) 'Towards a Unified Analysis of Gender and Kinship' in J. Collier and S. Yanagisako (eds) *Gender and Kinship: Essays Toward a Unified Analysis*. Stanford: Stanford University Press.

2 Gendering the Household: Some Theoretical Considerations

David Morgan

INTRODUCTION

I want to begin by recognizing the possible tensions between an analysis which starts from a gender perspective and one which begins with the household. Both perspectives have been important in the development of current sociological analysis and both perspectives have themselves undergone change. Recognition of possible tensions between the two perspectives has been present for some time (Stanley, 1992a; Arber, 1993; Anderson, Bechofer and Gershuny, 1994; Morgan, 1996) and this chapter aims to outline the bases of this tension and possible ways of going beyond it. At the simplest level it could be argued that gender represents a mode of classifying individuals (as when an array of data is broken down by sex) while households refer to some form of collectivity. Hence, there is always the danger that gender differences will be subsumed under an analysis which takes the household as the level of analysis. This simple methodological point takes on greater significance when it is argued that gender is not simply a matter of difference but is also a question of inequality (Evans, 1995; Morgan, 1996). Here, as Anderson *et al.* (1994) recognize, a household-based analysis may ignore differences in terms of power. This becomes especially important when, for example, reference is made to 'household strategies', an analysis of outcomes that may obscure the deployment of gendered power likely to produce such outcomes (Edwards and Ribbens, 1991; Wallace, 1993). In practice, however, this possibility of a tension between household- and gender-based approaches may possibly prove to be more fruitful than harmful. It can be recognized that both represent possible points of departure, thus retaining some of the gains in understanding that have been provided by an approach based upon households, while not losing sight of a gendered approach which sees gender in terms of both difference and inequality. Such a recognition will, it is hoped, further the gains made by both approaches. If, generally speaking, much household analysis has managed to avoid the dangers recognized by Anderson *et al.* (1994), a large part of the credit must go to feminist scholarship which, from the outset, highlighted gendered divisions within households. We may cite the work of the 'Resources within Households' group (Brannen and Wilson, 1987), work by Lydia Morris (1990) and Jan Pahl (1989) and briefer statements by Arber (1993) and Stanley (1992a). These analyses helped to ensure that the black-box of the household would remain partially open, that issues of power differentials would remain on the agenda and that the dangers of reification were correspondingly reduced.

There is little need at this point to go beyond listing the various ways in which gendered understandings of the household influenced research and theorizing. A major focus, of course, was upon divisions of labour between men and women within households, divisions in terms of the amount of domestic labour performed, the actual nature of the tasks performed and the way in which these shaped and drew upon commonsensical notions of male and female identities (Morris, 1990; Seymour, 1988). A major line of questioning here was around the extent to which there had been any significant shifts in terms of men's participation in domestic tasks. Other work focused upon the allocation and use of resources within the household, beginning with money but extending to consider issues to do with food, time and space (Charles and Kerr, 1988; Pahl, 1989; DeVault, 1991). There were also overlaps here with the developing analysis around the concept of care, the extent and the ways in which this was gendered and the various practices associated with informal care (especially of the elderly) within and between households (Finch and Groves, 1980; Stacey, 1981; Ungerson, 1990; Graham, 1991; Finch, 1994). An interesting illustration of a parallel development in both the analysis of household and the analysis of gender around the issue of care is provided by Hilary Graham (1991). While recognizing the strength of a feminist approach which highlighted gender as a major dimension in the analysis of care, she also recognizes the limitations of a series of studies which concentrated on unpaid care by relatives, which saw gender as the central social division, ignoring other divisions such as race and class. Her case study, focusing upon paid domestic service, not only introduces these other inequalities into the analysis but also calls into question conventional notions of a strongly bounded household. Domestic servants are both within and outside particular households to varying degrees.

Much of this work is still continuing and needs to continue. However, it can be reasonably maintained that, in Britain at least, there are few household-based analyses which do not take on board some kind of recognition of gendered differences and inequalities. A partial exception, here, may be made in the case of stratification studies where claims that the family or household is the unit of analysis do not always lead to a serious consideration of the interplays between class and gender within the site of the household (Morgan, 1996, see Chapter 2 for further elaboration). Generally speaking, household analysis is gendered analysis, and where it is not, there will always be a small chorus seeking to rectify this particular anomaly. Indeed, attention may be shifting to consider other household-based divisions, such as those concerning age and generation and, in particular, focusing upon the positions of children and young people within household practices (Allatt and Yeandle, 1991).

DEVELOPMENTS IN THE STUDY OF GENDER

It can be argued, however, that some degree of tension between gender and household will remain, despite the apparent degree of accommodation between the two found especially at the level of individual empirical studies. One important reason remains that the study of gender, significantly influenced by feminist scholarship, was largely encouraged by some kind of belief that the existing gender order was exploitative or unjust and should be changed (Oakley, 1981; Stacey, 1981; Maynard, 1990). Household studies were not necessarily informed by such a direct moral or political critique. Further, even where there has been some degree of accommodation between the two perspectives, it also has to be recognized that the study of gender, like the study of the household, has not remained static.

The recognition of gender differences within the household often took a relatively unproblematic approach to gender itself. Gender often tended to be an independent variable while various practices, values or attitudes relating to the household were dependent variables. Where gender interacted with other inequalities a more-or-less straightforward additive model was implied with the various subordinate statuses in terms of gender, class or ethnicity reinforcing each other in relatively straightforward ways. For example, Graham (1991: 73) writes: 'Gender, class and racial divisions emerge as integral and inter-connected structures within the organisation of everyday reproduction.' This usefully recognizes the complexities of the interconnections. Yet the primary elements (gender, class and racial divisions) would seem, in this context, to remain relatively stable and apparently unproblematic.

Nevertheless, parallel with and sometimes interacting with developments in household research, there were developments and debates within gender research and theorizing. These developments were numerous and came from diverse sources; taken together, they have important implications for the gendered analysis of the household.

1. Feminist versus Gender Research

Running through many of these debates and discussions was another tension about the relationships between feminist research and gender research. Was 'gender' research and talk about gender an attempt to undermine feminist research or to blunt its critical cutting edge through laying claims to academic respectibility? This might come about through the introduction of studies of men and masculinities (see point 6 below) or through the elaboration of theories of gender which paid little reference to questions of power and inequality. In practice many of these fears do not seem to be realized and much work appearing under the heading of 'gender' continues to be significantly informed by a feminist perspective (the journals *Journal of Gender Studies* and *Gender and History* are examples).

2. Difference versus Inequality

Linked to this there was a continuing tension between gender as difference and gender as inequality. It would probably be fair to say that the model of gender that influenced studies of the household emerged from a more general concern with social divisions and inequalities as well as feminist research and critique (for example Brannen and Wilson, 1987; Morris, 1990). An emphasis upon gender as difference tended perhaps to be more influential in cultural and literary studies. More finely nuanced discussions, of course, could begin to weave the themes of difference and inequality together, showing how the one influenced the other. This might prove to be especially important in the analysis of the household.

3. Gender as Structure

It has been noted already that gender is frequently seen as a property or characteristic associated with individuals. However, some of the major theoretical statements (such as Walby, 1990; Delphy and Leonard, 1992) would tend to focus on gender at a more structural level. Gender, or more likely 'patriarchy', is seen as a property of social formations or social orders, a product of historical processes rather than the aggregation of individual properties. While, it is argued, gender at a structural or systemic level will have implications for individual practices, these practices cannot simply be read off from more structural analyses of patriarchy. As in other areas of sociology, there is always a degree of tension between the two levels.

4. Dichotomy or Continuum?

Whether one is speaking about difference or inequality, gender tends most frequently to be understood in dichotomous terms. Scholarly representations combine with commonsense understandings in, for example, the analysis of an array of data 'by sex'. Studies of voting behaviour or attitude surveys would tend to be the clearest examples here. However, there are various strategies available which might undermine these dichotomous models. One strategy, to talk of a continuum of masculinity and femininity, has not often been taken up in British sociological analysis (in contrast to some social psychology) but remains a possibility. Perhaps the most common strategy is to explore gender criss-crossing other variables such as class, ethnicity, age, sexuality and so on. Another strategy might be to treat gender as a latent characteristic, a dependent rather than an independent variable, something that cannot be assumed from the simple presence of actors identified as males or females. This implies a more active understanding of gender.

5. Gender and Other Social Divisions

The recognition of interrelationships between gender and other social divisions has already been noted. This does not simply suggest that matters are more complicated. It also has implications for the way in which we approach gender or, indeed, any other division. While these different dimensions of social inequality might be used as building blocks, preserving the integrity of each, in order to develop more complex causal models of social difference and inequality, more fluid and more complex approaches may be suggested. Thus an alternative strategy might be to use these different divisions as primary colours which can be mixed in all kinds of shades. The act of mixing may be as important as the individual colours which are mixed.

6. Bringing Men Back In

At some point in these debates and developments it became increasingly recognized that gender was about men and women, rather than just women. Calls to 'bring men back in' came from a variety of quarters and with a variety of agendas and were received, equally, by a variety of responses ranging from whole-hearted enthusiasm to deep scepticism or outright opposition (Hearn and Morgan, 1990; Maynard, 1990). Such demands might be seen as part of a 'male backlash'; at the very least they had implications for the sharing out of research and teaching resources in a time of increasing financial stringency. Further, some of the calls to 'bring men back in' seemed to ignore the fact that men had almost always featured in feminist critical analysis. Analyses of patriarchy, for example, could hardly proceed without some analysis of the practices of men (Walby, 1990; Delphy and Leonard, 1992).

7. Gender and the Body

Discussions of gender have increasingly been linked to the developing area of the sociology of the body. It can be argued that feminist analyses were one of the main sets of stimuli to this developing area (Scott and Morgan, 1993). However, the implications of discussions of the gendered body have been rarely explored in the context of family and household studies, although the potential is there (Morgan, 1996). This is especially true when we link discussions of gender and the body to discussions of sexualities. Issues of care also frequently link bodily concerns with the analysis of the household.

8. Gender and Post-Modernity

Any of these overlapping themes and debates can be linked to current pre-occupations with postmodernity and, more recently, queer theory (Butler, 1990; Evans, 1995; Seidman, 1996). Debates within postmodernism also certainly have implications for the study of gender, favouring a more fluid, complex and ambiguous set of themes than was previously the case. There has been considerable debate as to whether these developments have the effect of undermining feminist analysis through dissolving patriarchy into a multiplicity of cross-currents and possibilities, or whether they may in fact provide genuine insight into the issues under consideration here (for a recent assessment, see McLaughlin, 1997).

CONSEQUENCES OF THESE DEVELOPMENTS

The consequences of these various converging themes for the study of gender may be outlined briefly. In the first place, there is a stress on gender as a process rather than as a thing. The idea of process can be understood at a variety of levels. Gender may be understood in historical terms as being shaped by long- or short-term developments in interaction with each other, such as distinctions between the public and the private, developments in labour markets, organization of households and so on. But it may also be understood as meaning more micro-interactive processes that take place on a day-to-day level between a variety of sets of others, significant or otherwise. An adolescent girl, for example, has some exchanges with her parents and brother before going out to visit some friends. She is subjected to some unwelcome attentions on the bus before she reaches her friend's house and spends the rest of the evening in the company of a group of girls. Meanwhile, her brother goes to meet some of the lads in the pub. There are a range of gender experiences here in this possibly stereotypical example, positive and negative, overt and covert.

Linked to this is the increasing use of the word 'gendering' (for a recent example see Davies, 1996). Again this underlines the idea of gender as a process rather than as a once-and-for-all achievement and may similarly be understood at a variety of levels. It may refer to a variety of organizational or institutional processes which define, directly or indirectly, particular contexts as gendered in certain ways. Examples are most readily found from the sphere of paid work and employment; bank employees, nurses and doctors, personnel managers and so on. Such gendering is not simply a question of the numbers of women or men at various levels; it is also the extent to which these positions, and the persons who occupy them, are defined in gendered terms. But the term 'gendering' may also apply to the work of the observer or the analyst. The research, perhaps informed by feminist scholarship, may see or understand particular situations as gendered where the formal understanding seeks to minimize the relevance of gender differences. Thus analyses of doctor-patient interactions may draw attention to gender differences where these have been unacknowledged in formal charters or patterned expectations (Roberts, 1985).

Yet again, this emphasis upon gender as a process is linked with the idea of 'doing gender' rather than simply *having* a gender (West and Fenstermaker, 1995; West and Zimmerman, 1996). This is associated with a more active understanding of gender, one which lays stress on the active, knowing agent as well as upon the constraints from immediate situations or historically shaped structures. Ideas of 'gender strategies' (Hochschild, 1990) or 'gender practices' (Morgan, 1996) may point in a similar direction.

Finally, there is the idea that gender is done or constructed in a multiplicity of sites which may or may not coalesce in some coherent overall pattern. As might be expected from the preceding arguments, while all or most sites may be expected to be gendered they may not be gendered in identical ways or to the same extent. We may therefore see the household as a site, perhaps a major site, in which gender, both in terms of difference and in terms of inequality, 'gets done'. At the same time the household is not just about gender and different households may be gendered in different ways and to varying extents, just as they may be classed, raced or aged.

GENDER AND HOUSEHOLD

Thus, recent developments in the analysis of gender which have culminated in a perspective on gender as processual, active and being accomplished in a variety of sites, have a range of implications for the study of the household. A point of departure might be to think of household practices and gender practices and the various ways in which these practices blend or flow into and affect each other. By household practices, I mean those relatively patterned and ordered human activities and interactions, together with the accounting procedures that accompany such activities, that take place within or in relation to households. By gender or gendered practices, I mean those practices which are defined, by the members themselves or by observers or by both, as being to do with the constructions of identities and differences between women and men. Thus, viewed from different perspectives, the same set of practices may be seen as being related to either household or gender or both in interaction. For example, vacuuming the floor may be seen as part of a set of practices that are necessary for the orderly maintenance of the household on a day-to-day basis as well as practices which are linked to gendered identities. From a household perspective such practices may be performed equally by a man or by a woman; from a gender perspective such differences may become crucial.

I would like to argue that the household is not simply any site for the doing of gender and gendered practices but it is a site of particular importance. The household may be defined as being particularly crucial for the day-to-day practices of gender since, firstly, a very large percentage of the population lives in households of one kind or another. Secondly, while the terms are not interchangeable, there is considerable overlap between the ideas of the household and those of the family.

While accepting that there are important differences between household and family, it is also the case that a large number of households consist of persons who are related to each other by ties of birth or marriage or their equivalent. Households may include persons who are not so related and family relationships certainly spread over two or more households;

nevertheless the overlaps continue to be important. It may be noted, for example, that family transitions are either the occasion for the formation of new households (marriage, divorce, leaving home, for example) or bring about changes in household composition (birth and death, for example). These are not the only occasions for the formation or change in the composition of households but they remain central ones.

At the same time, family relationships, and transitions leading to the formation of new or differently composed households, continue to be seen as themselves highly gendered. Legal and popular definitions of marriage and family life revolve around routinely understood differences between women and men and constructions of sexuality (Collier, 1995). Wedding ceremonies symbolize gendered differences and gender remains one of the major elements in the telling of family stories. Despite all the talk there might be about partners or parenting, the gendered nature of family terminology and practice remains secure. Of particular significance here is the interplay between gender and sexualities. While the analysis of households may point to a range of sexualities (gay and lesbian households for example), the analysis of family, and family transitions, tends to privilege a heterosexual model and to highlight the mutual reinforcement of gender and sexuality.

Family relationships, therefore, remain one of the major sites where gender gets done; gender is not incidental or formally irrelevant to family practices but, on the contrary, is built into these practices and routine understandings of them. Certainly many key family themes have gender at the heart of them; analyses of socialization practices and the experiences of childbirth and parenthood; divisions of labour between spouses over the life-course; patterns of divorce and reconstitution; domestic violence and abuse and so on. More complex is the extent to and ways in which constructions of gender within family relationships are crucial for the understanding of gender elsewhere. Does gender, as some would argue, 'begin at home' or does the family remain just one site, albeit an important site, for the construction and practice of gendered identities and gendered subjectivities? Or, yet again, is the family/household to be seen as a key, but not uniquely determining, patriarchal structure?

There are, however, complexities in the gendering of households. These in part arise out of the fact that household and family are overlapping but not synonymous terms. If families are strongly gendered, at least in ideological terms, households are less strongly gendered. Households may consist of people who are not related in family terms. It remains an open, and interesting, question as to whether households which are composed of persons unrelated by blood or by marriage are gendered in the same way or to the same extent as households which come closer to popular under-standings of families. These questions could apply, in different ways, to those individuals or households who would not normally consider them-selves to be 'family' (student residences or lodgers for example), as well as non-traditional households such as those based on gay or lesbian rela-tionships or some form of communal sharing.

Even if we were to confine our attention to what might clumsily be called family-households (including lone-parent households, reconstituted families, childless couples and so on) there is still the question as to which influences other than gender shape the interactions and practices within them. Often, for example, age interacts with gender to produce distinctive practices. In some cases, as in cross-class marriages (McRae, 1986), class may also be a relevant consideration, as may ethnicity.

One point worthy of further consideration stems from the complex dis-tinctions around the public/private division. This distinction has informed feminist scholarship in a variety of ways. In the first place, it has encour-aged sociological enquiry to shift from its preoccupations with life in the public sphere (employment, class and so on), where men and masculine themes seem to predominate, to giving equal weight to the private spheres of family, household and sexuality (Morris, 1990; Walby, 1990). Secondly, it has shown the complex ways in which this distinction has been woven around and often reinforces gender differences (Gamarnikow *et al.*, 1983). Finally, it has attempted to call the distinction between the public and the private into question and to show the links and continuities between the two spheres (Stacey, 1981; Maynard, 1990).

Generally speaking, family life is located on the private side of any line that modern societies might wish to draw here. This is not to say that there are not ambiguities and complexities with the drawing of this line, yet even recognizing these, there are strong societal presuppositions in locat-ing families in the private sphere, however this might be constituted.

Within this general ideological and cultural location of family life in the private sphere, there are further distinctions. One is that it is not simply family life in the abstract but especially family life as it is located in households, identified by the members as 'home'. The private sphere is constructed in its strongest form where relationships constituting families, practices denoting households and the complex economic and cultural symbolism associated with the home all converge (Crow and Allan, 1990).

From a gender perspective, the identification of home, family and household with privacy has generally been understood in negative terms. The private sphere seems to be especially resistant to wider changes in the gendered divisions of labour and assumptions about what constitutes women's or men's work. The supposedly safe haven of the family-based household is also identified as a site for violence against women and children while ideologies of privacy stand in the way of wider societal control over or investigation into these practices (Finklehor *et al.*, 1983). And, as a site of legitimate sexual expression, the marriage-based household may also provide further endorsement of prevailing patterns of gender difference.

Yet the family-based household may also be a site for innovation in gendered practices. It would seem that some changes have been taking place in the gendered divisions of labour within the household and in the divisions of parenting responsibilities between women and men. There is some evidence of an increasing desire on the part of men and women for more shared participation in parenting and domestic life together with signs that these desires are being translated into practice (Gershuny *et al.*, 1994). The limits of these innovations have been well explored but the fact that they can and do take place should also be recognized.

It may be that the idea of privacy also permits some innovation which can take place legitimately outside the informal controls of others, particularly in this case male work or leisure groups. Sue Sharpe's amusing image of the husband cleaning the house on his hands and knees in order to avoid scrutiny from the outside world is a striking image of the way in which the privacy of the home may allow some departure, in this case reluctant, from the conventional (Sharpe, 1984: 182). The language of strategies and negotiations, often applied to the analysis of households, may also highlight some of these possibilities for innovation in gendered practices and relationships. This language emphasizes process and change and is in keeping with the more fluid understandings of gender discussed earlier in this chapter.

Negotiations, of course, need not always be conflict-free and it may also be the case that households constitute important sites where pressure is placed upon men to modify their practices. The sources of such pressure may be various, including marriage to or cohabiting with a woman with feminist sympathies or the necessity of re-ordering domestic practices as a result of dual earning or, indeed, dual not-earning. We may also note, as a topic for further investigation, the extent to which children may themselves put issues of change in gendered practices on the domestic agenda through their exposure to various liberal or radical influences.

Much of this remains at a somewhat speculative level although the analysis of family planning and family limitation practices within households in the past may suggest some of the ways in which change is likely to come about. This is still a subject of some considerable debate, but it seems reasonable to suppose that deliberate birth-limitation strategies took place in households long before there was a readily available public discourse supporting these practices or institutions available to provide advice and information. Further such practices had implications for understandings of sexuality, for women in the labour market and for the gender order generally. Innovations in gendered practices may take place within the semi-private sphere of the family/household, but have implications for gender relationships in the wider public sphere.

It is possible, therefore, to begin to explore some more dynamic exchanges between gender and household and to develop perspectives that are fluid and which have a degree of openness about them. I shall attempt to take this argument a little further by way of a couple of illustrations: a specific focus on men in households and an examination of single-person households.

ILLUSTRATION: MEN IN HOUSEHOLDS

Part of the reformulation of a gender perspective has entailed the more explicit and detailed recognition of men as gendered actors (see Mac An Ghaill, 1996, for a recent overview of some of the key areas). This shift has made some impact on the study of households but could perhaps be developed further. Where men appear in household analyses they often appear as obstacles to change, especially in terms of the divisions of labour and responsibilities within the household. More traditional models of households will show men to be crucial actors in the formation of new households, the maintenance and reproduction of households and the formation of household identities through their position at the head. It was this that gave rise to the dominant position of men in stratification studies (Crompton, 1993). In all kinds of ways and from a variety of causes, the role of men in the formation, reproduction and identity of households has come under challenge (Heward, 1996).

Yet men still appear in households as possessors of power, economic and physical. Further, more recent research has suggested how men through their apparent emotional inexpressiveness call upon women for their emotional labour, thereby perpetuating gendered assumptions about the nature of women and men and, more generally, the gender order or patriarchy as a whole (for example Duncombe and Marsden, 1993). Such emotional servicing is, of course, found outside households but it probably remains true to say that its most complete expression is found within domestic contexts and that this has a high degree of public legitimacy.

There is much evidence to support this particular image of men in households and the way in which their positions there contribute to the maintenance of gendered assumptions and identities. This may, of course, be especially the case where more traditional public ways of proving oneself to be a man become either less available or less legitimate. Recent concentration on the emotional divisions of labour seem to be especially valuable in highlighting what men get out of family and domestic life while also pointing to ways in which their positions are maintained (Hochschild, 1990; Duncombe and Marsden, 1993). Further, such concentration on the emotional meaning of domestic life for men may also provide clues as to why change often appears to be so slow and uneven.

However, it is doubtful whether this is the whole story. I have suggested that households, through their semi-private status, might become sites for gender innovations, for men as well as women. Here it may be important, as a research strategy, to concentrate on cases where men are clearly involved in household practices. While Dallas Cliff's sample of early retired men shows relatively little in the way of innovation (Cliff, 1993) there are some hints in Wheelock's (1990) account of unemployed men and, more strikingly, Barker's (1994) discussion of lone fathers. Barker's small sample is not confined to 'new men'; he in fact divides them into pioneers and patriarchs on the basis of responses to some attitudinal questions. He concludes (page 249):

> Thus, whilst this study has suggested that lone fatherhood is not the last – or the first – haunt of the New Man, it has also suggested that lone fatherhood is one of the sites within the patriachal relations of society of interesting developments in parenting and masculinities.

It might also be noted here that there has probably been an over-concentration on men as fathers in the family literature and less on men in other capacities in domestic life. Indeed, even discussion of men as fathers tends to concentrate (certainly in the public imagery) on fathers in relation to relatively small children. We know less about fathers in relation to adolescent children (but see Sharpe, 1994) while relationships between fathers and adult children need to be extrapolated from studies dealing with kinship relationships (Finch and Mason, 1993). These would include other family-based identities such as brother, son, husband and uncle. There has been some study of men as carers (Arber and Gilbert, 1989; Applegate and Kaye, 1993) but relatively little on men as the 'cared-for', especially where that care is particularly intensive or long term. Finally, we need more information on men in households which are not constituted on the basis of conventional family ties (Weeks *et al.*, 1996).

One way of thinking about men in households may be to stress the variable quality of their involvement in household and domestic life. It has long been recognized that the extent and ways in which 'family' is a central life interest varies for men as well as for women (see Edgell, 1980, for example). This degree of involvement may vary according to work commitments (or the ability of men to deploy work commitments as 'legitimate excuses' (Finch and Mason, 1993), to stages in the life-course or to personal inclinations. However, it is likely that the idea of the orderly life-course, perhaps one of the major features of late-nineteenth- and early-twentieth-century Britain (Anderson, 1985), is itself being eroded as a result of shifts in employment, the positions and expectations of women and family life in general. The concentration, in recent years, on the situations of young working-class men (and women), making or not making the transition from home to work and from family of origin to family of procreation is a reflection of the weakening of the central life-course model. The situation of such individuals often calls into question clear-cut notions as to what it means to 'belong' to a household or, more simply, to be 'in' a household. And that ambiguity about household membership and attachment may also reflect on gendered identities filtered through class and age.

It may be, as Gershuny *et al.* have suggested, that the household is the site of change that has yet to work its way fully through the system (Gershuny *et al.*, 1994). While the general picture that we have is one of considerable innovation and the elaboration of complex coping strategies on the part of women in the household and relative stability or even resistance on the part of men, this is a picture which, while it may be consistent, is hardly stable. To what extent can men resist change in the face of increasing threats to the stability and identity that family life was once supposed to provide for both men and women? If men are, in some cases or under some circumstances, beginning to change, what kinds of negotiations in terms of gendered identities are taking place? Put another way, we are looking at the interplay between the everyday practical negotiations around the division of labour within households on the one hand and wider, shifting or contested, understandings of masculinity on the other. This is to be seen as an interchange: changing or broadening models of masculinity may give legitimacy to changes being negotiated within the household, while these changes in household practices themselves constitute part of the shifting understandings of masculinity and femininity in the wider society.

ILLUSTRATION: SINGLE PERSON HOUSEHOLDS

The growing number of single-person households is beginning to attract some media and scholarly attention. The 1996 edition of *Social Trends* highlighted the finding that 'more than a quarter of households in Great Britain in 1994–5 consisted of one person living alone, almost double the proportion in 1961' (*Social Trends*, 1996: 49). A headline in the *Independent* warned that 'The English Face Lonely Future in Solitary Homes' (7 March 1995). A later issue of the same newspaper had a more optimistic-sounding discussion by Cal McCrystal (12 March 1995) making use of the earlier sociological phrase (originally used in connection with kinship studies in advanced industrial societies) 'intimacy at a distance' (Finch, 1989: 29). This cites evidence that suggests a third of all households in the UK will be single-occupancy types in six years' time. Even now, Greater London has one in four persons aged 16–59 living on their own (Family Policy Bulletin, December 1994).

The sociological analysis of single-person households faces a number of difficulties. In the first place, the very title presents problems for definitions of households that include some element of sharing. Following from this, many of the sociological problems which involve questions of interaction and social relationships seem to be excluded through a strict focus on single-person households. The same would also seem to apply to questions of gender. Beyond analysing the breakdown of single-person households by gender (a distribution which itself varies according to age) is there a great deal more that can be said?

At the most elementary level it may be asked whether men and women manage their lives in single-person households differently. Put another way, the question is whether the single-occupancy status is the prime consideration, modifying even apparently basic considerations such as gender, or whether gender continues to reassert itself. Are people in single-person households more or less likely to be innovative in gendered practices in their relationships with others outside their households? Answers to these questions will probably highlight the limitations of an exclusive focus upon households. As the use of the phrase 'intimacy at a distance' suggests, living in single-person households does not mean an absence of social or sexual contacts. The question, therefore, shifts to some extent to consider relationships between households. How do people maintain some kind of balance between separation and intimacy? What can the different patterns of usage of time, space, money and food tell us about gendered relationships across and between households? Are we pointing to a more fluid understanding of the boundaries of households and hence a more complex relationship to the construction of gender identities?

Further complexities arise when it is stressed that single-person households are not all of one piece. Three main categories suggest themselves:

- The never married, who choose neither to marry nor to cohabit but who possibly maintain long-standing relationships with another person of the opposite or the same sex;
- Divorced separated or 'un-partnered' individuals. Some of these may chose to remain in the 'single' status; others may actively seek new relationships and may see this as some transitional stage;
- Widowed persons, who have experienced periods of married or cohabiting life over a fairly long period of time.

Of course there are all kinds of variation on these themes but they serve as a reminder of the importance of considering patterns of entry into – and possible exit from – the single-person household status. This again emphasizes the importance of adopting a more fluid understanding of household as a process rather than as a thing and hence overlapping with the developments in the analysis of gender.

At the moment 'single-person households' are 'good to think with' in that they not only stretch and enlarge our understanding of households, but also have impacts upon constructions of gender. Does the fluidity shown in the growth of single-person households imply, at least for the younger cohorts, a greater fluidity in understandings of gender and gendered strategies? Or are shifts in the gender order themselves major factors in the shaping of single-person households?

CONCLUSIONS

Despite the tensions that exist between studies of the household and studies of gender, there has often been a partial resolution at least at the level of particular studies. Within British sociology, gender was a major theme in the analysis of households, almost from the beginning. This included discussions of gender as difference as well as of gender as inequality, although it is likely that the emphasis was more upon the latter.

However, the analysis of gender has itself developed in ways which have yet to be fully incorporated into the analysis of households. Some of these key themes in the analysis of gender have included the recognition of gender as involving men as well as women, a stress on gender as a process rather than as a thing and a more complex understanding of gender in inter-action with other social differences. At the same time we recognize that households, similarly, are not static entities. They have change built into them, as individuals leave or are added and as the wider society and net-works within which these households are located itself undergoes change. Consideration of the range of household forms in late modernity, including the rise of single-person households, permits further reflection on the com-plexities of household processes and the fluidity of their boundaries.

There are various ways in which these parallel and interacting changes in understanding may be brought together. The 'auto/biographical' turn in many areas of social enquiry (Stanley, 1992b) represents one way in which the shaping and re-shaping of gender identities may be traced over the life-course as individuals move in and out of different household forms and clusters of experiences. Households, and the movements between them, may be seen as contributing to the shaping of gender, just as gender, seen as part of a flow of life interacting with other social distinctions, may be seen as shaping the character of households. Similarly, some discussion in terms of household and gender practices may assist in thinking about the dynam-ics of their interrelationships as we move towards the end of the century.

REFERENCES

Allatt, P. and Yeandle, S. (1991) *Youth Unemployment and the Family: Voices of Disordered Times.* London: Routledge.

Anderson, M. (1985) 'The Emergence of the Modern Life Cycle in Britain'. *Social History*, 10, 1, 69–87.

Anderson, M., Bechofer, F. and Gershuny, J. (eds) (1994) *The Social and Political Economy of the Household.* Oxford: Oxford University Press.

Applegate, J.S. and Kaye, L.W. (1993) 'Male Elder Caregivers' in C.L. Williams (ed.) *Doing "Women's Work": Men in Non-Traditional Occupations.* Newbury Park Ca.: Sage.

Arber, S. (1993) 'Inequalities within the Household' in D. Morgan and L. Stanley (eds) *Debates in Sociology.* Manchester: Manchester University Press.

Arber, S. and Gilbert, N. (1989) 'Men: the Forgotten Carers'. *Sociology*, 23, 1, 111–18.

Barker, R.W. (1994) *Lone Fathers and Masculinities.* Aldershot: Avebury.

Brannen, J. and Wilson, G. (eds) (1987) *Give and Take in Families.* London: Allen & Unwin.

Butler, J. (1990) *Gender Trouble: Feminism and the Subversion of Identity.* London: Routledge.

Charles, N. and Kerr, M. (1988) *Women, Food and Families.* Manchester: Manchester University Press.

Cliff, D. (1993) 'Under the Wife's Feet: Renogotiating Gender Divisions in Early Retirement'. *Sociological Review*, 41, 1, 30–53.

Collier, R. (1995) *Masculinity, Law and the Family*. London: Routledge.

Crompton, R. (1993) *Class and Stratification: an Introduction to Current Debates*. Cambridge: Polity.

Crow, G. and Allan, G. (1990) 'Constructing the Domestic Sphere: the Emergence of the Modern Home in Post-war Britain' in H. Corr and L. Jamieson (eds) *Politics of Everyday Life: Continuity and Change in Work and the Family*. London: Macmillan.

Davies, C. (1996) 'The Sociology of Professions and the Profession of Gender'. *Sociology*, 30, 4, 661–78.

Delphy, C. and Leonard, D. (1992) *Familial Exploitation*. Cambridge: Polity Press.

DeVault, M. (1991) *Feeding the Family: the Social Organization of Caring as Gendered Work*. Chicago: Chicago University Press.

Duncombe, J. and Marsden, D. (1993) 'Love and Intimacy: the Gender Division of Emotions and "Emotion Work"'. *Sociology*, 27, 2, 221–42.

Edgell, S. (1980) *Middle-Class Couples*. London: Allen & Unwin.

Edwards, R. and Ribbens, J. (1991) 'Meanderings around "Strategy": a Research Note on Strategic Discourse in the Lives of Women'. *Sociology*, 25, 477–90.

Evans, J. (1995) *Feminist Theory Today: an Introduction to Second Wave Feminism*. London: Sage.

Family Policy Studies Centre (1994) *Bulletin*. December. London: FPSC.

Finch, J. (1989) *Family Obligations and Social Change*. Cambridge: Polity.

Finch, J. (1994) 'The Concept of Caring: Feminist and other Perspectives' in J. Twigg (ed.) *Carers: Research and Practice*. London: HMSO.

Finch, J. and Groves, D. (1980) 'Community Care and the Family: a Case for Equal Opportunities'. *Journal of Social Policy*, 9, 4, 487–514.

Finch, J. and Mason, J. (1993) *Negotiating Family Responsibilities*. London: Routledge.

Finkelhor, D., Gelles, R.J., Hotaling, G.T. and Straus, M.A. (eds) (1983) *The Dark Side of Families*. Beverley Hills: Sage.

Gamarnikow, E., Morgan, D., Purvis, J. and Taylorson, D. (eds) (1983) *The Public and the Private*. London: Heinemann.

Gershuny, J., Godwin, M. and Jones, S. (1994) 'The Domestic Labour Revolution: a Process of Lagged Adaption' in M. Anderson, F. Bechhofer and J. Gershuny (eds) *The Social and Political Economy of the Household*. Oxford: Oxford University Press.

Graham, H. (1991) 'The Concept of Caring in Feminist Research: the Case of Domestic Service'. *Sociology*, 25, 1, 61–78.

Hearn, J. and Morgan, D. (eds) *Men, Masculinities and Social Theory*. London: Unwin Hyman.

Heward, C. (1996) 'Masculinity and Families' in M. Mac An Ghaill (1996).

Hochschild, A. (1990) *The Second Shift*. London: Piatkus.

Mac An Ghaill, M. (ed.) (1996) *Understanding Masculinities*. Buckingham: Open University Press.

McLaughlin, J. (1997) 'Feminist Relations with Postmodernism: Reflections on the Positive Aspects of Involvement'. *Journal of Gender Studies*, 6, 1, 5–16.

McRae, S. (1986) *Cross-Class Families*. Oxford: Oxford University Press.

Maynard, M. (1990) 'The Re-shaping of Sociology? Trends in the Study of Gender'. *Sociology*, 24, 2, 269–90.

Morgan, D. (1996) *Family Connections: an Introduction to Family Studies.* Cambridge: Polity Press.

Morris, L. (1990) *The Workings of the Household.* Cambridge: Polity Press.

Oakley, A. (1981) *Subject Women.* London: Martin Robertson.

Pahl, J. (1989) *Money and Marriage.* Basingstoke: Macmillan.

Roberts, H. (1985) *The Patient Patients: Women & Their Doctors.* London: Pandora.

Scott, S. and Morgan, D. (eds) *Body Matters.* London: Taylor & Francis.

Seidman, S. (1996) *Queer Theory Sociology.* Oxford: Blackwell.

Seymour, J. (1988) 'The Division of Domestic Labour: a Review'. Working Papers in Applied Social Science, No. 13. Manchester: University of Manchester.

Sharpe, S. (1984) *Double Identity: the Lives of Working Mothers.* Harmondsworth: Penguin.

Sharpe, S. (1994) *Fathers and Daughters.* London: Routledge.

Social Trends (1996) Annual Review. London: HMSO.

Stacey, M. (1981) 'The Division of Labour Revisited or Overcoming the Two Adams' in P. Abrams *et al.* (eds) *Practice and Progress: British Sociology, 1950–1980.* London: Allen & Unwin.

Stanley, L. (1992a) 'Changing Households? Changing Work?' in N. Abercrombie and A. Warde (eds) *Social Change in Contemporary Britain.* Cambridge: Polity Press.

Stanley, L. (1992b) *The Auto/Biographical 'I'.* Manchester: Manchester University Press.

Ungerson, C. (ed.) (1990) *Gender and Caring: Work and Welfare in Britain and Scandinavia.* Brighton: Harvester.

Walby, S. (1990) *Theorising Patriarchy.* Oxford: Blackwell.

Wallace, C. (1993) 'Reflections on the Concept of "Strategy"' in D. Morgan and L. Stanley (eds) *Debates in Sociology.* Manchester: Manchester University Press.

Weeks, J., Donovan, C. and Heaphy, B. (1996) 'Families of Choice: Patterns of Non-Heterosexual Relations. A Literature Review'. Social Science Research Papers, No. 2. London: South Bank University.

West, C. and Fenstermaker, S. (1995) 'Doing Difference'. *Gender & Society*, 9, 1, 8–37.

West, C. and Zimmerman, D. (1996) 'Doing Gender'. *Gender & Society*, 10, 1, 125–51.

Wheelock, J. (1990) *Husbands at Home: the Domestic Economy in Post-Industrial Society.* London: Routledge.

Part II
Gendered Care

3 Men in the Household: Caring Fathers

Vincent Duindam

INTRODUCTION

Fathers, as important caregivers for their children, and men doing substantial tasks in the household more generally, are a rare phenomenon. As D. Morgan states:

> ... most of the evidence points to very slow changes in the direction of men's participation ... Most of the findings are, therefore, relatively pessimistic although perhaps we should begin to look more closely at those men who are attempting to take on greater responsibilities within the home. (Morgan, 1992: 136)

Precisely this argument was the motivation to undertake the present study. There are a number of studies on 'caring fathers' available now from several countries: examples inlcude the United States (Radin, 1982; Pruett, 1983), Sweden (Lamb *et al.*, 1982a), Australia (Russell, 1987) and Israel (Sagi, 1982). In the literature a number of possible determinants of care work by men have been pointed out. Both the views of men and women and their present social context appear to be important. In addition, there has been much debate about the family backgrounds of caring fathers. One of the questions is whether they are imitating their own inspiring father, or compensating for his lack of involvement. Two determinants of a father's functioning as a major caregiver in intact families seem to emerge: (a) the parents' perceptions of the fathering they had experienced as children, and (b) financial-employment factors; particularly fathers' problems in obtaining jobs, mothers' economic activity and maternal career aspirations (Radin, 1994: 44).

In this chapter I present the results of a study on 182 caring fathers in the Netherlands. This group of fathers cannot be called representative of 'the Dutch father'. In this study, the research team were particularly aiming at 'caring' fathers. In the Netherlands generally men hold full-time jobs. Only between 2 and 5 per cent of the fathers work part-time in order to care for their children. Although it is now more common for mothers in the Netherlands to do paid labour, a substantial number of women leave their jobs when they become mothers. Most mothers who do work, work in part-time jobs; often a few hours per week. Caring fathers and their female partners, however, have a similar investment in paid labour: both of them hold substantial part-time jobs (about 30 hours per week). These women and men are also highly educated, they have 'emancipated' views on the division of tasks in the household and they are politically oriented to the left. Another difference with the general population of parents in the Netherlands is that the women are as highly educated as their partners and that their income per hour is not significantly less than that of their partners (Duindam and Spruijt, 1997).

In the remainder of this chapter, I present firstly the background to the research study and the methods used in it. Subsequently, a number of descriptive quantitative results from the study will be given. Then the results of qualitative research will be presented. In particular, the gains of being a caring father, the role of the partner, problems at work and ideas about career and domestic tasks will be discussed. Finally, I will try to discover which variables are associated with different amounts of care giving within this group of men and will take into consideration different areas that turned out to be relevant in previous studies (Lamb *et al.*, 1982b; Radin, 1982; Sagi, 1982; Pruett, 1983; Russell, 1987).

THE RESEARCH CONTEXT

The aim of the present study is to provide insight into the motivations and backgrounds of caring fathers. This project is financially supported by both Utrecht University in the Netherlands and the Dutch Family Council. It was hoped that the research on men and care would be stimulated by the project, and that stereotypes may be lessened.

Respondents were contacted in a number of different ways. Twenty nine per cent responded to an advertisement in the Dutch feminist monthly *Opzij* (which may be translated as 'out of my way, her way'). These fathers knew the names of other fathers. The snowball method was used to send a questionnaire to 226 men, 182 of whom filled it in and returned it. This amounts to a response rate of 81 per cent. In order to recruit appropriate participants to the research a set of criteria were used to define a father as 'caring': part-time work now (or in the recent past) and/or having taken parental leave and/or flexible working hours. Only one father that responded could not be called 'involved' according to these criteria. In addition, in-depth interviews were conducted with 19 men. Almost all of them are heterosexual men with a partner. It should be stressed that in this study the perspective of the father was the central focus. In the question-naire however, there were also questions about the partners. These were answered by the men too, which may lead to some distortions.

Key Characteristics of the Respondents Quoted in Chapter

The average age of the men was 38.2 years, and that of their (female) part-ner 36.7 years. The mean number of children these fathers have is 1.9. During the general elections of 1990, 95 per cent of the fathers voted. Their sympathy rested with the left-wing factions in parliament: 95 per cent of them supported these parties. The men are very highly educated: more than 85 per cent of them finished a School of Higher Vocational Education or took a degree at University. Eighty-two per cent of the fathers

Table 3.1   Characteristics of the Respondents Quoted in this Chapter

Respondent Identifier	Age	Hours p.w.	No. children	Occupation and level
13	40	unkn	2	unknown
19	37	30	3	education, high
20	43	32	2	civil servant, high
28	38	32	1	education, high
41	34	16	2	social work
43	39	30	2	business, high
68	64	24	1	business, high
75	38	32	2	social work
77	37	26	3	business, high
81	35	30	4	education, high
88	42	19	2	education, high
89	38	34	1	civil servant, high
91	46	27	3	social work
106	41	29	2	education, high
119	42	34	2	education, low
128	34	28	2	business, low
131	36	30	3	social work
135	32	40	1	civil servant, low
147	43	32	2	social work
158	37	32	2	business, high
167	33	26	2	social work
175	45	47	2	education, low
177	37	31	4	education, high
179	43	34	3	education, high
181	38	6	3	skilled labour

work part-time, mainly substantial part-time jobs. Interestingly, although there are significant differences, their partners have a similar labour-participation level. About as many fathers (n = 39) as mothers (n = 42) took parental leave. Twenty-five per cent of the men, and 20 per cent of the women, work in business. The income-situation of the men and their partners is also comparable: there is no significant difference in what the men and women earn per hour.

We will now turn to the qualitative part of the research. Important themes were:

- the gains of being a caring father
- the role of the partner
- problems at work
- ideas about career and domestic tasks.

Interviewees are identified after each quote by a unique identifier number.

THE ADVANTAGES OF BEING A CARING FATHER

A deeply established idea is that men who do 'women's work' lose status. Even their very masculinity may be questioned by doing work that is defined as 'women's work' (for example, Morgan, 1992). A further line of thought is that domestic tasks do seem very heavy and burdensome. This kind of work should be equally divided between women and men: men should take their share of the 'trouble'. However, in this study we wanted to know what the men liked about their (caring) situation. What motivated them? Being a caring father seems to be rewarding particularly in the following three respects:

1. It leads to a direct relationship with your children, which is much deeper and more rewarding than a mediated relationship. Eighty-six per cent of the fathers indicated that they appreciate their relationship with their children very much. They talk about 'tenderness', 'cuddling', 'being a witness' and 'sharing important things'.

   'I am able to witness our children's development myself, and not through the accounts of my wife.' (41)

   'All those things my father missed, like observing your child, feeling her rhythm when you are with her all day.' (135)

2. It leads to a sense of a more complete life of combining caring with paid work: the best of both worlds. Thirty-two per cent of the fathers indicate

that their being a caring father makes their lives more rich and complete. Respondents say it makes them 'a more complete person', 'not slaves to their work'. It gives 'insight into yourself', into 'your own youth'.

> 'Having the time for day-to-day activities with the children. Enjoying the ordinary things, for which the hurried career leaves no room.' (13)

> 'It invites creativity, playfulness, spontaneity. In short: one does not always have to be such a stiff, grown up person'. (179)

3. It appears to lead to a better relationship with the partner for 20 per cent of the fathers who mentioned their partner. They stressed the good relationship between them; the fact that there was much contact between them, and a good feeling of sharing the caring. The arrival of the child had led to a new bond between them. Also they thought it important to create room for their partner.

> 'An equal and therefore happy relationship with my wife.' (175)

Powerful Partners: the Strategies of the Women

Most of the respondents agreed that the ideas of their partner pertaining to the division of tasks had influenced them (n = 114) and her actual influence may even be greater. As an example of this one father who claimed not to be influenced elsewhere remarked: 'The division of household chores has, over the years, come about in particular through confrontations with my partner.' (106)

Some of the men who acknowledge the influence of their partner stress her role in becoming conscious of the issues concerning the combining of caring and career:

> 'She was one of the people who re-educated me in matters relating to work, the household and upbringing.' (119)

> 'Without her influence I definitely worked 150 per cent.' (28)

Other men, however, make clear that they and their partners take the same views on these issues. They state they have arrived where they are now together. Maybe the partner has accelerated the process, some add: 'When the division of tasks is at stake our noses have been pointing in the same direction from the very beginning. We continuously check up with each other to see whether this is still the case.' (89)

Many men give examples of the ways in which they have been influenced by their partners. Their statements have been the basis for an attempt to find out what strategies their partners use. The following elements seem to be important:

- In an early stage, sometimes even before the birth of the first child, very clear agreements were made pertaining to the division of tasks. In some cases these arrangements took a conditional form. Without an agreement there were to be no children.

  'She has indicated that she only wanted children if the caring tasks were to be divided up.' (128)

  Subsequently, the woman saw to it that the agreements were kept.

  'I am to prepare nice dinners too. She is certain to make sure that my attention for the household does not decline ...' (77)

  Usually she put issues of household tasks on the agenda.

  'She brings up this issue of the division of tasks more often than I do, whenever, in her eyes, things go wrong. In actual practice she has to defend her time more often. Then we discuss our basic assumptions: what is a fair distribution of the tasks?' (131)

- In this whole process partners are very clear and persistent. They know what they want and they do not give up. Many respondents said that equal sharing was completely taken for granted by their partners.

  'Her insistence on arriving at actual agreements pertaining to the division of tasks.' (75)

  At the same time she makes clear that she appreciates what is going well.

  'She stimulates me in being a father and a househusband through her positive words of appreciation and through her demands ...' (43)

- She intends to give her partner room by trying not to keep too tightly in control of things herself. This is a most important point. Shortly we shall see that she succeeds in this: the men hardly come up with this theme when asked about conflicts relating to the division of tasks.

  'On the one hand she expected me to share everything with her in a fair way, on the other hand she herself did not claim her role as a mother too much.' (147)

She tries to make visible those tasks her partner obviously does not see.

'She is able to show what 'hidden' or 'invisible' tasks are part of taking care of children and the household. In a word, she made clear to me that these tasks can be more exhausting than a full-time job outside the home.' (135)

On occasion she imposes sanctions when her partner does not meet his commitments.

'Her persistence in seeing to it that the agreements are kept helps me to meet my commitments. When I come home at 6.05 p.m. instead of 6.00 p.m. everybody is already having their dinner.' (177)

We can conclude that these women coach and stimulate their partners in all kinds of ways in taking a fair share in the caring tasks. They talk, discuss, and negotiate. Conditions are agreed to, and commitments are made. Progress is guarded, supervised and appreciated. If necessary, sanctions are imposed. What is hidden is made visible. Space is created for the partner to perform his tasks. This does not happen in a very rigid way, however: talents and preferences are taken into account by these couples when dividing chores. In brief, most of the men seem to have a powerful partner.

It may also be instructive to look at relational conflicts. Forty-seven per cent of the respondents indicate that there are hardly any conflicts about the division of tasks. Forty-three per cent indicate that there are (or have been) problems about this issue once in a while. Six per cent state there are conflicts about this almost all the time. We can conclude that more than half the men have or have had at least some conflicts about the division of tasks. The following conflicts were reported as occurring the most:

1. My partner is not readily satisfied with my performance within the home (38 per cent);
2. My partner does not leave me enough room to do things in my own way (27 per cent);
3. I feel overloaded by my partner (17 per cent), and
4. My partner does not easily leave things within the home to me (6 per cent).

Most of the female partners do not have many problems in leaving things within the home to their men. This may be part of the explanation for the involvement of their male partners.

THE WORK SITUATION

Seventy-six per cent of the whole group say they have experienced obstacles when trying to realize their caring fatherhood. The obstacle mentioned most (41 per cent) is the work(ing) environment. The category 'in myself' also scores highly: 30 per cent of the obstacles. The examples respondents give here relate to internalized norms pertaining to a career-orientation and to resistance to household chores: 'My orientation of achievement and my being a caring father conflict with each other.' One father said about household chores: 'It is hard to come up with discipline in this busy job that is not structured for you by other people. At times the work is boring, one is never finished, and all kinds of more attractive things are waiting, making eyes at you.' (181)

Most of the fathers (more than 80 per cent) find their career important or very important. However, if they had to choose between being employed full-time or being a househusband, full-time active within the home, a number of them (28.3 per cent) would opt for the latter option. This is very interesting, because it means that some of the fathers estimate both domains very highly at the same time. So the idea that the more a father is involved with his career, the less he can be bothered about caring within the home, may have to be refuted.

Almost all problems encountered had to do with the arranging of part-time work, flexible working hours or parental leave, and with the resistance of employers, superiors and – less often – colleagues against this. Many men felt the strong pressure to work full-time, or even more. 'I had to convince the management that 32 hours instead of 40 was a possibility. At the same time the 8 hours for this government funded institution should not be jeopardized.' (20)

A few men were confronted with a superior who strongly advised them to drop the idea of working part-time. One of them was even obliged to take a month to think the matter over. In addition, a number of respondents mentioned the practical arrangements of part-time work or flexible working hours. Also the prevention of working overtime, or working on days reserved for parental leave were cited as further obstacles. Some fathers were looked upon as disloyal; there were complaints that they were not available enough: 'People found it hard to accept that I stayed at home when one of the children was ill.' (120) There were also problems with arranging parental leave, calamity leave, and places at day care centres: 'My employer initially denied the existence of parental leave. As an executive of the ABVA (Labour Union) I raised hell.' (51)

The fathers were also asked whether they (had) tried to change arrangements in the work place. The most favoured strategy was one of consultation and negotiation with superiors and colleagues. Various elements were brought to the fore: 'be clear in what you want'; 'make a concrete proposal', 'keep in touch and keep negotiating'. 'Try to convince them and if they adopt a flexible attitude to you, you will show appreciation'. A number of other fathers stressed the importance of being clear so as to leave no doubt: 'be assertive', 'make demands', 'play it hard'. 'Present your plans not as open for discussion, but as final'. (43)

'I used my parental leave as a crowbar. I worked 12 months, 32 hours a week and I simply showed that it is possible.' (135)

What strategy somebody can employ will always depend upon their particular position and opportunities available. One father who had just experienced an unfavourable job application now argued in favour of caution:

'Cautiously sound out what opinion your future employer has about part-time work. Do not force anything. Certainly do not come up with it during your interview for a job.' (102)

Contrast this with the following remark: 'I had a rather blunt attitude. They needed drivers and they wanted me but I would not drop my demands.' (70)

Some men mentioned 'performing well' as a strategy. (14) 'Showing that you are not disloyal'; 'I have indicated that I want to be evaluated on the basis of my output'; 'Always keep one step ahead.' This strategy appears to be rather exhausting since one has to work hard in so many domains.

A number of fathers mentioned a strategy to make their working hours more flexible. To compensate for performing caring tasks during the daytime they would work some evenings. In addition, they made sure they could be reached by phone by colleagues or customers. A few men had their right to work part-time – for instance, when a child was expected – recorded at the beginning of their engagement with an employer.

Finally, some fathers saw that their only option was to tender their resignation and to accept another job:

'In my last job (personnel manager at Phillips) I "struggled" for many years in vain to get a part-time position. When I could not succeed in this I changed my strategy and looked for a job elsewhere in which I could work part-time. Three years ago I found it.' (81)

RESISTANCE TO HOUSEHOLD CHORES *VERSUS* FEELING APPRECIATED

Most of the men (55 per cent) indicated that they did not feel any particular resistance to doing more household chores. Since a rather large minority of the fathers did in fact feel this resistance, it would be interesting to look into their motives. Moreover, the issue is very important because many studies show that a change in role patterns between women and men stops or slows down here. A problem seems to be that many women and men do not feel appreciated enough for this kind of work. Therefore the respondents were asked to indicate whether they felt they got enough appreciation from their partner for their activities with the children and in their household activities. In addition to this they were asked the same question about their partner. The results indicate that more appreciation is felt for activities with the children than for household activities. In the perception of the men, moreover, their partners experience less appreciation than they themselves do – in particular with respect to household tasks. The more resistance to household activities a man has, the less his partner feels appreciated for her own household activities. The resistance that men have towards work in the household is to be found along three lines:

1. Their initial idea that it is women's work.

    'Cleaning the windows: everybody can see it!' (91)

    'Initially one finds it feminine to use the vacuum cleaner or to make the beds ...'(88)

2. The way they themselves have been brought up, and, as a consequence, not seeing what should be done.

    'I do not see what has to be done; I never learnt to look at household chores, so I do not see them.' (158)

3. Finding it less important.

    'In contrast to taking care of the children, household tasks are rather tiresome ....' (19)

How did the fathers deal with their resistance to household work? Many men spontaneously mentioned the role of their partner. Often they discussed the issue with her, negotiated, and at times quarrelled. Some men complied, or partially complied with the wishes of their partner after confrontations. Most of the men stressed that they thought it to be no more than fair *vis-à-vis* their partner to take their share in the household chores. 'Oh well, it grows. One sees the necessity. One also sees that it is fair in relation to one's partner.' (68) Most of the men stress that it simply has to be done: 'pull yourself together', 'get it over and done with', 'bite the bullet' is the drift of their argument. A number of the fathers indicate that they are very pleased with the cleaning lady they have hired in to do some of the chores. Forty-one per cent of them have a cleaning lady. It was striking that only one or two of the fathers (who experienced resistance) tried to see the value of working in the household. We shall quote one of the exceptions:

> 'In itself household tasks do not really make a nice activity, but I see them as part of the choice of wanting to be a "caring father". So I tried to make something nice of it anyhow, I developed my own style.' (167)

VARIABLES ASSOCIATED WITH PATERNAL INVOLVEMENT

I will now attempt to discover which variables are associated with different amounts of caregiving *within* this group of fathers. The research team expected to find significant results in the following areas: the present social context of the fathers, their value orientation and their family of origin. In the quantitative element of the research a number of correlations were established between these variables and hours of caring.

- A number of measures relate rather directly to the work situation. Caring for more hours is significantly associated with less often being employed, working fewer hours per week (in paid labour), earning less per week, and having a lower family income. In addition, we find a negative correlation between caring more hours and being the main breadwinner.
- More care by fathers is also significantly and negatively related to paid help in the household. A number of measures that might have been expected to differ significantly, did not, in fact: they were the occupational level, and, importantly, the father's income per hour.
- Most fathers did meet obstacles in their attempts to realize an involved fatherhood. In this respect there was no relation between the amount of obstacles and the number of caring hours. Nor was this the case with the flexibility in their working hours. If we look at their family situation all fathers seem to form a homogeneous group. Their age is about the same (38.2), the mean number of children is almost two, and the mean age of their (eldest) children does not differ significantly. Being married or cohabiting did not make a difference. There is a difference in the number

of tasks that fathers perform in the household. Fathers who care more hours perform more tasks.

- When we turn to the partners of these fathers we find a number of significant differences. More caring hours by father is associated with more hours in paid labour by mother. In addition more, care by fathers is negatively related to caring hours by mothers. Further, more caring hours by fathers are related to high priority of work for mothers, and with her having less flexibility in her working hours. No differences were found in her educational level, occupational level, income per hour, employment by the government, nor in her political views or religious conviction. It should be kept in mind, however, that this group of women is homogeneously highly educated, politicially left-wing and not very religious.

- In considering the value orientation of the men, their internalized norms and their opinions, the men were questioned about their political views, religious convictions, and views on paid labour and care work. The significant differences we found had to do with feeling responsible for the income *versus* feeling responsible for the domain inside the home. More hours of care are associated with feeling less responsible for the income situation and more responsible for the domain inside the home. There was another significant finding: more hours of care are associated with opting for being a full-time househusband rather than opting for full-time paid employment. A number of measures did not make a significant difference. Whether the man or the woman first started to talk about wanting to have children did not make a difference neither did the political views or religious conviction of the men.

- Finally, one of the relevant questions seems to be: are these men imitating their own (caring) father or are they compensating for a lack of involvement on behalf of their own father? The great majority of caring fathers do not see their own father as a positive model. Fewer than 7 per cent of the 182 men who participated in this study state that they were inspired by their own father. However, men inspired by their father do care more hours: 18.32 hours per week (compared with 13.72). And we find a positive correlation between father's caring hours and his having had an inspiring father.

There are, perhaps, a number of different paths that lead to caring fatherhood: the father having had a caring father himself, which, in recent decades, has not often been the case, could lead to identification with him and a continuation of the caring attitude. This can be seen in a minority of cases (7 per cent). If there had not been an inspiring father, however, sons may have found other ways of becoming a caring father. One hypothesis is that the presence of younger siblings could possibly place an elder child in the position where it can learn to care. A second hypothesis would be that the presence of an older brother would give the opportunity to identify with him. If fathers are mainly absent maybe elder brothers can take their place. This could help the younger boy to develop a stable masculinity, which in its turn could prevent fear of 'female' work (Chodorow, 1978). And thirdly, possibly an elder sister could play a role in 'coaching' her younger brother in caring work (almost all the men come from traditional families). On the basis of the available material we have had to reject these three hypotheses, except for the last one: more caring hours by a fathers is positively related to the presence of an elder sister.

CONCLUDING REMARKS

We have studied a group of fathers who can be defined as 'caring fathers'. They take more time for their children and for household chores than is usually the case in the Netherlands. In particular, the gains of being a caring father, the role of the partner, problems at work and ideas about career and domestic tasks have been discussed.

The obstacle mentioned most is the work(ing) environment. Almost all problems in this area had to do with organizing part-time work, flexible working hours or parental leave, and with the resistance of employers, superiors and – less often – colleagues against this. The importance of flexibility in working hours was also demonstrated in an Australian study (Russell, 1987). Arrangements for taking leave were shown to be relevant in a Swedish study (Lamb *et al.*, 1982b).

Apart from this, the value orientation of the men themselves appears to play a role. They mention their own resistance against household chores, for instance. Some men in addition have a hard time in combining their ideas about caring with their ideas about a career. Other researchers have linked up these views, attitudes and opinions with the socialization history of respondents: what norms are internalized during the life-course? Factors such as political views and religious attitude can all make a difference. Special focus is usually on gender role beliefs. Modest support is generally found for a relationship between egalitarian gender role beliefs and the amount of care work by men (Baruch and Barnett, 1981; Lamb *et al.*, 1982b; Feldman *et al.*, 1983; Barnett and Baruch, 1987).

In this study partners appear to be very influential. This may have to do with the fact that their involvement in paid labour is very similar to that of the caring fathers: a high level of participation, and a substantial part-time job. In addition, women appear to earn approximately the same per hour as their male partners. It should be noted that this makes the partners an exceptional and very interesting group. The picture arises of a group of powerful women: they know what they want and they go for it. In a number of studies the level of power/relative resources of the female partner is the most important predictor of care work by husbands (Ericksen *et al.*, 1979; Huber and Spitze, 1983; Russell, 1986; Starrels, 1994). In fact in almost all the countries studied so far, the role of the female partner seems to be very relevant. We can see this in the United States (Radin, 1982; Pruett, 1983), in Sweden (Lamb *et al.*, 1982) and in Australia (Russell, 1987). This leads Norma Radin to the conclusion that mother's desire for a career is an important factor 'propelling' families into paternal child-rearing arrangements (Radin, 1982).

Further, the family of origin of the men has been discussed. According to some theories, caring men imitate their own father with whom they have been able to identify in a personal way, because he was an available and positive model. Based on Chodorow's theory (1978), predictions about the backgrounds of caring fathers would appear to be obvious. One would expect that their own father (the grandfather) had been at home a great deal; that he had been a close and positive identification model, and for this reason his son had been able to identify with him in a very personal way. This would lead, in turn, to a stable gender identity and to the development of caring qualities. However, fewer than 7 per cent of the 182 men who participated in this study, report that they have been inspired by their own father (though these few men do care more hours per week). Other researchers seem to have come to the same conclusion. In most studies (Grønseth, 1975; Finkelstein and Rosenthal, 1978; De Frain, 1979; Eiduson *et al.*, 1982; Pruett, 1983; Radin and Goldsmith, 1985; Barnett and Baruch, 1987), the active and involved fathers have had to miss their own father, either because there was no (longer) a father present, or because he was hardly ever at home. Consequently, these fathers did not have happy memories of their own fathers. There were only a very few studies that could confirm the predictions based on the imitation-theory: Manion (1977) and Sagi (1982). This has led some researchers to replace the imitation hypothesis by a compensation theory. Most research attention has gone to the relationship that fathers had with their own father and mother. The role of siblings is not often discussed. Yet caring fathers may have learnt to do so by interacting with younger brothers and sisters. Or, alternatively, they may have been taught to care by their elder siblings.

We attempted to discover which factors were associated with different amounts of caregiving within the group of fathers. It was presumed that both the present social context of the fathers, their value orientation and their family of origin would be associated with the number of hours they cared per week. This could be confirmed by quantitative data. Significant correlations were found with

- whether the father was employed, the number of hours spent in paid labour;
- his feeling responsible for the income *versus* the household, his preference for paid labour *versus* caring; and
- his having grown up with an elder sister.

This last finding was surprising. The influence of sibling relations has scarcely been studied in relation to caring fathers. In addition, the relation between the number of caring hours per week and a father having been inspired by his own father almost reached significance.

Finally, both in the quantitative and the qualitative datasets the partner appeared to be very important. The number of 'male caring hours' was significantly (and positively) related to her finding her own work important, spending (more) time in paid labour, and spending less time caring. This finding is a recurrent theme in studies on caring fathers. However, we should keep in mind: 'Mothers may leave the gate open, but fathers have to wish to walk through it for shared caregiving to ensue' (Radin, 1994: 44).

REFERENCES

Barnett, R. and Baruch, G. (1987) 'Determinants of Fathers' Participation in Family Work'. *Journal of Marriage and the Family*, 49, 29–40.

Baruch, G. and Barnett, R. (1981) 'Fathers' Participation in the Care of their Pre-school Children'. *Sex Roles*, 7, 1043–55.

Baruch, G. and Barnett, R. (1986) 'Fathers' Participation in Family Work and Childrens' Sex-role Attitudes'. *Child Development*, 57, 1210–23.

Chodorow, N. (1978) *The Reproduction of Mothering: Psychoanalysis and the Sociology of Gender*. Berkeley: University of California Press.

Duindam, V. (1991) *Ouderschapsarrangement en geslachtsidentiteit* [Parenting Arrangements and Gender Identity]. Utrecht: Lemma.

Duindam, V. (1993) 'The Concept of "Socialisation": Criticisms and Alternatives' in M. de Ras and M. Lunenberg (eds) *Girls, Girlhood and Girls' Studies in Transition*. Amsterdam: Het Spinhuis, 25–37.

Duindam, V. (1995) 'Mothering and Fathering: Socialisation Theory – and Beyond'. *Nordic Journal of Women's Studies*, 2, 1–14.

Duindam, V. and Spruijt, E. (1997) 'Caring Fathers in the Netherlands'. *Sex Roles*, 36, 3/4, 147–68.

Eiduson, B., Kornfein, M., Zimmerman, I. and Weisner, T. (1982) 'Comparative Socialization Practices in Traditional and Alternative Families' in M.E. Lamb (ed.) *Nontraditional Families: Parenting and Child Development*. Hillsdale, N.J.: Lawrence Erlbaum.

Ericksen, J., Yancey, W. and Ericksen, E. (1979) 'The Division of Family Roles'. *Journal of Marriage and the Family*, 41, 301–13.

Feldman, S., Churnin Nash, S. and Aschenbrenner, B. (1983) 'Antecedents of Fathering'. *Child Development*, 54, 1628–36.

Finkelstein Keshet, H. and Rosenthal, K.M. (1978) 'Fathering after Marital Separation'. *Social Work*, 23, 11–18.

Frain, J. de (1979) 'Androgynous Parents Tell Who They Are and What They Need'. *The Family Coordinator*, 28, 237–43.

Grønseth, E. (1975) 'Work-sharing Families: Adaptations of Pioneering Families with Husband and Wife in Part-time Employment'. *Acta Sociologica*, 18, 202–21.

Hochschild, A. (1989) *The Second Shift: Working Parents and the Revolution at Home*. New York: Viking Penguin.

Huber, J. and Spitze, G. (1983) *Sex Stratification: Children, Housework and Jobs*. New York: Academic Press.

Lamb, M.E., Frodi, A.M., Hwang, C.-P., Frodi, M. and Steinberg, J. (1982a) 'Effect of Gender and Caretaking Role on Parent–Infant Interaction' in R. Emde and R. Harmon (eds) *Attachment and Affiliative Systems: Neurobiological and Psychobiological Aspects*. New York: Plenum.

Lamb M.E., Frodi, A.M., Hwang, C.-P. and Frodi, M. (1982b) 'Varying Degrees of Paternal Involvement in Infant Care: Attitudinal and Behavioral Correlates' in M.E. Lamb (ed.) *Nontraditional Families: Parenting and Child Development*. Hillsdale, N.J.: Lawrence Erlbaum.

Manion, J. (1977) 'A Study of Fathers and Infant Caretaking'. *Birth and the Family Journal*, 4, 174–79.

Morgan, D. (1992) *Discovering Men*. London: Routledge.

Pruett, K.D. (1983) 'Infants of Primary Nurturing Fathers'. *The Psychoanalitic Study of the Child*, 38, 257–81.

Radin, N. (1981) 'Childrearing Fathers in Intact Families: Some Antecedents and Consequences'. *Merrill-Palmer Quarterly*, 27, 4, 489–514.

Radin, N. (1982) 'Primary Caregiving and Role-Sharing Fathers' in M.E. Lamb (ed.) *Nontraditional Families: Parenting and Child Development*. Hillsdale, N.J.: Lawrence Erlbaum.

Radin, N. (1994) 'Primary-Caregiving Fathers in Intact Families' in A.E. Gottfried and A.W. Gottfried (eds) *Redefining Families: Implications for Children's Development*. New York: Plenum Press.

Radin, N. and Goldsmith, R. (1985) 'Caregiving Fathers of Preschoolers: Four Years Later'. *Merrill-Palmer Quarterly*, 31, 375–83.

Russell, G. (1986) 'Primary Caretaking and Role-sharing Fathers' in M.E. Lamb (ed.) *The Father's Role: Applied Perspectives*. New York: Wiley.

Russell, G. (1987) 'Fatherhood in Australia' in M.E. Lamb (ed.) *The Father's Role: Cross-Cultural Perspectives*. Hillsdale N.J.: Erlbaum.

Sagi, A. (1982) 'Antecedents and Consequences of Various Degrees of Paternal Involvement in Child Rearing: The Israeli Project' in M.E. Lamb (ed.) *Nontraditional Families: Parenting and Child Development.* Hillsdale, N.J.: Lawrence Erlbaum.

Segal, L. (1990) *Slow Motion: Changing Masculinities, Changing Men.* London, Virago.

Starrels, M. (1994) 'Husbands' Involvement in Female Gender-Typed Household Chores'. *Sex Roles,* 31, 473–91.

4 Gender Roles and Food in Families

Susan Gregory

INTRODUCTION

This chapter examines the ways in which gendered roles and responsibilities are understood and negotiated within the family setting with specific reference to the production and consumption of food and meals. It is based upon a study which examined the effect on the family of one member's change in diet, and focused upon specific kinds of change in diet: a slimming diet, becoming a vegetarian or being advised to change diet as part of treatment for a medically diagnosed condition.

Research by social anthropologists has alerted us to the way that, in many different kinds of societies, ritual events are often marked and confirmed through the consumption of food (Douglas, 1984; Fieldhouse, 1986). Levi-Strauss (1966) saw food preparation as an 'indicator of civilisation'. As many theorists, particularly feminist theorists, have drawn the home and the family into the centre stage of enquiry into social life, those activities that tend to take place within the household have begun to be examined in detail. After childcare and parenting, the provision of food and the organization of meals are a pivotal feature of home life.

The significance of diet, food and eating for the organization of social life has long been recognized by many other disciplines within the social sciences, and most recently by sociologists (Delphy, 1979; Murcott, 1983; Mennell, 1985; Charles and Kerr, 1988; DeVault, 1991; Mennell *et al.*, 1992; and many others). The location of the family as a crucible for the formation and reinforcement of social values has also been recognized across cultures and generations (Backett, 1982; Blaxter and Paterson, 1982; Fieldhouse, 1986), as has the role of meals and eating in families (Delphy, 1979; Blaxter and Paterson, 1982; Charles and Kerr, 1986).

Lifestyle factors, such as diet and eating habits, have, in the West, been pinpointed as strategic to individual health, and form a major component of health policy recommendations, certainly in the UK (see for example the *Health of the Nation* discussion document 1993). The behaviour changes frequently recommended in these documents, although targeted at the individual, are most likely to be seen to be the responsibility of those most closely associated with the organization and preparation of food and meals (Wilson, 1989). As many studies have shown, this is usually a woman and usually 'the wife or mother' (Murcott, 1983; Charles and Kerr, 1988; DeVault, 1991; Mennell *et al.*, 1992).

FOOD, FAMILIES AND GENDERED RESPONSIBILITIES

The way in which women feel and respond to the pressure of these kinds of messages is complex and not at all straightforward. Murcott has reported on women who, despite family pressures and restrictions over what they cook and who for, assert that 'it is a pleasure to cook for him' (Murcott, 1983: 89). Charles and Kerr (1988) have described an understanding from women respondents of what a 'proper' meal should consist – cooked meat with two vegetables – learned through trial and error of what family members are prepared to tolerate. DeVault (1991) draws attention to the multiple aims that 'feeding the family' might have for a wife and mother. She suggests that to engage in domestic tasks can be seen as a woman not only fulfilling a female role, but also actively endorsing, on a day-to-day basis, her gender identity.

The setting for these activities, the family, is often portrayed as the safe and appropriate place for love, caring and parenting, but also containing appropriate roles for its members (Barrett and McIntosh, 1982). This is embodied in an ideology which Bernardes (1987) suggests, whilst identifying the family as a social group, clearly sets out the roles of 'mother', 'father', 'child', 'wife', husband', and the appropriate social behaviour to be displayed within those roles. These beliefs provide a simple but idealistic notion of what the family 'should' be, and disguises the complex and dynamic realities of social life (Bernardes, 1985). It is also the case that notions of gender and understandings of how to define and understand family life are inextricably linked (Morgan, 1996).

Food and eating practices provide a significant pivot upon which many assumptions about family life balance and are made real. The family and the roles assumed by its members are demonstrated and reinforced through day-to-day activities. Within the private world of the family, it is in what women do, and to an extent in what men do not do, that these gender roles are evident (Graham, 1985; West and Zimmerman, 1991; DeVault, 1991).

The activity which takes place most significantly, although not exclusively, within the family and which to a large part defines the setting and prescribes the roles, is that of caring (Graham, 1983; Ungerson, 1983; Leonard and Speakman, 1986). Caring in its various forms could be said to have two aims: to complete a necessary and practical activity, whether cooking a meal for the family or bathing an elderly relative, but also to establish and endorse gender and other roles. The popular conflation of the product of the female reproductive system (pregnancy and childbirth) with the activities assigned to the home (domestic work and childcare) place the responsibility for 'caring' firmly in the hands of women.

The interrelationship between gender and the family is embodied in the responsibilities undertaken by women through domestic and childcaring tasks. The responsibility for domestic tasks has been well documented (for example Oakley, 1985; Morris, 1992) and many have made the point that responsibility for household tasks does not imply control over its form or content (Charles and Kerr, 1988). The provision of meals may be seen as a housewife's responsibility, but which food she cooks may not be what she would prefer (Charles and Kerr, 1986; 1988; McKie *et al.*, 1993) Also, whilst the way in which domestic tasks are both divided up and completed may have changed and become less clear cut, the responsibility for ensuring the tasks are undertaken, and to a particular standard, remains implicitly or explicitly, largely that of women.

Mason (1987) notes that notions of responsibility changed over time for couples in later life, but more in terms of how it was construed than what was actually done. In households where domestic labour had been divided on strictly traditional lines, men began, over time, to 'help' their wives with specific tasks. Thus a sense of continuity was maintained over where responsibilities lay, despite changes in activities. In this way women may not see themselves as restricted in opportunity or subservient to their partners and families, but specify practical reasons of convenience or expertise for choosing to undertake domestic tasks, or stress idealistic motives, such as love, pleasing others and guarding against selfishness, for wanting to care for the family (Barratt and McIntosh, 1982; DeVault, 1991).

Responsibility for food and meals bring together all of these factors: family life, gender roles, women's responsibility for the health and well-being of family members, at once satisfying notions of healthy eating, proper parenting, and 'doing gender' (West and Zimmerman, 1991). What will be eaten, how it will be prepared and who will do the preparing may be subject to negotiation between family members, and the potential for such negotiation may vary through the life cycle, but is rarely explicit or formally recognized (Charles and Kerr, 1988; DeVault, 1992).

Activities connected with food and meals not only reveal individual preferences and prejudices about the taste and type of food product, but, more importantly, highlight the social processes which are frequently played out around the meal table, such as the socialization of children, the development of independence of young people and the reinforcement of gender roles.

THE FAMILY AND DIETARY CHANGE

The Study Design and Participants

The study, which took place between April 1993 and September 1995, was designed in three stages: the first used unstructured focus groups, the second gathered data through semi-structured questionnaires and interviews, and the final stage sent out postal questionnaires. The first two stages used an open structure which encouraged participants to use their own words and ideas. The third stage was made up of questions informed by responses to the previous stages. Whilst the final stage results make no claim to be representative of the general population of family members in Britain, the study provides evidence to suggest that the first and second stage results were not idiosyncratic to a relatively small group of people in the south of England.

Participants in all stages were required to have had the experience of changing diet for a specific reason, or to have lived in a home where such a change had taken place. The second stage aimed to recruit more than one member of the family, one of whom was the person who had changed diet and one we have termed the 'home manager'. The term home manager is used to describe the person who has the primary responsibility for domestic tasks, especially those relating to food and eating. Ten focus groups were held with between three and eight participants in each. The members of 75 families were interviewed, and over one thousand people responded to the third stage questionnaire.

Most of the participants were heterosexual couples with and without dependent children living at home. Most in fact had had children, and of these some had young children, some school-aged children and others adult children. Some participants were newly married or living together, whilst others had been in long-term relationships. Their ages ranged from early twenties to over 60. Just a few were less conventional, such as adults returning to live with parents due to ill health.

For the purposes of this chapter, the results that are of particular interest are those that demonstrate the ways in which members of families organize and understand their shared and individual activities. Two themes emerged from the data which illustrate how family members, and particularly the female home manager, understood their roles within the context of their everyday lives. The first of these, gender roles and notions of the family, shows how the ways in which family members talk about and organize food-related activities indicate how they understand 'the family'. The second theme, the role of the home manager, as defined earlier, shows how central this role is to the organization of family activities and especially those related to food and eating. It was clear that, certainly within the families participating in this study, although it was not unusual for family members – husbands, partners and children – to join in with food-related tasks, this was rarely routine and regular. Despite changes in the domestic division of labour, within this study these domestic tasks remained the responsibility of women.

GENDER ROLES AND NOTIONS OF THE FAMILY

The focus of the study was the integration and management of a change in diet, rather than definitions of family as such. Nevertheless, activities connected with food and meals, and how they were experienced and explained, demonstrated ways in which participants understood the concept 'the family'. Morgan (1996: 182) has suggested that 'the home, both as an address and as a site for domesticity, is a key element in the construction of a self'. The participants of this study described activities which were conducted together as a family group, or on behalf of the family as a group. Through these activities they conveyed their understandings of 'the family' as a social entity, and as a way of identifying themselves as individuals and as part of a group. Although there were differences between the more 'conventional' families and those less so, all seemed to have ideas of what was usual or unusual in terms of the roles played by individual members. These ideas were conveyed through descriptions of how families were expected to operate and the way food and eating practices facilitated a sense of family. What was clear was that this sense of family was sustained by notions of gender. In presenting data all the names have been changed to pseudonyms.

Gendered Organization

Data from this study demonstrates the ways the families divided up tasks around food and eating on gendered lines, with one member of the family, usually the wife or mother, primarily responsible for the production and consumption of meals. It was most likely that she undertook virtually all of the tasks, accompanied or assisted occasionally, but not routinely, by

another family member. It should be stressed that there was little evidence
that this division of labour was arrived at through formal discussion and
agreement, and most people, when asked how meal and food related activities were organized, tended to explain arrangements in practical terms:

> Int: ... you don't share, cook together?
> Wife: Not cook together, but more so now that I'm working Sundays,
> P... might come into the kitchen and say can I do something, but it
> doesn't happen very often because he's usually a lot later than I am.
> (Townsend. Couple, both employed, 3 teenage children, wife: coeliac)

> Wife: Well I find it works [shopping alone]. The main reason is the
> nature of my work. I work part-time, so I could go to the shops every
> day, but I chose to go twice a week because I like fresh food in... But
> also it is a method of controlling the family budget.
> (Holtby. Couple, both employed, 2 teenage children, wife: slimmer)

However, some participants were aware of how practicalities could indicate or challenge gender stereotypes. Mrs Trollop, a slimmer in her early
fifties without children, said: 'When we were first married it was the
woman's job to do that and it's been the same ever since'. Mrs Dumas,
who was in her late fifties and severely disabled with multiple sclerosis,
commented that 'I used to do the cooking, like every wife does, now it's
all down to G... [her carer husband]'. In contrast, Mrs Carter, in her late
thirties, employed with two young children, noted that her husband 'would
love to do more shopping, I know that's unusual in a husband, but if I send
him he'll come home with all sorts of things that won't make up a meal.'
Many of the women saw shopping and cooking as their domain,
whether they liked it or not:

> Wife: That's right, yes. He wouldn't enjoy doing everyday cooking any-
> way, ... I don't think. I don't either but I have to.
> (Carter. Couple 36/50, both employed, 2 young children,
> wife: slimmer)

> Wife: That's right, all they have to do is walk in and it's there. He rings
> me when he leaves work and it's on the table when he walks in. Isn't
> that wonderful?
> (Dickens. Couple 49/49, both employed, no children at home,
> wife: slimmer)

Mrs Bronte, who had a husband (with MS) and son both in full-time
employment was quite clear. 'It's my job... An old fashioned custom, but
that's the way it is.' However, it was not unusual for husbands to see this

'duty' as a pleasure that their wives enjoyed. For example, Mr Poe (a coeliac) said of his wife, who was also in full-time employment, 'But P. always liked cooking anyway. I could see that with some women I would have been a problem.'

Thus even where these kinds of domestic tasks were shared or roles were reversed, the arrangement was frequently seen *in relation* to a norm which saw women as the appropriate person to take responsibility.

Eating Together

Charles and Kerr (1988: 17) have reported on the place of food in family occasions whether celebratory or everyday, and have argued that 'food practices help to maintain and reinforce a coherent ideology of the family throughout the social structure'. Mennell *et al.* (1992: 115) have noted that eating together and sharing food – commensality – has been seen as an activity which 'among a group ... defines and reaffirms insiders as socially similar', in a range of social settings. The belief that eating together as a group was an ideal that a family should aspire to wherever possible was mentioned or implied by many of the participants of this study, despite work and school pressures.

> Wife: Right, breakfast is a bit hit and miss at the moment, we just select it on the hop really, getting ready for school and work. Lunch is shared with members of the family who are here, we'll sit down to table and eat. My daughter has a lunch box at school. Evening meals we all wait for each other to sit round the table, because we feel it's really important for families to share meals together and we make a special event of it. Usually breakfasts at weekend we share, Saturdays and Sundays and lunches and dinners, we all share them.
>
> (Edwards. Couple 30s/40s, husband: employed, wife: housewife, 2 young children. Family: vegetarian)

Participants commented on its presence:

> 'It's a social thing, it's a practical thing, a shape to the day and you finish by half past six.'
>
> (Sachs. Couple late 40s, both employed, 2 teenage children, husband coeliac)

> 'I think it's very important part of family life. I think sharing food is a wonderful pastime and it's conversation.'
>
> (Archer. Couple 50s/60s, husband semi-retired, wife part-time employed/ME)

They also commented upon its absence: a woman talking about a period in her life when she was a single parent said

> 'I tend to feel that there is something missing there for the boys and me really, the fact that we didn't eat as a family unit all the time.'
>
> (Binchy, couple 48/52, both employed, 2 independent children living at home, female partner: ME)

Mrs Archer felt that 'I think it's sad that people don't do it.'

Thus eating together was seen as an opportunity to communicate and share the day with the rest of the family, and reinforce the family group and each member's place in it. In the family where a daughter (in her mid-thirties) suffering from ME had returned to her parents' home due to her ill-health a flexible arrangement allowed the daughter to join her parents for shopping and cooking when she did not feel up to catering for herself, but to make her own arrangements when she could. Nevertheless, her mother saw this in relation to her daughter's status as an adult who was no longer required to routinely conform to family mealtimes:

> 'Oh, yes, yes. I mean S's an adult, so she makes her own mind up what she eats and things like that. If she was a child it would be different.'
>
> (Byatt. Couple, early 60s, father retired, mother part-time employed, daughter 36: ME)

THE ROLE OF THE HOME MANAGER

The role of the home manager, and the ways in which this role was acted out by members of these families seemed strategic to how the participants conceptualized their families. The role of the home manager was implicitly seen as female, particularly in the more conventional families, despite a few instances of role reversal. Again, much of what the home manager undertook was expressed in terms of practicalities, but incorporated an underlying expectation of caring and responsibility for others in the family.

Organizing Family Tasks

In just one family the husband, who worked part time on a self-employed project, was totally responsible for all tasks connected with food and eating, including the often invisible task of provisioning. His domain was the kitchen and he was concerned about ensuring a healthy balanced diet for the family, expressed concern over junk food, or food being wasted, and even complained, mildly, that his food management and culinary efforts were rarely noticed by the family.

This exception suggests that the role of the home manager brings with it feelings of responsibility which transcend gender. Nevertheless, the study shows that this example is the exception rather than the rule. It was the lived experience of the family, and particularly the home manager, that provided indicators of how the family and its members' roles were understood. Domestic tasks tended to be conducted by women, and at the very least co-ordinated and buttressed by them.

Most female home managers shopped alone or with young children, or, if accompanied by an adult member of the family, this was not regular or routine. Cooking also tended to fit around the work needs of the male partner. Again, the notion of practicality frequently formed the basis for explanations for the arrangement:

Wife: In the beginning, when we first met he felt guilty about not helping me do the shopping because when he was on his own he felt it was something that was shared. He felt he shouldn't let me do it all on my own, but then I said, well, sometimes I can get round quicker on my own, I feel.

> (Binchy. Couple living together 48/52, both employed, two independent children living at home, female partner: ME)

Wife: Pretty much me without exception. We sound like a very stereotyped family don't we?... One, because he's usually at work and as I say he does work some pretty ridiculous hours, and he can cook, he is not particularly brilliant but a lot of it is a lack of practice. He certainly doesn't have a problem with doing the cooking, but he is also very slow.

> (Bolton. Couple 32/31, husband employed, 3-month baby, both vegetarian)

Nevertheless, some families could be flexible and some participants reported circumstances where meal preparation was undertaken by other family members. This was not, however, often a routine arrangement and seemed to rest upon the personal preference of the family member who was taking over the task.

Wife: The day I work..., so it tends to be my husband, purely because he does enjoy cooking, and because the children are so time consuming, baths, bedtime, things like that. That seems to be my role. And he's preparing the meal.

> (Wolff. Couple 32/31, both employed, wife: part-time, 2 young children, husband: MS)

Wife: If we go at weekends, he always comes with me, but during the week then, obviously, he's at work and, only because he's one of these unusual men that likes shopping. There are a lot of men who don't like shopping. They will do anything to get out of shopping.

> (Dickens. Couple 49/49, both employed,
> no children at home, wife: slimmer)

There were just a few families who divided food-related tasks on clear gender lines with husbands who, where food was concerned, did not venture into the kitchen.

Wife: He makes a mean boiled egg!! When I used to have breakfast at the weekend he would, rather than cereal or toast I might have a boiled egg and toast, that is before I dieted, and he used to do that. Breakfast is the only thing though, boiling eggs.

> (Dickens. Couple 49/49, both employed,
> no children at home, wife: slimmer)

Husband: No, not for me, I don't get involved in those things [shopping], so I wouldn't know.
Wife: I told you, only since he's been at home and I've been out, he's learned how to boil water, and I'm not kidding when I say that at all.

> (Travern, Couple 59/60, husband retired, wife part-time
> employed, no children at home, husband: diabetes)

Caring for the Family's Health

Many home managers, when talking about changing diet, whilst frequently expressing their views in practical terms, demonstrated a strong sense of responsibility for the health and well-being of the family. This was particularly the case where the female home manager was totally responsible for food and meals. A number of women participants who were recruited through a series of slimming clubs had, as a part of their weekly meetings, been given information and advice about the nutritional value of foodstuff, and the value of preparing food in a 'healthy' way (that is, how it could be cooked and served). This information was frequently seen as something that should be used for the benefit of the whole family. As one wife and mother of two teenage children said:

> 'I felt that apart from me eating better it was doing a favour for the family because I gave them what I eat.'

> (Holtby. Couple, both employed, 2 teenage children,
> wife: slimmer)

Others realized the mutual benefit the slimming diet had for both them-selves and their families:

> Wife: I suppose because I am now more aware than I ever was before about the content and the calories of the week's meals that the children, the family must benefit as well. As I say, I've never eaten much junk food, but I must admit that they have, because they like their chips, but I'm very conscious now of what they have to eat. ... I may well like to slip back to my old ways but I think if I do it's not doing the children any good, so I have to keep on the straight and narrow ... They're going to go on and bring their own families up one day I assume.
>
> (Rhys. Couple 41/50, both employed, 2 teenage children, wife: slimmer)

> Wife: No initially I was wondering whether it was right for the children, but on the whole I'm sure that the change has benefited them as well ... My husband has lost nearly a stone and a half himself
> Int: Right, this is alongside your diet?
> Wife: Because I think, like most men in the house, they eat what they are given, well my husband does anyway, he's very easy going.
>
> (Dickens. Couple 49/49, both employed, no children at home, wife: slimmer)

The process of incorporating these new ideas about nutrition and healthy meals did not always meet with a positive response and a number of home managers mentioned the difficulties they faced:

> Wife: Yes, I think I tried to change their diet considerably as well. Tried to make it more healthy as I learned more about it. I tried to introduce them to more healthy eating. Well, they don't like eating food without meat and they tend to like a fair amount of meat.
> Int: Have you talked to them about it?
> Wife: Oh yes, till they shut off, now I think they are bored to tears with it all.
>
> (Binchy. Couple living together 48/52, both employed, 2 independent children living at home, female partner: ME)

The attempts at introducing these ideas into the family meals, in order to benefit both themselves and their families varied in terms of the level to which family members were consulted. Many substituted what they saw as 'healthy' food – low fat; low calorie – into existing meals. Some tried this substitution without mentioning it to the family, to see whether they would just happily accept the change. Some discussed it with the family, and many mentioned, with some resignation, an awareness of the limited scope they had in making changes. This suggests that the responsibility for the health of their families was not always accompanied by a sense of control which might allow them to make arbitrary decisions about the content of family meals. Medical diets attracted very strong feelings of responsibility from home managers. Much of that responsibility was manifested in what they were prepared to do to ensure the dietary requirements are followed.

> Wife: Yes, and that really makes me cross, because I think, if I've put in an effort and try and do what's good for him, I think, well, the least he could do is just leave something out that's not really good for him. And that really irritates me … Also I get the feeling that all the good I've done in the week, it's gone in one evening.
>
> (Bronte. Couple 50s/60s, husband self-employed,
son employed, husband: ME)

> Wife: Yes I didn't want her to lose out on anything. I found it quite hard to begin with, but you soon get used to it.
>
> (Rushdie. Couple 49/50, 2 teenage children,
daughter: diabetes and vegetarian)

Watching and Waiting

It is the role of the home manager which plays a pivotal part in caring for the family. This is the person who tends to be at the forefront of negotiating changes and shifts in emphasis and perspective in terms of what members do or do not do. Certainly what seems clear is that notions of how the family is defined are ascertained and verified through roles and responsibilities which are understood rather than discussed. The 'watching and waiting' mentioned by Hilary Graham (1984) as fundamental to domestic activities are part of a process of negotiating continuity and change to which women are most attuned. For women this can often mean being aware of family members' needs and preferences and conducting a complicated balancing act made up of intuition and perseverance:

> Int: So, effectively, the person who made sure you stuck to your diet was your wife?
> Husband: Yes, I mean I can go out and eat something I shouldn't, but there's never anything on the table that she knows I shouldn't eat. …
> Wife: I have actually heard it said by the guy who diagnosed A …, who was an eminent gastroenterologist, he said that the person who comes off worst on a coeliac diet is a coeliac mother. If you have coeliac child

you would manage the diet for the family, it's a mother's instinct, I manage it because A …'s on it, but if you had to manage it for yourself, you sacrifice. Not sacrifice yourself, your concern for your own well being is that you will go without. You know, I've made a cake for my daughter, but not bothered for myself. You know, it's that stubborn mother thing.

> (Sachs. Couple late 40s, both employed, 2 teenage children,
> husband: coeliac)

Wife: My concern was the fact that I realised that we were eating so much fat. The whole family was eating too much fat … Well, I started to think about heart problems in men and I could see that my husband would be falling into that high risk category, so that concerned me.

> (Blyton. Couple mid 40s, husband employed, wife housewife,
> 2 teenage children, wife: slimmer)

In this study gender remains fundamental to roles and responsibilities within the family, and particularly to the role of the home manager. Although a number of the families were flexible over food-related tasks, the majority found the women doing the provisioning, the shopping, the cooking. Tasks associated with the role of home manager, especially those related to food, embodied notions of caring, love and affection, all of which tended to be seen as 'naturally' the domain of women, and realized through everyday lived activities. These activities, whilst practical, nevertheless embody the nature of the family and the gendered meanings that activities connected with food and meals can have for the participants.

CONCLUSIONS

The literature discussed in this chapter draws attention to the complex and dynamic nature of the family and the way that activities around food, diet and meals demonstrate social roles and identities. Whilst food may be essential for survival, it also plays a strategic part in the organization of family life and, as such, contributes to how people understand and act out their social roles. Notions of caring place women centrally within the family and the activities which take place within that setting. Whilst seen by some as a site for frustration and oppression, the family is seen by many women of all ages as safe, fulfilling and an appropriate place to function. I have suggested that it is in the day-to-day experience of living within the family that people attach meaning to their roles and responsibilities, and, by examining that setting, light is shed upon how this takes place.

The data presented here support much of the literature, in that the participants, both women and men, seemed to have clear ideas of the gendered nature of food related activities, whilst seeing this from a very practical perspective. So when a woman undertakes all or most of the shopping in her own time rather than family time, it is because it is convenient, because she works part time, or works near the shop, or her husband works long hours. When a man chooses to cook meals for the family on a regular basis, it is because he is a good cook or enjoys cooking, or his wife is disabled and unable to cook.

The two themes explored here as a vehicle for discovering how people understand their roles and responsibilities – gender roles and notions of the family, and the role of the home manager – locate women as central actors. When asked about how they organized food-related tasks, their practical terms revealed beliefs about what was expected of family members as wives and husbands, as men and women. There was some variation in the level to which the domestic tasks were shared, but the way in which that sharing was understood was gendered. Within that flexibility, many women mentioned how unusual it was for husbands to want to do or enjoy doing shopping or cooking, and many saw themselves as the person who undertook the tasks no one else wanted.

It was over meals that the notion of the family seemed to be most firmly manifested with many describing the value of meeting together over a meal to share the day's events. The introduction of a new diet – the central feature of this study – brought with it new ideas and demands which could generate uncertainty. The slimmer who produced family meals introduced new foods to the family, whilst monitoring the responses, and balancing both her own and her family's preferences with the amount of work that might generate.

The role of the home manager could be seen to be central to the negotiation of everyday activities such as shopping, cooking and meals. Attempts to influence the content of family meals and the monitoring of medical diets could be seen to be routine to their roles within the family. Thus not only was the production of family meals ultimately their responsibility, but this was part of caring for the health and well-being of all the family. The lived experience of providing food and meals for the family embodies social understandings of gender roles. Caring, as a gendered activity, is acted out, not only through the practical activity of shopping and cooking, but also in the way that women take responsibility for that caring role, and family members rarely question that gendered division of labour.

The introduction to this edited collection has drawn attention to the close association between 'gender' and 'the household', despite the multiple meanings that tend to be associated with these two concepts. This study has illustrated ways in which those meanings are negotiated and understood. David Morgan, in Chapter 2, describes an interactive process, with the household as a strategic site for shaping and 'doing' gender, and gender, in turn, shaping and forming households. Everyday activities related to food, meals and eating provide a setting within which that process operates. It was rare, in this study, to hear women complain of being oppressed by their family roles. Nevertheless there were powerful examples of both women and men fulfilling conventional gender roles which were seen as natural and inextricable.

REFERENCES

Backett, K. (1982) *Mothers and Fathers: a Study of the Development and Negotiation of Parental Behaviour.* London: Macmillan.

Barrett, M. and McIntosh, M. (1982) *The Anti-social Family.* London: Verso.

Bernardes, J. (1985) 'Family Ideology: Identification and Explanation'. *Sociological Review*, 33, 2, 275–97.

Bernardes, J. (1987) ' "Doing things with Words": Sociology and "Family Policy" Debates'. *Sociological Review*, 35, 4, 679–702.

Blaxter, M. and Paterson, E. (1982) *Mothers and Daughters: a Three Generational Study of Health Attitudes and Behaviour.* London: Heinemann Educational Books.

Charles, N. and Kerr, M. (1986) 'Issues of Responsibility and Control in the Feeding of Families' in S. Rodmell and A. Watt (eds) *The Politics of Health Education.* London: Routledge and Kegan Paul.

Charles, N. and Kerr, M. (1988) *Women, Food and Families.* Manchester: Manchester University Press.

Delphy, C. (1979) 'Sharing the Same Table: Consumption and the Family' in C. Harris (ed.) *The Sociology of the Family: New Directions for Britain.* Sociological Review Monograph 28. Keele: University of Keele.

DeVault, M.L. (1991) *Feeding the Family: the Social Organisation of Caring as Gendered Work.* Chicago: University of Chicago.

Douglas, M. (1984) *Food in the Social Order: Studies of Food and Festivities in Three American Communities.* London: Russell Sage.

Fieldhouse, P. (1986) *Food and Nutrition: Customs and Culture.* London: Chapman Hall.

Graham, H. (1979) 'Prevention and Health: Every Mother's Business: a Comment on Child Health Policy in the Seventies' in C. Harris (ed.) *The Sociology of the Family: New Directions for Britain.* Sociological Review Monograph 28. Keele: University of Keele.

Graham, H. (1983) 'Caring: a Labour of Love' in J. Finch and D. Groves (eds) *A Labour of Love: Women, Work and Caring.* London: Routledge and Kegan Paul.

Graham, H. (1984) *Women, Health and the Family.* London: Harvester Wheatsheaf.

Graham, H. (1985) 'Providers, Negotiators and Medicators: Women as Hidden Carers' in E. Lewin and V. Oleson (eds) *Women, Health and Healing: Towards a New Perspective*. London: Tavistock.

Health of the Nation (1993) Discussion Document. London: HMSO.

Leonard, D. and Speakman, M.A. (1986) 'Women in the Family: Companions or Caretakers?' in V. Beechey and E. Whitelegg (eds) *Women in Britain Today*. Buckingham: Open University Press.

Levi-Strauss, C. (1966) 'The Culinary Triangle'. *New Society*, 1, 66, 937–40.

McKie, L., Wood, R. and Gregory, S. (1993) 'Women Defining Health: Food, Diet and Body Image'. *Health Education Research: Theory and Practice*, 8, 1, 35–41.

Mason, J. (1987) 'A Bed of Roses? Women, Marriage and Inequality in Later Life' in P. Allatt, T. Keil, A. Bryman and B. Bytheway (eds) *Women and the Life Cycle: Transitions and Turning-Points*. London: Macmillan Press.

Mennell, S. (1985) *All Manners of Food: Eating and Taste in England and France from the Middle Ages to the Present*. Oxford: Basil Blackwell.

Mennell, S., Murcott, A. and van Oterloo, A. (1992) *The Sociology of Food: Eating, Diet and Culture*. London: Sage.

Morgan, D.J.H. (1996) *Family Connections*. London: Polity Press.

Morris, L. (1990) *The Workings of the Household*. London: Polity Press.

Murcott, A. (1983) ' "It's a pleasure to cook for him": Food, Mealtimes and Gender in some South Wales Households' in E. Gamarnikow, D. Morgan, J. Purvis and D. Taylorson (eds) *The Public and the Private*. London: Heinemann.

Oakley, A. (1985) *The Sociology of Housework*. London: Basil Blackwell. Second Edition.

Ungerson, C. (1983) 'Why do Women Care?' in J. Finch and D. Groves (eds) *A Labour of Love: Women, Work and Caring*. London: Routledge and Keagan Paul.

West, C. and Zimmerman, D.H. (1991) 'Doing Gender' in J. Lorber and S.A. Farrel (eds) *The Social Construction of Gender*. London: Sage.

Wilson, G. (1989) 'Family Food Systems, Preventive Health and Dietary Change: a Policy to Increase the Health Divide'. *Journal of Social Policy*, 18, 2, 167–85.

5 Using Gendered Discourses in Negotiations: Couples and the Onset of Disablement in Marriage

Julie Seymour

INTRODUCTION

Much of the recent social science literature on households has emphasized the way in which the distribution of resources and behaviours between individuals within those households is contested (Seymour, 1992a; Brannen and Wilson, 1987; Duck, 1983; Duck, 1986; Duncombe and Marsden, 1993). Many research perspectives no longer view household members simply as constituting a unit, but consider how people respond as discrete actors within that unit. From these perspectives, household activities and processes such as the division of domestic labour are examined as actions through which participants reveal the operation of power relations within the household (Berk, 1985; Mason, 1989; Seymour, 1992b). While numerous studies have focused on the operation of gender relations between heterosexual couples (but see Blumstein and Schwartz, 1983; Dunne, 1996 for a discussion of gay and lesbian households), other researchers have considered alternative forms of power relations, for example those based on age, and taken an inter-generational viewpoint (Morrow, 1996).

This research focus on power in households can appear to challenge ideologies of home life as a 'peaceful haven' (Allan and Crow, 1989: 8) for those who share living space. To view household members, particularly those in intimate relationships, in terms of the operation of power relations may seem to be at odds with popular conceptions of marriage, yet, as Clark (1991: 165) has commented,

> husbands and wives, beneath a veneer of 'coupleness', are often not so much partners in a joint enterprise, as competitors in a handicap race, rivalling each other for the prize of access to a variety of scarce resources: domestic servicing, material support, care, nurturing and affection.

Researchers who focus on issues of power such as Foucault (1980) consider it to be an integral aspect of *all* social relationships whether they are intimate or more distant and hence, it will be evident between household members. In addition, Foucault argued that power in relationships could best be revealed by adopting a micro-perspective which examined individuals' behaviours and this emphasis on the everyday interaction of individuals has strengthened the case for the application of this level of analysis to the domestic unit. Drawing on this approach, household researchers have attempted to examine the day-to-day reality of intimate relationships and, researchers of marital behaviour have gone on to compare this with the ideology of companionate marriage.

The aim of this chapter is to examine this construction of marital partners as 'competitors' by focusing on a study of the way in which couples responded to one particular life event; the onset of disablement of one member through sudden injury or chronic illness (Seymour, 1994). One key aspect of the study was to consider the coping strategies (that is the behaviours and attitudes) adopted by individuals in response to this event and to examine how the strategy of one member of the couple compared with that adopted by their spouse/cohabiter. In some couples, the adoption of differing coping strategies led to situations of potential conflict which had to be resolved. In this chapter, I will look at the manner in which these couples negotiated with each other to address this potential conflict and how some individuals were able to achieve the continuation of their preferred coping strategy despite opposition from their husband/wife/ cohabiter. In the context of these specific negotiations around disablement, the operation of power relations becomes transparent and in particular the 'bargaining tools', which individuals employed in order to achieve their desired outcome. This study therefore acts as a heuristic device or window on the issue of power and its negotiation by intimate couples.

RESEARCHING NEGOTIATIONS AS A SITE OF
THE OPERATION OF POWER

Marital negotiations are clearly a site in which power is exercised and, for researchers, allow the consideration of the variety of dimensions of power. For such research, an approach which draws on the work of Foucault (1980) provides several appropriate conceptual tools with which to work. First, as previously mentioned, the relational approach to power and the related micro-perspective justifies the examination of household processes and intimate relations from the standpoint of each of the individuals involved. Secondly, by adopting a dynamic processual view of the exercise of power, that is as something people actively employ rather than simply possess, the potential to exercise power is perceived as available to both members of a partnership rather than belonging solely to one member owing to hierarchical status categories such as, in this study, male/female or disabled person/carer. As a result, each member in the relationship is portrayed as an active agent within the household. It is important to note at this point that Foucault's work has been strongly criticized, particularly by feminist writers, for neglecting the structural inequalities which underlie gendered and other social relations. Writers such as Braidotti (1986) and Davis *et al.* (1991) consider he overemphasized the role of individuals as agents and did not pay enough attention to the influence of enduring social divisions such as gender and age on interactions between individuals. It is necessary to acknowledge the criticisms of these writers but also to recognize that Foucault's emphasis on agency allows power to be viewed in a more fluid manner than would be feasible if social structures of dominance such as gender were used in a fixed and non-negotiable manner. Finally, and most importantly for the purposes of this study, Foucault's emphasis on the way in which power is exercised through the use of discursive practices (ways of talking and thinking about topics) allows a consideration of the manner in which individuals may draw on particular discourses to advance their position in negotiations. Again this perspective allows a fluid interpretation of the concept of power because dominant or prevailing discourses are not viewed as static arguments which predict the outcomes of household activities at all times; for example, in relation to gender, by providing a crude hierarchical justification which would allow the male member of a partnership to say 'I should be able to carry out my preferred behaviour simply because I am the man.' Instead, such discourses are actively employed when their utility is revealed to the individuals who can draw on them to advance their personal case (Sarup, 1993: 74). This perspective implies a focus on agency by allowing for the creative use of power by particular individuals in specific locations. However, the discourses which may be drawn on include socially constructed ones which operate at a broader level than that of discrete households, emphasizing the continued presence of structural constraints.

By recognizing the structured inequality of the dominant discourses but also the ways in which, as individual agents, both men and women can utilize them, researchers of the household are attempting to examine the empirical value of Gidden's (1984) theory of structuration regarding the relationship between structure and agency. This investigation is proving particularly fruitful in studies which focus on the process of negotiation between individuals where, as suggested above, the interplay between structure and agency become particularly evident. With regard to their own research on family caring responsibilities, Finch and Mason (1993: 173), consider that investigating negotiations between household members allows a (rare) 'empirical example of the processes through which structure and agency relate'. Thus while providing specific findings about social interaction within and between households, researchers in this area are also scrutinizing the relationship between empirical study and developing social theory.

Stages of the Negotiation Process

Before discussing the specifics of the negotiations between the couples in the study, it will be useful first to itemize the component parts which make up the negotiating process. One dictionary definition of the act of negotiation is 'to treat (that is discuss, deal with, arrange terms) with another in order to make a bargain, agreement or compromise' (Cassell's English Dictionary, 1982). Such a definition is useful because it highlights the discrete parts of the process of negotiation. First, there is a decision as to whether to become involved in some form of engagement with another party. Individuals may choose, or indeed may choose not, to become involved in explicit negotiations with others and will vary in the way in which they engage or interact with the relevant individual(s). For example, engagement could consist of a casual conversation, a formal meeting, a family gathering, mediation by third parties or written communication. Finch and Mason in their work on family negotiations (1993) stress that the form of negotiations is as important as the outcome. That is, we must look at procedure as well as substance.

Secondly, in this consideration of the stages of negotiation, there will be an outcome of the process, a resolution, although this may not be mutually satisfying to both parties. Finally, there is an implicit assumption that individuals will bring to the negotiating process, a range of bargaining tools, whether they be personal or social, with which to influence the negotiations. These bargaining tools include discursive practices but they can also involve material resources and personal attributes (Bradley, 1996). While welcoming the return to examinations of the material inequalities of gendered relations which Bradley and others (Davis *et al.*, 1991) have developed in their research on social resources in the household, the focus of this chapter is somewhat narrower and will consider only the extent to which gendered discourses are utilized as bargaining tools in negotiations between couples. Discourses of gender are clearly one form of asymmetrical structures from which individuals can draw but as this chapter will show they are often cross-cut with other aspects of the particular substantive area being investigated. This is entirely to be expected since, as Lyotard (1984) has suggested, individuals are best conceptualized as the nodes of a social network through which multiple discursive practices intersect and, as such, individuals may participate in many such practices simultaneously (Sarup, 1993: 156).

THE NEGOTIATION OF COPING STUDY

The data reported on in this chapter come from an ESRC-funded study of 'The Negotiation of Coping: Disablement, Caring and Marriage'. The study was small-scale, qualitative and longitudinal. The sample consisted of 16 heterosexual couples (14 married, two cohabiting) where one member had recently experienced the onset of disablement through injury or chronic illness. All such members had been treated within the same District Health Authority. The couples were interviewed three times within the period of a year. These interviews took place at approximately one month, six months and one year after discharge from hospital or the diagnosis of chronic illness. On each visit two researchers were involved so that both members of the couple could be interviewed, first together in a brief joint interview followed by a separate but simultaneous individual interview.

A small-scale study such as this cannot claim to represent the full range of experiences of couples where one member becomes disabled. Nor is it suggested here that the frequency with which various coping mechanisms were used by the couples interviewed are typical of others. The purpose of the study was rather to elucidate the processes of negotiation employed by couples and to analyse the kinds of resources that can be brought into play in these processes.

The study focused on recent and unexpected physical (but non-terminal) health conditions which resulted in individuals sustaining a physical impairment. It excluded mental health conditions. It included both conditions of sudden onset, most frequently caused by road traffic accidents but also including conditions such as cardiac arrest, and the recent development of chronic illness including neurological, renal and rheumatological conditions. In total nine interviewees had undergone the sudden onset of their condition (six males, three females) while seven had recently developed chronic illnesses (three males, four females).

The focus of the study was on younger disabled people; within the health service this definition is used to refer to people between the ages of

18 and 65. Within the study, interviewees' ages varied between 27 and 64 years. The length of marriage ranged from two to 39 years. Ten of the marriages were the first for both individuals, the remaining six couples were variously in their first, second or third marriages or partnerships. Fourteen couples had children, although they lived at home in only 11 cases. The children's ages ranged from toddlers to adults. The couples chosen possessed a range of financial resources.

The interviews were all taped, transcribed and then coded using the Ethnograph computer package. These transcripts were then examined for emerging analytic themes. The framework of analysis arising from the first interviews was significantly suggested by the interview schedule and focused largely on variations in the recent sequence of events and the initial choices of coping styles by interviewees. However, due to the longitudinal nature of the research, it was possible to adopt a more grounded theory approach to the design of subsequent interview schedules and the analysis of the data collected from the second and third interviews. As a result, the themes which emerged included those deemed important by the interviewees and led to a greater focus on the nature of the marital relationship and the costs of enlisting support from others as well as the expected consideration of intra- and inter-couple similarities and differences.

In presenting direct quotations, the names of interviewees have been changed to protect their confidentiality. In addition, we were quickly made aware in our interviews that the labels of disabled person and carer often used in the research literature were not those with which the people we interviewed identified. As such it has been necessary to devise some other form of distinguishing reference between members of a couple when providing quotations without resorting to the inappropriate medical term patient. Since during the recruitment procedure, we first contacted the individual who had experienced injury or chronic illness, it was decided to refer to them as the key contact. Their spouse or cohabiter are referred to as partner. In quoting verbatim, the conventions *I* for Interviewer, *F* for female and *M* for male have been employed.

The Negotiation of Coping project was one of seven which made up the ESRC and Joseph Rowntree Foundation-sponsored Management of Personal Welfare Initiative which aimed to take a multi-disciplinary approach to the interface between individual coping responses and structural resources in both personal and community responses to various forms of stress (Titterton, 1992; Hearn, Popay and Edwards, 1998; Williams, Popay and Oakley, 1999). The Negotiation of Coping study attempted to combine developments in the psychological literature relating to the coping process with aspects of welfare research which focus on material circumstances and structural disadvantage. Before describing the data however, it is necessary to outline briefly the concepts and earlier studies on which the Negotiation of Coping study was based.

CONCEPTUALIZATIONS OF GENDER AND RELATIONSHIPS IN THE COPING LITERATURE

The Negotiation of Coping study drew initially on the psychological literature of coping, particularly the interactive model of Lazarus and Folkman (1984). These authors originally categorized coping strategies as either problem-focused or emotion-focused (Lazarus and Folkman, 1984; Folkman *et al.*, 1986). Problem-focused efforts are directed at doing something constructive about the conditions of threat or harm and include active coping, planning, suppression of competing activities and seeking instrumental support. In contrast, emotion-focused strategies are concerned with regulating emotions arising from the situation. Typical examples of such strategies are enlisting emotional support, positive reinterpretation, acceptance, denial and adoption of religious beliefs (Folkman *et al.*, 1986). While drawing on this literature, the study aimed further to develop work on coping with regard to issues of gender and coping within relationships. It was also concerned with examining the role of material resources such as income or type of house on the coping process. One early finding was the way in which material resources were used alongside asymmetrical gender discourses to produce a situation where the couple would pay someone (usually another woman) to provide substitute labour in cases where it was the female partner who had acquired an impairment. Clearly, those able to 'buy in' instrumental support (such as help with bathing or cleaning the house) had available financial resources, while other couples mentioned not enlisting such support due to its cost. This coping strategy was however, cross cut by gender dynamics since, in all cases, the practical support bought in was to replace that which could no longer be performed by the female spouse/cohabiter. In no cases was payment made to replace practical tasks previously carried out by the male member of a couple who had since become disabled; in such cases, the female partner often simply increased the number of tasks she undertook. These examples of buying-in substitute female labour suggested the use of a dominant discursive practice which constructs the performance of certain domestic tasks (particularly intimate personal care such as bathing but also housework) by men as gender-inappropriate (West and Zimmerman, 1991; Seymour, 1992b). Its use enabled some males in the study to access financial resources and provide substitute female labour rather than have to perform such tasks themselves.

Coping and Gender

One strand of early studies of coping strategies focused on differences in the coping mechanisms employed by men and women, relating problem-focused and emotion-focused approaches to gender (Billings and Moos, 1981; Hamilton and Fagot, 1988; Vingerhoets and Van Heck, 1990). The research suggested that men more frequently adopted pragmatic problem-focused coping strategies whereas women were more likely to use emotion-focused coping styles and to seek social support. This practical/emotional categorization has resonances with the 'doing/being' dichotomies often refered to in discussions of gender differences (Seymour, 1992b). Explanations in the literature for such gender-specific coping preferences included exposure to different kinds of stressors, variations in the way situations were appraised by women and men and whether particular coping strategies result in the same outcome for both sexes (Vingerhoets and Van Heck, 1990).

This strand of research has recently been criticized by Dobash and Dobash (1992) for being gender blind in the construction of the measuring instruments employed. A more substantial criticism of such work addresses the way that gender was conceptualized in these studies as simply one of a number of independent social variables which define the resulting coping strategies employed. Hamner, Hearn and Bruce (1999) state that instead of this view, gender should be seen as a fundamental social division which underpins social life and influences all interactions. Adopting this perspective of gender as an interactive process means, for example, that when Pearlin and Schooler (1978) stated that women have lower levels of coping resources and adopted less effective coping responses to alleviate stress, researchers should focus on female access to such resources as a symptom of the operation of gender relations, rather than see it as a definition of the coping strategies of all women. This processual conceptualization of gender meant that one aim of the Negotiation of Coping study was to investigate the concepts of gender and coping in a more complex manner than had occurred in the previous psychological literature. The researchers would consider what role is played by gender in the negotiation of coping including the forms these negotiations take, on the bargaining tools used by male and female members of a couple and on the extent to which the eventual outcome of these negotiations is mutually satisfying to both spouses/cohabiters.

Coping within Relationships

The strong influence of the discipline of psychology in the area of stress and coping means that many of the studies on coping focus on the individual; there have however, been attempts to incorporate other family members into the research. One such stream of work is Family Systems Theory, a functional approach, which considers the dynamics and interactions of all family members following a stressful event. This Systems perspective tends however, to conflate the experiences and coping responses of individuals within the family (Turk and Kerns, 1985; Chowanec and Binik, 1989). Family Systems Theory assumes that all family members, or indeed practitioners or researchers, will make the same assessment as to what constitutes dysfunction; a consensus view of the household which, as mentioned in my introduction, has been strongly disputed (Brannen and Wilson, 1987).

Research on coping by couples has tended to be on heterosexual couples and less so on gay and lesbian couples (but see Donlau *et al.*, 1985; Nicholson and Long, 1990; Shelby, 1992). Couple studies have been carried out on the effect, usually psycho-physiological, of a life event on the spouse/cohabiter. Such analysis is different however, from considering how married or cohabiting people cope as a couple. In this last case, consideration is given to the processes of dealing with a life event as one member of a relationship and how such coping is negotiated. This approach is in line with developments in research on carers which focuses on the duality (Twigg, 1994) of the caring/cared-for relationship rather than viewing those involved only as discrete individuals. It also allows for an examination of the extent to which individuals are prepared to prioritize their relationship rather than their personal needs (Coyne and Smith, 1991).

In the Negotiation of Coping study such a choice would arise when an individual's preferred coping strategy conflicted with that adopted by their spouse or cohabiter. For example, if one individual responded to a stressful situation by denying its existence, a tension could arise if their spouse/cohabiter wished to seek instrumental support from formal or informal sources and therefore needed to explicitly address the situation.

Such tensions did not arise within all relationships in the study. Indeed, a number of the couples we spoke to adopted similar or complementary coping strategies in response to particular aspects of disablement. In the latter case, although coping strategies of spouses/cohabiters differed, this difference often aided or complemented individual coping responses. This occurred in the case of Mr and Mrs Billingsbey, a couple in their fifties, both of whom were uncomfortable with Mr Billingsbey providing help with bathing for his wife. The situation was resolved to mutual satisfaction by Mrs Billingsbey accessing public bathing facilities and therefore enabling her husband to continue in paid employment and finance her use of these facilities rather than provide her with personal care. For another couple of a similar age, Mr and Mrs Hexton, the provision of personal care by a husband to his wife was less problematic as they had a history of shared bathtimes. These two cases show that it is not the adoption of particular coping strategies *per se* which affect the impact of an unexpected stressor on intimate couples; the researcher cannot, nor should wish to, produce a blueprint for behaviour to be used in such situations. However, as stated above there were occasions in the study where the coping strategies adopted by individuals in a relationship proved to be problematic. This took place when members of a couple carried out contrasting or conflicting coping strategies, that is where the coping strategies of one or both spouses/cohabiters actively hindered those of the other or resulted in significant conflict. In these cases, coping strategies needed to be negotiated between couples and this was carried out in a variety of ways.

NEGOTIATING COPING STRATEGIES WITHIN MARRIAGE/COHABITATION

The methodology of the study, conducting three interviews with each couple, proved particularly suited to exploring the issue of negotiating coping strategies. By having more than one interview, the researchers were able to establish particular areas where negotiation was apparently necessary and ask informants what they had done in relation to this area. This is preferable to asking prescriptive questions such as 'What do you think you would do in the case of ...?' which some studies of coping strategies have done (cf. Stetz *et al.*, 1986). In addition, having both joint and separate interviews allowed us to ask about individual styles of coping but also to observe interactions between the couple which provided further data as to the negotiation of these strategies (cf. Seymour, Dix and Eardley, 1995). At this point, it is probably appropriate to reiterate that couples were responding to the onset of physical impairment or chronic illness as it impacted on a number of areas of their lives (finance, parenting, employment, social life, and so on). That is, each individual may be carrying out several coping strategies and, as a result, couples may have had to carry out a number of different negotiations as they addressed the compatibility of their strategies in different life areas.

The process of negotiation will only occur where there is perceived to be a tension between spouses'/cohabiters' coping strategies and where individuals consider that addressing this tension is more important than suppressing one's own preferred coping strategy (Coyne and Smith, 1991). Where neither of these conditions occur, the negotiation of coping strategies is unlikely to even reach the engagement stage.

No Engagement

Where coping strategies are predominantly similar or corresponding (as with Mr and Mrs Hexton being able to give and receive personal bathing care), there is presumably no need for the couple to enter into negotiations. Although the performance by both members of the couple of some coping strategies may prove problematic in the long term, for instance if both individuals continually deny the existence of a health condition (Roskies and Lazarus, 1980), the issue here is not one of negotiation. Similarly, if strategies are complementary, as with Mr and Mrs Billingsbey utilizing and paying for public bathing facilities, there is no tension to be negotiated. In the study, where there were contrasting coping strategies which could result in potential tension, or in the case of conflicting strategies, actively hinder individual's preferred form of coping, there were still couples where no engagement took place. Here we have to understand as Finch and Mason (1993: 66) point out in their focus on forms of negotiation '... what the presence or absence of talk *means* in the context of specific negotiations?' (author's emphasis). How does it illuminate power relations in the partnership? Non-engagement may occur due to a wish to avoid raising an issue of potential conflict which may jeopardise the relationship. One important consideration here for the Negotiation of Coping study was which member of the couple decided not to pursue the issue of personal preference of coping strategy owing to the possibility of disruption to the relationship.

For example, one couple in their twenties, Mr and Mrs Ford, appeared to avoid addressing issues which were potentially conflictual, despite encouragement from their GP. When interviewed Mrs Ford described how she was unable to engage her husband in discussion:

I. Do you think he feels the same way?
F. I don't know. We don't talk about it really much. The doctor keeps telling us off. 'You must discuss these things.'

She continued:

F. Simon doesn't like discussing things very much anyway. I suppose he's a *typical feller*. I mean, we're that busy as well now, so they tend to be more practical things that we discuss when we're around. ... so I suppose it's a case of being too busy, which is a poor excuse but...

(Mrs Ford, partner, 3rd interview, my emphasis)

Finch and Mason (1993: 77) suggest that the ability to stay out of a discussion is an indication of power. They also found in their research on family caring responsibilities that in cases where there was no discussion, that is no engagement, the outcome tended to be strongly gendered with women becoming the carers of other family members. It can be suggested that constructions of masculinity which discourage talking about personal issues can combine with structural features of marriage/heterosexual relationships as patriarchal institutions in which male preferences take precedence to result in a situation whereby the lack of engagement will usually lead to an outcome in which male members of a couple benefit.

Engagement

The concept of negotiation is often related to talking or discussions. In the study, this was the manner in which some, but not all, couples resolved questions of differences in coping strategies. The issue is complicated in that talking is, in itself, a coping strategy; it is mostly related to enlisting emotional support. The question arises as to how one negotiates the lack of emotional support from a spouse/cohabiter if he or she will not engage in conversation (see Duncombe and Marsden (1993) for a discussion of this area). Indeed, it appeared that for one or two of the couples who were experiencing conflicting coping strategies, a self-assessed deterioration in the quality of their relationship meant that they were also those least likely to be engaging in conversation with their spouse/cohabiter and therefore were unable to negotiate this conflict. Again, drawing on the work of Finch and Mason (1993) it has been shown that negotiations can be either explicit or implicit; that is they may take place openly in specific discussions or they may arise through less frank means. The couple in the study with the most explicit negotiations held overt and focused examinations of the advantages and disadvantages of specific forms of action. These conversations were encouraged by the skills learnt by the female key contact on a counselling course. Thus Mrs Corton described how:

F. ... we came back home and went through all the pros and cons, the finances and what would be better and what wouldn't, and what might be the outcome and what wouldn't, and we just kept on talking it through until we came to a conclusion. I suppose doing the counselling course might have helped with that because I can prioritise more easily and not let us wander off into another area.

(Mrs Corton, key contact, third interview)

Noticeably, this couple, both in their forties, were cohabiting and their current relationship was not the first long-term partnership for either member. Mrs Corton explained that she was aware of elements of being a couple, such as emotional support, which she considered necessary and which had been missing in her previous relationships. As a result, she was prepared to address them explicitly in the current partnership. The explicit nature of the negotiations between this couple may reflect a pre-existing more equitable division of power relations in the relationship than was the case for Mr and Mrs Ford (above) and may also contribute to a similarly more equitable division in subsequent actions rather than the gendered outcomes which Finch and Mason (1993) state tend to occur when there is less discussion of issues. Some couples had much less explicit negotiations but nevertheless were communicating with each other. For example, Mrs Petworth was less inclined than was her husband to use talking as a means of dealing with her experiences. Mr Petworth wished to discuss with his wife the fact that he had been, as he put it, 'bloody impossible' but said that when he raised the topic, 'She always says "Don't be so stupid" when I do'. He had been able to communicate with his wife via a book he was writing of his experiences of which he said:

M. It ultimately became – it sounds soft, not a love letter - but I would come up to this theme in my notes, which she reads. And she sometimes would say, 'What have you written this bit for, do you think I don't know that?'

(Mr Petworth, key contact, first interview, my emphasis)

This last example shows that although explicit discussion of particular coping strategies may be considered inappropriate (or too painful) by couples at specific times, they are still able to enter into some form of (implicit) negotiation to reach an outcome which is acceptable to both members of the marriage/cohabitation. Interestingly, many couples mentioned that since the onset of the impairment or chronic illness, they had become aware of an enhanced sense of immediacy. As a result, they would tackle issues which occurred straight away and would be more likely to raise them with their spouse/cohabiter earlier than perhaps previously they may have done. In addition, they were less likely to prolong arguments or sulk. This alteration in the timetabling of negotiations was associated with a positive reappraisal of their relationship and a sense that, as one woman put it:

F. It's not a rehearsal, this.

(Mrs Leafield, partner, third interview)

Resolution

If negotiations are entered into, then it is likely that some form of resolution will emerge. This may, however, not always be mutually agreeable to both members of the couple. Of the 12 couples in the study who experienced contrasting or conflicting styles, the preferred coping strategy was able to be continued by more men than women (eight to four), more 'carers' than disabled spouses (nine to three) and also by those who expressed low commitment to the relationship. These findings mirror those of an earlier study of long-term spouse carers (Parker, 1993) which suggested that gender was a key dimension in spouse negotiations, but one which interacted both with perceived notions of dependency related to disablement and the self-assessed quality of the relationship.

In a situation where a resolution is reached which is less satisfying to one spouse/cohabiter than the other, it can be assumed that the least satisfied member of the couple was in a weaker negotiating position. That is, they were less able to argue for the continuation of their preferred coping strategy or the cessation of their spouse/cohabiter's strategy than was the other member of the relationship. The ability to negotiate successfully a personally favourable resolution depends on the bargaining tools which are brought to the process.

Bargaining

The bargaining tools which individuals bring to negotiations within marriage/cohabitation can be specific to the relationship or may reflect wider dynamics of the social world in which that marriage/cohabitation takes place; that is, they can be personal or socially constructed. Bradley (1996: 105) drawing on Giddens, suggests that such bargaining tools can be best conceptualized as resources and may be either material or personal resources or discursive practices. She identifies economic resources, positional resources, symbolic resources (in which she includes discursive practices), domestic resources, sexual resources and personal resources. The last three resources in particular she considers have allowed women to exercise power in the domestic sphere or personal relationships. From the study data, it was occasionally difficult to disentangle what Bradley (1996) calls personal resources (the use of individual character and qualities to exercise control) from other less individualized resources. For example, was a male member of a couple's ability to negotiate a satisfactory resolution for himself due to his character or gender? Yet in many instances, there were examples of the employment of socially constructed bargaining tools used by our interviewees in their negotiations. These included: status as key contact or partner; gendered discourses including position as family 'knowledge holder', particularly in relation to health matters; commitment to the relationship; and the effect of wider family dynamics such as the presence of family members able to provide support. Different aspects of the identity of those in the study intersected with each other (such as male key contact) and acted to strengthen or weaken the negotiating position of particular individuals.

GENDERED DISCOURSES AS A BARGAINING TOOL

To focus specifically on the use of gendered discourses as a bargaining tool, we found that they were, as Foucauldian theory suggests, not utilized simply as a static structural position, that is 'I am the man/woman and therefore can continue my preferred strategy'. Instead they were used by the interviewees in a sophisticated manner within the negotiating process to enhance their personal case, that is, to enable them to have their preference accepted as arising from a legitimate (rather than selfish) excuse. Finch (1989) has discussed legitimate excuses in relation to people explaining why they were unable to carry out certain (caring) behaviours. In contrast, in this study, people were employing legitimate excuses to enable them to continue with their preferred coping strategy in the face of opposition from their spouse/cohabiter.

Gendered discourses as a bargaining tool were utilized differently by the men and women in the study and variously in tandem with other socially constructed discourses reflecting the interviewees' involvement with multiple discursive identities and practices. Twice as many men than women (eight compared with four) seemed able to negotiate a personally favourable resolution and this seemed to be the case whether or not they were key contacts or partners. Some men explicitly used a gendered discourse involving acceptable masculine responses to emotional demands in order to justify not supporting their wives'/cohabiters' preferred coping strategy; for example, three men described how they 'disappeared' when their wives sought emotional support as they felt unable to provide it. One man said of his wife's response:

> *M*. I think there was tears and things … but away from me, because she knows I'm awful when women cry. I can't cope with women crying.
> (Mr Ossington, key contact, third interview)

In such cases, being unable to carry out an action is more acceptable than being unwilling to do so (Finch and Mason, 1993) especially if the situation is complicated by ideological expectations on the part of a wife/ cohabiter that the male should respond positively to the female member of the couple's attempts to enlist emotional support. The absence of such anticipated support can have a deleterious effect on the person so denied (Pagel *et al.*, 1987).

In contrast, of the four women who successfully negotiated their preferred coping strategy, three were partners, that is the member of the couple who had not experienced a physical impairment or chronic illness. This suggests that for women, gendered discursive frameworks about family health which result in women being perceived as acting appropriately as family carers (and therefore in possession of, or rightly seeking, some specialist medical or health knowledge) may in some cases, increase their bargaining power. This seemed to be the case in relation to information-seeking behaviour. Interestingly, this problem-focused behaviour was more commonly adopted by the women in the study group than by the men. Hence, while the psychological literature suggests that women are more likely to adopt emotion-focused strategies than men (Billings and Moos, 1981), the findings of this study show that there are certain problem-focused strategies which women are able to adopt if it is recognized by their husband/cohabiter that they have a legitimate, social rather than personal, excuse for doing so. In this case, a problem-focused strategy is gender-appropriate for women. Thus, for our interviewees, it appeared that if information-seeking behaviour needed to be negotiated with husbands or male cohabiters, women were able to draw on the socially constructed, gendered responsibility of women for the health of their families (Graham, 1993) to argue their case successfully.

Hence, Mrs Knowles cited one instance where her husband had felt she had been too forthright in demanding information about appropriate equipment for him and told her she should have 'let it ride'. Her response to him was:

> *F*. I can't do that because I'm involved in this as much as you are.
> (Mrs Knowles, partner, third interview)

This gendered discourse was also used by women to justify using this information-seeking coping behaviour with health and welfare professionals as shown in the following example:

> *F.* [Referring to medication] I've asked you know ... I mean it wasn't Andrew that was asking, it was me.
>
> He's been examined (in hospital ward) and everything else while I've been there. But I mean, at the end of the day, if they don't want me there, if they say so, I still wouldn't go, so it makes no difference.
>
> They tried shoving me out of the hospital. They said, 'Oh, we're going to do this [carry out a medical procedure during which they expected her to leave the bedside cubicle]' and I said 'That's alright' [and stayed with her husband].
>
> It's pointless it getting explained twice [medical procedure]. After all, it's me that's got to look after him, so I may as well know what's going on.
>
> (Mrs Leafield, partner, first interview)

Powerful as these gendered discourses were, the commitment of individuals to the marital relationship was perhaps the ultimate bargaining tool. Where the quality of the relationship was described by interviewees as problematic before the onset of impairment or chronic illness of one member, difficulties could be exacerbated by conflicting coping strategies. For one couple, the husband employed the threat of leaving the marriage to allow him to continue his preferred strategy. This case acts as a reminder that coping with the onset of disablement is not a process occurring in a vacuum but takes place as part of the continuing story of the marital/cohabiting relationship. Hence Finch and Mason (1993: 79) state 'negotiation can only be understood with reference to the biographies of the individuals involved and the history of their relationships, as they have developed over time'.

CONCLUSION

By drawing on the results of a study of the Negotiation of Coping with the onset of disablement, this chapter has developed the research on gender and the coping process by examining the negotiation of coping strategies between men and women and the way this reflects power relations within marriage/cohabitation. It has shown that individuals use discourses of gender, not just as static biological categories in heterosexual relationships but in an interactive way as providing a number of symbolic resources which can be drawn on to provide bargaining tools in the negotiating process. These discourses can take the form of culturally appropriate masculine or feminine behaviour or socially constructed gender roles/responsibilities. While drawing on these discourses may appear to be personally useful to individuals, particularly women, in the sphere of micro-power relations, it should be remembered that gendered relations are constructed to the disadvantage of women and so the personal gain may ultimately be a Pyrrhic victory. For while Finch and Mason (1993) have shown how family negotiations are an example of the processes through which structure and agency relate and hence how people are able to retain their individualism in family life or marital relationships, they have also noted that drawing on socially constructed ideologies can have the effect of consolidating gender differences. For example, while drawing on gendered discourses of female responsibility for family health matters may help the information-seeking behaviours of particular women, it serves at the same time to reinforce the view of such activities as appropriately female.

In this way, individuals as agents both draw on and contribute to the structures in which they live (Giddens, 1984). Empirical research on negotiations in households is providing examples of the ways in which this process – structuration – is carried out and is, excitingly, attempting to apply to the social world a concept which some commentators had considered was purely theoretical.

The narrow focus taken within this chapter on the role of discursive practices in negotiations is not intended to privilege this type of bargaining tool above the use of material resources and personal attributes highlighted by Bradley (1996) and other writers. Elsewhere I have discussed the use of these other social resources in the negotiation process (Seymour, 1994). Indeed, this return to a focus on the role of material issues for couples is a useful counterpoint to contemporary writers, among them Giddens (1992) himself, who have sometimes neglected these aspects in their discussions of the construction of late-twentieth-century intimate relationships. The emphasis in this chapter on the negotiation of coping between two members of an intimate couple has also shown that in studies of caring, researchers need to look at the totality of relationships rather than viewing the user and carer as separate entities. This is because, as part of this process, people are not only specifically negotiating their coping strategies but also more generally negotiating the form and continuation of their relationship with intimate others. In this study, by drawing on the well-conceptualized dimensions of coping in the psychological literature but then expanding the focus of the research to incorporate developments within sociology relating to households and intimate relationships, the tendency to consider people as isolated individuals is avoided and the emphasis is placed on interpersonal relations and structural constraints. This multi-disciplinary approach is also being adopted by psychologists in this area who are showing an increasing interest in interpersonal dynamics and relationship-focused coping (Coyne and Smith, 1991). In relation to issues of gender, power and the household there is much to be hoped for by this interdisciplinary collaboration.

REFERENCES

Allan, G. and Crow, G. (eds) (1989) *Home and Family: Creating the Domestic Sphere*. London: Macmillan.

Berk, S. (1985) *The Gender Factory: the Apportionment of Work in American Households*. London: Plenum Press.

Billings, A. and Moos, R. (1981) 'The Role of Coping Responses and Social Resources in Attenuating the Stress of Life Events', *Journal of Behavioural Medicine*, 4, 139–57.

Blumstein, P. and Schwartz, P. (1983) *American Couples*. New York: William Morrow.

Bradley, H. (1996) *Fractured Identities: Changing Patterns of Inequality*. Cambridge: Polity Press.

Braidotti, R. (1986) 'The Ethics of Sexual Difference: the Case of Foucault and Irigaray', *Australian Feminist Studies*, Summer, 1–13.

Brannen, J. and Wilson, G. (1987) *Give and Take in Families: Studies in Resource Distribution*. London: Allen and Unwin.

Cassell's (1982) *Cassell's English Dictionary*. (4th ed.) London: Cassell.

Chowanec, G. and Binik, Y. (1989) 'End Stage Renal Disease and the Marital Dyad: an Empirical Investigation', *Social Science and Medicine*, 28, 9, 971–83.

Clark, D. (ed.) (1991) *Marriage, Domestic Life and Social Change: Writings for Jacqueline Burgoyne*. London: Routledge.

Coyne, J. and Smith, D. (1991) 'Couples Coping with a Myocardial Infarction: a Contextual Perspective on Wives' Distress', *Journal of Personality and Social Psychology*, 61, 3, 404–12.

Davis, K., Leijenaar, M. and Oldersma, J. (1991) *The Gender Of Power*. London: Sage.

Dobash, R. and Dobash, R.E. (1992) *Women, Violence and Social Change*. London: Routledge.

Donlau, J., Wolcott, D., Gottlieb, M. and Landsverk, J. (1985) 'Psychological Aspects of AIDS and AIDS-related Complex: a Pilot Study', *Journal of Psychosocial Oncology*, 3, 39–55.

Duck, S. (1983) *Friends for Life: the Psychology of Close Relationships*. Brighton: Harvester Press.

Duck, S. (1986) *Human Relationships: an Introduction to Social Psychology*. London: Sage.

Duncombe, J. and Marsden, D. (1993) 'Love and Intimacy: the Gender Division of Emotion and "Emotion Work". A Neglected Aspect of Sociological Discussion of Heterosexual Relationships', *Sociology*, 27, 2, 221–41.

Dunne, G. (1996) *Lesbian Lifestyles: Women's Work and the Politics of Sexuality*. Basingstoke: Macmillan.

Finch, J. (1989) *Family Obligations and Social Change*. Oxford: Polity Press.

Finch, J. and Mason, J. (1993) *Negotiating Family Reponsibilities*. London: Routledge.

Folkman, S., Lazarus R.S., Dunkel-Schetter, C., DeLongis, A. and Gruen, R. (1986) 'The Dynamics of a Stressful Encounter: Cognitive Appraisal, Coping and Encounter Outcomes', *Journal of Personality and Social Psychology*, 50, 992–1003.

Foucault, M. (1980) *Power/Knowledge: Selected Interviews and Other Writings 1972–1977*. Brighton: Harvester Press.

Giddens, A. (1984) *The Constitution of Society: Outline of the Theory of Structuration*. Cambridge: Polity Press.

Giddens, A. (1991) *The Transformation of Intimacy: Sexuality, Love and Eroticism in Modern Societies*. Cambridge: Polity Press.

Graham, H. (1993) *Hardship and Health in Women's Lives*. London: Harvester Wheatsheaf.

Hamilton, S. and Fagot, B.I. (1988) 'Chronic Stress and Coping Styles: a Comparison of Male and Female Undergraduates', *Journal of Personality and Social Psychology*, 55, 819–23.

Hamner, J., Hearn, J. and Bruce, E. (1999) 'Gender and Welfare' in Williams, F., Popay, J. and Oakley, A. (eds) *Welfare Research: a Critique of Theory and Method*. London: UCL Press.

Hearn, J., Popay, J. and Edwards, J. (eds) (1998) *Men, Gender Divisions and Welfare*. London: Routledge.

Lazarus, R.S. and Folkman, S. (1984) *Stress, Appraisal and Coping*. New York: Springer.

Lyotard, J.-F. (1984) *The Postmodern Condition: a Report on Knowledge*. Manchester: Manchester University Press.

Mason, J. (1989) 'Reconstructing the Public and the Private: the Home and Marriage in Later Life' in Allan, G. and Crow, G. (eds) *Home and Family: Creating the Domestic Sphere*. London: Macmillan.

Morrow, V. (1996) 'Rethinking Childhood Dependency: Children's Contributions to the Domestic Economy', *The Sociological Review*, 58–77.

Nicholson, W. and Long, B. (1990) 'Self-esteem, Social Support, Internalized Homophobia and Coping Strategies of HIV + Gay Men', *Journal of Consulting and Clinical Psychology*, 58, 6, 873–76.

Pagel, M., Erdly, W.W. and Becker, J. (1987) 'Social Networks: We Get By with (and in Spite of) a Little Help from our Friends', *Journal of Personality and Social Psychology*, 53, 793–804.

Parker, G. (1993) *With This Body: Caring and Disability in Marriage*. Buckingham: Open University Press.

Pearlin, L. and Schooler, C. (1978) 'The Structure of Coping', *Journal of Health and Social Behaviour*, 19, 2–21.

Roskies, E. and Lazarus, R. (1980) 'Coping Theory and the Teaching of Coping Skills' in D. Davidson and S. Davidson (eds) *Behavioral Medicine: Changing Health Lifestyles*. New York: Brummer/Mazel.

Sarup, M. (1993) *An Introductory Guide to Poststructuralism and Postmodernism.* Second Edition. London: Harvester Wheatsheaf.

Seymour, J. (1992a) ' "No Time to Call my Own": Women's Time as a Household Resource', *Women's Studies International Forum*, 15, 2, 187–92.

Seymour, J. (1992b) 'Unsexed by Failure: Gender and the Division of Domestic Labour'. Unpublished Ph.D. thesis, Department of Sociology, University of Manchester.

Seymour, J. (1994) *The Negotiation of Coping: Disablement, Caring and Marriage.* End-of Award Report to the Economic and Social Research Council, May 1994.

Seymour, J., Dix, G. and Eardley, T. (1995) *Joint Accounts: Methodology and Practice in Research Interviews with Couples.* Social Policy Reports, 4. York: University of York, Social Policy Research Unit.

Shelby, R.D. (1992) *If a Partner has AIDS: Guide to Clinical Intervention for Relationships in Crisis.* London: Harrington Park Press.

Stetz, K., Lewis, F. and Primomo, J. (1986) 'Family Coping Strategies and Chronic Illness in the Mother', *Family Relations*, 35, 515–22.

Titterton, M. (1992) 'Managing Threats to Welfare: the Search for a New Paradigm of Welfare', *Journal of Social Policy*, 21, 1, 1–23.

Turk, D.C. and Kerns, R.D. (1985) *Health, Illness and Families: a Life-span Perspective.* New York: John Wiley and Sons.

Twigg J. (ed.) (1994) *Carers: Research and Practice.* London: HMSO.

Vingerhoets, AD J.J.M. and Van Heck, G.L. (1990) 'Gender, Coping and Psychosomatic Symptoms', *Psychological Medicine*, 20, 125–35.

West, C. and Zimmerman, D. (1991) 'Doing Gender' in J. Lorber and S. Farrell (eds) *The Social Construction of Gender.* London: Sage.

Williams, F., Popay, J. and Oakley, A. (eds) (1999) *Welfare Research: a Critique of Theory and Method.* London: UCL Press.

Part III
Gendered Time and Space

6 A Fight for Her Time: Challenges Facing Mothers who Work in Hospital Medicine

Janet Stephens

INTRODUCTION

Early studies on time and time use focus on the relationship of time to work, and how economic pressures shape people's responses to time, a well-worn maxim being 'time is money' (Moore, 1963; Blyton, 1985). More recently, Adam's innovative work on the issue of time has high-lighted the multiplicities of time that make up our daily lives. Adam (1989, 1995, 1996) argues that in social science analyses it is necessary to understand time in all its multiplicities; personally we are not aware of time as being one-dimensional. For example, when a woman's working day is over her roles may change from that of worker to being a mother, a friend or someone following a hobby. However, at all times we are all those people; it is just that we become them at differing times, potentially with different people and in various locations. Women are part of the general economic life through their attachment to the labour force; however, the types of dependent-related activities that women carry out 'are not so much time measured, paid, spent, allocated and controlled as time lived, given and generated' (Adam, 1996: 157). Adam has developed a concept of 'timing', that there is a good or bad time for action which is temporally located in the personal and social history of a person. The ability to 'time' appropriately means that control over life-course decisions and their con-sequences is retained. For many women, however, an increasing level of dependants' demands over the life-course undermines their ability to retain control.

This chapter draws on Adam's concept of 'timing' to understand how a sample of professional women hospital doctors make sense of their lives when they move from full-time to part-time working as a response to becoming mothers. Their experiences, including the conflicts and their resolutions were explored as the doctors step outside the dominant and most valued temporality of the organization (full-time work). The first section sets out the wider theoretical framework within which the research project is located. Next the methodology of the research is briefly outlined. The empirical sections of the chapter focus on issues of hospital medicine as a career (earned time); childcare and domestic 'help' (bought time); and leisure ('stolen' time). The discussion concludes that as a 'mother' there is a cultural and moral imperative for women to respond to dependants' demands in Western society. Their own allocations of time and time use are subsumed beneath partner's and dependants' demands, reducing the ability to retain control over life-course decisions and their consequences.

RESEARCHING MOTHERS IN THE PROFESSIONS – THEORETICAL FRAMEWORK

The general framework of the project draws on a dual systems societal concept to understand how capital and patriarchy relate to impact on individuals (Cockburn, 1983, 1988; Walby, 1986, 1990; Witz, 1990). Walby (1986: 54) forcefully argues that patriarchy has to be understood as a system of structures through which men oppress and exploit women. Her model of patriarchy includes patriarchal relations in the state, male violence and sexuality. She especially emphasizes the importance of the power of patriarchy in the home and in the sphere of paid work. She argues that 'the primary mechanism which ensures that women will serve their husbands is their exclusion from paid work on the same terms as men'. The use of patriarchy as a key element of analysis is problematic due to the various interpretations of the term. Cockburn has said that it is sometimes used by default, because of the lack of a more precise, accurate term. However, Cockburn (1991) argues that partriarchal relations permeate relationships in all work situations, and in all domestic situations. Thus, 'the sex/gender system is to be found in all the same practices and processes in which the mode of production and its class relations are to be found' (p. 195). Whilst Cockburn's (1983) study focused on the printing industry, her analysis is also applicable to other professions and occupations. Cockburn distinguishes, for example, the importance of male power in an economic way, where men's higher earning power and promotion in industry is predicated on women's provision of domestic services.

   In the professions the total commitment demanded by and able to be given by men, to such a 'greedy institution' (Coser, 1974) is only possible because their female partners are willing to act as assistants to further their careers (Fowlkes, 1980; Finch, 1983; Apter, 1993). I have developed elsewhere the idea of women acting as 'honorary chaps' in the professions until they become mothers (Stephens, 1996). The dominant ideology which locates *all* women primarily in the domestic sphere after the birth of their children, I have argued, is the single most important factor in accounting for women's failure to gain and retain their place in top jobs. The move from full-to part-time work was made as a response to the impact of motherhood on professional women. The hospital organization is a total temporal institution, that is, it is covered by staff on a 24-hours-a-day, 52-weeks-a-year, basis. Junior hospital doctors normally work up to 80 hours a week and for the trainee doctors in this sample, part-time work means a 40-hour working week. The tension caused by dual ideologies for mothers who work, the ideology of 'professional' and the ideology of 'mother', lead to conflicts which she has to resolve by giving 'enough' time to be visibly successful in both. It is the societal force exerted by the ideology of mother which means that the responsibility for the well-being and harmony in the domestic sphere ultimately lies with the mother (Phoenix and Woollett, 1991).

This chapter draws on research which aimed to unravel three interwoven aspects of women's lives. These aspects or strands of everyday life (Davies, 1990) are components of the identity of the women doctors interviewed for this study. The first two are those of being a mother and working as a professional. The third strand of their identity, that of following a part-time programme in a profession, has distinct problems related to the medical profession which are set out below in the section on the *Flexible Training Scheme*, but which are applicable more widely across other professions and occupations in which long hours are the norm.

EARNED TIME – GENDERED CAREERS

'Timing' of career and family formation is of vital importance to women who are seeking to work part-time and yet further their careers. For those mothers who work in medicine, there are twin driving forces – the motivation to achieve consultant status in their chosen specialty, and the motivation to establish and successfully maintain a family unit (McRae, 1990). Authors such as Beechey and Perkins (1987) and Dex and McCulloch (1995) have identified a general process of downward career mobility across occupations when women return to work after time out for childbearing and rearing. For many women their childbirth and childrearing years clash with an intense career period when young professionals are expected to undertake post-graduation education, in-house training or specialized professional examinations. Following Adam (1992, 1995) ideas of timing linked to career and family have been developed. 'Good' timing can be the key to success, 'bad' timing can mean an excess of 'waiting' time and subsequently 'lost' time. 'Perfect' timing requires a delicate synchronization of decisions and outcomes in both spheres of family formation and career progression. Hantrais (1993) argues that because women experience and control time differently from men, the gendered nature of time needs to be a component of research into the workings of the household as well as the workplace. Men in Western society are seen to have their prime function in the world of work where time is task-led. Time can be allocated according to a sensible definition of time needed to fulfill set tasks and jobs. However, if the time allocated falls short then 'overtime' is available to be drawn on because the centrality of worktime for men is anticipated and accepted by partners and employers (Elchardus, 1991).

For women who work, time is also divided into work-time and therefore similarly task oriented, but additionally, because of the ideology of 'mother', there is an imperative for her to respond to dependants' demands (Davies, 1990). It is here that difficulties arise. Time cannot be allocated in the same way as task-led time when it is needed for caring for a sick baby, organizing school activities, or caring for elderly parents. Caregiving is seen as women's work and women's control over their own time is subsumed beneath partner's and dependants' demands on their time. Hochschild (1990: 37) describes this caregiving, or emotion work, as 'women's continual attunement to the task of striking and restriking the right emotional balance between child, spouse, home and outside job'.

THE FLEXIBLE TRAINING SCHEME

The women doctors in the sample for this research were participants on the *Flexible Training Scheme for Doctors and Dentists with Family Commitments or Disability*, a part-time training programme designed to meet the specific needs of hospital doctors at a distinct point in the life-course. Originally entitled the *Part-time Training Scheme for Women Doctors*, the scheme was set up by the National Health Executive in 1969 as a response to the perceived demographic challenge faced by the Executive as employers. Seeking to retain their investment in highly trained staff, women were encouraged to return to the labour market after a career break for childrearing. The Flexible Training Scheme is an acknowledgement that both men and women (although as the original title suggests, it was thought that women would have a greater need for the scheme) had special needs at distinct points in their career. It was intended to facilitate their continued training, on a part-time basis, to consultant status. Within the National Health Service there has always been provision to work (rather than train) part-time, an option mostly taken up by women and overseas doctors (Dowie, 1987). In medicine the move off the training track is generally viewed as professional suicide. The result is career stagnation, as one senior registrar explained to me:

> Yes, well it's very difficult in medicine because the only other alternative would be to work at what they call clinical assistant sessions ... there's no promotion and no training involved, you could do them for ten years and at the end of it you are no better off than at the beginning.
>
> (Senior Registrar, Genetics, 4 children)

To the users of the *Flexible Training Scheme* this is a valuable route through the training grades whilst being able to spend time with dependants. However, although the National Health Service Executive has a stated commitment that by the year 2000, 5 per cent of all staff will work on a flexible basis, in the region of Wales, the location for this research, the figure stands at just 1 per cent, the lowest in the United Kingdom.

METHODOLOGY – A LIFE-TIME PERSPECTIVE

Qualitative research methods were used to study how women doctors make sense of their professional and familial lives. Through semi-structured interviews themes such as strategies for managing long-term career and family progression were explored. Qualitative interviews highlighted the contradictory and complex nature of this sample's attitudes and actions, and allowed the women to describe and reflect on their processes of decision making and the temporal sequencing of their decisions. A particular intention was to explore the lived realities of their lives and to uncover the consequences of their decision-making processes. All the doctors interviewed were working part-time in the medical profession in Wales at the point of data collection as an outcome of their becoming mothers. The table below provides characteristics of the research sample and indicates which specialty they worked in, their grade, whether their partner was also working in medicine, and the number of children they had.

Table 6.1   Characteristics of the Research Sample

Specialty	Grade	No. of Children	Partner Medic	Location/ Comments
Anaesthetics	SR	One and pregnant	Yes	Cardiff Subsequently transferred out of region
Anaesthetics	Reg	Two	Yes	Bangor Withdrawn from *FTS* to session work
Community Health	SR	Three	Yes	Swansea Withdrawn from *FTS* to job share
Genetics	SR	Four	Yes	Cardiff Made up to Consultant
Histopathology	SR	One	No	*Cardiff
Obstetrics and Gynaecology	SR	Two	Yes	Cardiff
Oncology	SR	One and pregnant	Yes	Cardiff
Paediatrics	SR	Three	Yes	Bangor
Paediatrics	Reg	One	Yes	*Cardiff
Psychiatry	SR	Three	No	Cardiff Made up to Consultant
Psychiatry	SR	Two	No	Swansea
Psychiatry	SR	Two	Yes	Swansea
Psychiatry	Reg	Two	Yes	Carmarthen
Psychiatry	SHO	One	Yes	Cardiff
Public Health	SR	Four	Yes	Newport/Gwent
Public Health	Reg	Two	Yes	Swansea
Radiology	SR	Two	Yes	Cardiff

*Denotes inward transfer from other Regional Health Authority
Key to Grades: SR = Senior Registrar; Reg = Registrar; SHO = Senior House Officer

THE INTERVIEWS

Location of the interview setting was left to the convenience of the women. Each interview was recorded and later fully transcribed. The length of each interview was between one hour and two and a half hours' duration, and each was timed with consideration to the doctors' work or childcare timetables. Some took place in hospital settings and one in my own office, but most took place in the doctors' homes with their children present.

All the interviews provided rich and valuable data with those in the home giving an extra dimension. Many interviews carried out in the home setting are accompanied by background noises: musical toys being wound up, apologies for interruptions to feed or change babies, the spin of the washing machine, and the children's voices themselves. For example, one newborn baby's gurgling happiness is evident at the start of the interview, which eventually becomes impatience, and then insistence that it was time for the interview to finish. I took the hint and closed the interview with thanks for both mother and child's time, reflecting on how aspects of others' timing permeate the whole research process!

Analysis was carried out as an on-going process to identify and develop themes and issues which were presenting through the data. It was important to me to learn about common issues such as the problems of part-time working in a total temporal institution, and childcare decisions for professional women. This was aided through familiarizing myself with the data by transcribing the taped interviews myself, and coding and indexing the data. From the data, emergent themes and issues were identified. In relation to the concept of 'timing', from analysis of the data the issues of career and family progression, household management, and leisure are examined in this chapter.

EARNED TIME – THE FLEXIBLE TRAINING SCHEME AND MEDICINE AS A CAREER

Timing of career progression in medicine is relatively straightforward to plan on an ideal-type uninterrupted career pattern, as there are distinct building blocks needed to gain promotion to the next grading. So, for example, all junior doctors know that they need to gain their Part I professional exams before they can apply for the next grade up, from registrar to senior registrar, and so on. For many women, though, the ability to plan a career is diminished, because the family unit follows the timing demands of the male partner's career. Across occupations, women generally tend to follow the geographic mobility demands of their husband's career (Apter, 1993; Brannen *et al.,* 1994). In medicine, moving to different locations, including overseas, for a new rotation is seen as part of the job. When whole families are uprooted this can cause difficulties, as one doctor explained to me.

> ... and then every time you move you're moving with a family, you can't just sort of bunk in a flat if you've got two little children to cope

with and that really was the pits ... if I've got one criticism of the whole shebang its the social disruption at the junior levels.

(Registrar, Public Health, 2 children)

If the timing of a career within hospital medicine can be conceptualized as a relatively straightforward enterprise, the timing of family formation is not so straightforward: modern *contraception* techniques may be sophisticated and reliable – *conception* can be more haphazard and less predictable (Fox, 1989). Career planning and family planning are inextricably linked for women who continue their career during childrearing years. For those mothers who work in the professions, there are twin driving forces – the motivation to be successful and maintain a family unit (McRae, 1990). Using 'good' timing, women training in the medical profession can combine a move in career with a return to work after childbirth – however this demands an absolutely professional approach to family planning. The ability to time childbirth appropriately means that control over career progression is retained. 'Good' or 'bad' timing has not been an explicit preoccupation of authors who examine differing life-course histories, however, aspects of timing are certainly implicit. For example, research into women who return to work after a career break have identified a process of downward career mobility when women return to work in such circumstances (Martin and Roberts, 1984; Beechey and Perkins, 1987; Dex and McCulloch, 1995). Such studies indicate the negative aspects of taking time out of career building. Negative aspects of timing clearly impact on career progression and family formation. Being able to space childbearing and career progression so that the one complements the other is extremely difficult. One doctor was able to time both exactly as she wished:

That's when I had my first child, so I started onto that scheme. I then became pregnant with my second child ... do you see what I mean how it was all planned? I know that lots of women can't but I can, I can conceive very well, and I think you do have to, I mean its awful but you do have to organise that sort of thing, but when you've got a career you almost have to plan down to the month when you do.

(Senior Registrar, Psychiatry, 3 children)

The above example of career progression and family formulation was in fact the only one in the collected data which displayed such 'perfect' timing. More commonly, an actual pregnancy was the impetus for initial enquiries about the mechanics of working part-time within the National Health Service. Timing of children and timing of career progression are linked then, as both form the basis for the overall success or failure of the doctor in achieving the end goal of reaching consultant status in her specialty.

The biggest difficulty that all the women encountered was synchronizing their need to use the scheme with coordinating the move from full-time to part-time working. The Administrator of the course, who herself had worked part-time for a while during her career, agreed that you really need to know about eighteen months in advance that you will conceive, in order to synchronize all the stages of getting onto the *Flexible Training Scheme* with the birth of a child. One of the doctors in the sample, a senior registrar who had one young child and was pregnant at the time of the interview argued:

> Unless you apply for it the day the miss your first period I can't see that you have any realistic hope of getting on to it when you actually need it, which is when they're very small.
>
> (Senior Registrar, Oncology, 1 child and pregnant)

Once on the Scheme, doctors are responsible for the management of their own work-related time. It is important to remember, that as junior doctors, although they are defined (and paid) as 'part-time' workers this can mean an input of up to 40 hours. Although classed as a part-time worker by the NHS, childcare cover is classed by the care providers (and has to be paid for) as full-time. Therefore, the doctor, as skilfully as she is able, has to organize all family members' timetables; she becomes the juggler seeking to keep all plates spinning at once, tending to each as it sways off its course before it falls (Forman, 1989). Aids to timing successfully the practicalities of everyday life are discussed in the following sections which focus on two aspects of 'bought' time: childcare and domestic 'help'.

BOUGHT TIME: CHILDCARE

Bought time or enabling time refers to types of childcare utilized by families to 'free' women up for work. In this study I asked all the women who mostly organizes the home sphere and related responsibilities. All the women answered that they felt they were primarily responsible for organizing the domestic sphere. This was often given as a rational explanation due to both partner's employment status:

> There has been this implicit assumption that because I am here more then I make sure things are covered at home and he makes sure he gets to work.
>
> (Public Health, Senior Registrar, 4 children)

Morris (1995) has shown that the traditional division of domestic labour holds firm across class and despite employment status. This was again reinforced as questions related to costs of childcare elicited responses to the effect that it is often paid for out of the woman's salary, it is seen as her area of expertise and she is usually left in control of the type of child-care used.

> ... obviously we discussed it but I think I had more clear ideas in my mind about what I wanted than my husband did, I had thought it through more clearly than he had and he didn't even look at the nursery prior to my child going there but he trusted me to find the best that we could.
>
> (Senior Registrar, Histopathology, 1 child)

Because the mother has the primary task of finding and deciding on what type of childcare to use and, specifically, whom to employ, when arrangements go wrong then it is up to the mother to sort things out:

> That's where good childcare comes in, knowing that the arrangements you've made, you are happy with them because if you're not then you are worrying and you can't concentrate.
>
> (Senior Registrar, Paediatrics, 3 children)

Childcare arrangements are made by the mothers as it is *their* peace of mind and *their* work that is impacted on if this is not well organized, as another doctor explained:

> Well you know, I couldn't work if I thought he wasn't happy ... and there was a bad period where he would cry and not want to stay which was pretty awful but I was literally only a couple of hundred yards away from him, which was why we chose that nursery in the first place, and I could always pop over and very soon he settled down.
>
> (Senior House Officer, Psychiatry, 1 child)

As mothers tend to take main responsibility for childcare, this suggests that men do not have, or are not expected to have, the same concerns about childcare as women. The preferred type of childcare for most mothers is kin networks (Brannen *et al.*, 1994). However, many more women are now prepared to utilize professional childcare services, despite their prohibitive cost, to enable them to return to work. For the women in this study, kin networks were not available owing to geographical mobility demands. This means that professional families often buy in or contract out services and employ nannies, childminders or private nurseries. The mothers explained that they changed the type of childcare they employed to be compatible with the changing needs of their children. When the children were first born women tended to stay at home themselves or use nannies, when they were older childminders were more commonly used to care for children outside regular school hours. I found one example of a nanny share.

Multiple types of childcare are used especially when siblings are at different ages. For example, one Senior Registrar with two children, one in full-time education and the other pre-school age, simultaneously used four different types of childcare. First, a childminder was employed to take the children to school when the mother was at work in the mornings. Second, formal education is clearly the most used type of childcare for all children, in this case playgroup for the younger child, and primary school for the older child. Unusually in this study, this doctor also had local kin support as her parents had moved their home to live near their grandchildren. The grandparents collected the children from playgroup and school. The fourth type of childcare used was the services of a regular babysitter when the parents went out in the evening. Grandma and Granddad stood in for the considerable leftovers of holidays, sickness, dental appointment and so on. With all the childcare provision that this Senior Registrar uses she still firmly believes that she is ultimately responsible for them and argued:

> I can't see the point of going through having two kids and then not looking after them, I can't see it.
>
> (Psychiatry, Senior Registrar, 2 children)

This doctor has formulated a detailed childcare plan which will change as her children's needs change, for example, when the younger child enters full-time education. However, despite such a detailed plan incorporating four different types of childcare she sees the responsibility for its organization as remaining with her.

BOUGHT TIME: DOMESTIC 'HELP'

All the doctors interviewed saw themselves as responsible not only for organizing childcare provision but responsible for the successful management of domestic chores. Prior to family formation they had all worked full-time in a job which demanded an input of up to 80 hours a week. They moved to part-time working practice in order to spend more time with their children. However, with childcare responsibilities came the responsibility for household management. Thus household cleaning, shopping, and so on were understood by these women as part of the package because of the increased amount of time they spent in the domestic sphere.

I asked the doctors in my sample if they transferred good managerial practice which they used in their paid work role into the domestic sphere by
delegating certain jobs to others. If, for example, they bought time by free-
ing themselves from the ironing, washing windows, or other tasks. Many
of them did engage paid domestic labour which they saw as assistance for
them, rather than assistance for both partners to ensure the efficient running of a shared household.

> Like ironing, I hate ironing, but yes I strongly believe in delegating jobs
> to other people, my husband wasn't fussy [on hiring domestic help] but
> then he didn't do any housework did he, he has no idea how long iron-
> ing takes actually.
>
> (Senior Registrar, Oncology, 1 child and pregnant)

As Table 6.1 above shows, most of the women's partners were themselves
in jobs which demanded a long working day, and so household tasks were
contracted out or bought in rather than being shared by both partners. A
Senior Registrar justified her use of bought domestic help, arguing that
housework was a negative and wasted use of a precious resource:

> I mean I'm not going to spend my time that I have actually got with the
> children doing cleaning, I'm not prepared to do that ... because the time
> I have is very precious.
>
> (Senior Registrar, Psychiatry, 3 children)

It is a curious fact that women become defensive when asked if they
employ an outsider to do the family's ironing, washing windows and so on,
however sensible such an act of time management it would appear to be.

> I think I felt I never liked the idea of having someone in. I thought you
> should always be able to do it yourself really, I should be able to clean it
> myself at least once a week ... I felt guilty about asking her to come,
> you still believe that you should be doing everything that a full-time
> mum is doing.
>
> (Senior Registrar, Radiology, 2 children)

For these women, this attitude would again appear to be tied up with the
notion of where the ultimate responsibilty lies for the welfare of the family
unit. Their responses reflected the notion that part of the mother's 'job' is
to provide a clean and attractive home environment whilst the male partner is following career demands and providing financial security.

The majority of women, however, took an instrumental attitude to the
domestic sphere and split it into jobs they accepted and others which they
rejected as being outside the remit of mother; they bought in services to

cover domestic chores in order to use their non-paid-working time to spend with their children. Some defined time with their children as needing to be 'quality' time and were resentful of having to do housework when their time at home was so limited. From the data, the women doctors' time was actually split between paid work and child-centred activities. Interestingly, none of the women in this sample used paid care to pursue their own leisure activities.

STOLEN TIME – AUTONOMOUS LEISURE OR CHILD-CENTRED ACTIVITIES?

Deem (1986) argues that leisure is a highly gendered activity. For men, an hour less at work means an hour extra leisure time. For women, because the demarcation lines between leisure and work are so difficult to define, an hour less spent on paid work means an hour more for other, most often child-centred, activities. From the interview data, when asked about time for themselves, most of the women doctors replied that they did not have any autonomous leisure activities at all. The specific leisure activities they had enjoyed prior to childbirth, were often seen as inappropriate now, such as mountain climbing or hill walking.

> Yes, we've had to give up most things because we liked doing things where you could not easily involve young children ... we did try walking with him in a rucksack but he didn't like it so that was the end of that.
>
> (Senior Registrar, Oncology, 1 child and pregnant)

When children are of varying ages and engage in extra-curricula activities mothers have to be extremely inventive to keep up with dependants' demands on their time. The following extract gives insight into one registrar's weekend:

> ... if all four of you are doing stuff outside work that becomes a major problem. We were giving a concert on Saturday which meant you rehearse in the afternoon and give a concert in the evening, plus one of my children goes to orchestra on Saturday morning so by the time we get up and I have [a smallholding] as well, so I have to milk the goat and do the chickens and the geese and then you take the one to orchestra and the other one goes to start the party ... it all gets a bit frantic but there we are.
>
> (Registrar, Public Health Medicine, 2 children)

The above extract highlights how this professional woman's leisure time and autonomous interests are very much linked to her two children's out-of-school time activities. Her smallholding though was her 'oasis' which she found extremely satsifying to keep. This 'leisure' pursuit was unique among the doctors, most had given up autonomous activities until their children were older.

With one exception where a partner was unemployed at the time of data collection, all the doctors in my sample were married to men who also had demanding jobs, most often to other doctors. Their partners worked long hours and so, because these women were working part-time and spent more time with the children their leisure time became inextricably linked to their children's. None of the women used paid childcare time for their own leisure activities. Non-paid-working time was most often spent 'ferrying' children to and from their activities.

> Well the age spread of the children is ten, five and twenty months so they have very different demands, which means evenings tend to get taken up and [working longer hours] would mean cancelling something or not being able to take them to something and I thought that wasn't fair on them.
>
> (Senior Registrar, Paediatrics, 3 children)

The doctors' leisure time, or at least that time when they were not in paid employment, was spent in a supervisory or support role, for example taking the children swimming or organizing and helping with children's concerts, or supporting school sports activities.

CONCLUSIONS

This chapter has explored the gendered nature of time for a sample of women hospital doctors who are training part-time as a response to their familial position. Such negotiations can be viewed negatively from a career progression point of view, but in fact are seen positively by the women because of the extra time made available to spend with children. As a consequence the women in this sample have the main responsibility for the management of the domestic sphere. Thus although they achieve a valued aim of spending more time with their children, they are burdened with the entire responsibility for the domestic sphere, which was not an intended outcome (Hochschild, 1990). Many will transfer their work skills to delegate household chores and so buy themselves extra time for child-care activities. They develop a more instrumental view of time use in the home, as they actively want to spend time with their children but see time spent on housework as wasted, and a negative use of their time. Because they divide their time between paid work and childcare, they are less able to 'steal' time for their own leisure activities, but give them up or adapt them to suit their children's abilities and needs.

It is important not to overlook the central importance of calendrical and clock time as part of the pragmatics of daily life (Adam, 1996). For the family unit to function successfully, sleeping, eating and getting up times have to be negotiated and established so that paid work and school times can be adhered to (Edwards, 1993). The pivotal point here rests on those factors operative in the construction of the individual family member's daily 'time-table'. Women's timetables tend to be constructed around the needs and demands of dependants: partners, children and elderly parents. Women's daily time allocations for different tasks are determined by deferring to dependants' time-tables which are perceived to take priority over the mother's (Hantrais, 1993). After all, her *primary* role is to care for and attend to her children's and partner's needs. Because the dominant ideology concerning the 'family' in contemporary Britain locates the wife/mother/daughter as the prime familial carer (Richardson, 1993) then her own work, needs and leisure are seen as secondary to others. Availability and use of time therefore can be seen to be gendered. If it is accepted that time is socially constructed and that it is externally determined for women through partners' and children's timetables, then it follows that women cannot use time as a taken-for-granted commodity – rather it has to be 'earned', 'bought' and even 'stolen'. The gendered nature of time and how women struggle to allocate it in ways that allow them to be visibly successful in their public and private lives are therefore central to understanding how professional women combine their working lives with their domestic lives.

REFERENCES

Adam, B. (1989) 'Time and Health Implicated: a Conceptional Critique' in R. Frankenberg (ed.) *Time and Health*. London: Kluwer.

Adam, B. (1995) *Timewatch: the Social Analysis of Time*. Cambridge: Polity Press.

Adam, B. (1996) 'Time for Feminist Approaches to Technology: Nature and Work' in J. Pilcher and A. Coffey (eds) *Gender and Qualitative Research*. Aldershot: Avebury.

Apter, T. (1993) *Professional Progress: Why Women Still Don't Have Wives*. London: Macmillan.

Beechey, V. and Perkins, T. (1987) *A Matter of Hours: Women, Part-Time Work and the Labour Market*. Cambridge: Polity Press.

Blyton, P. (1985) *Changes in Working Time: an International Review*. London: Croom Helm.

Brannen, J., Meszaros, G., Moss, P. and Poland, G. (1994) *Employment and Family Life: a Review of the Research in the UK (1980–1994)*. London: Thomas Coram Research Unit.

Cockburn, C. (1983) *Brothers: Male Dominance and Technological Change*. London: Pluto.

Cockburn, C. (1991) *In the Way of Women: Men's Resistance to Sex Equality in Organizations*. Basingstoke: Macmillan Education.

Coser, R.L. (1974) *The Family: its Structure and Functions*. London: Macmillan.

Davies, K. (1990) *Women, Time, and the Weaving of the Strands of Everyday Life*. Aldershot: Avebury.

Deem, R. (1986) *All Work and No Play?: a Study of Women's Leisure*. Milton Keynes: Open University Press.

Dex, S. and McCulloch, A. (1995) *Flexible Employment in Britain: a Statistical Analysis*. Equal Opportunities Commission, Discussion Paper No. 15. Manchester: Equal Opportunities Commission.

Dowie, R. (1987) *Postgraduate Medical Education and Training: the System in England and Wales*. London: King Edward's Hospital Fund for London.

Edwards, R. (1993) *Mature Women Students: Separating or Connecting Family and Education*. London: Taylor and Francis.

Elchardus, M. (1991) 'Flexible Men and Women: the Changing Temporal Organisation of Work and Culture', *Social Science Information*, 30, 701–26.

Everingham, C. (1994) *Motherhood and Modernity: an Investigation into the Rational Dimension of Mothering*. Buckingham: Open University Press.

Finch, J. (1983) *Married to the Job*. London: Allen and Unwin.

Finch, J. and Mason, J. (1993) *Negotiating Family Responsibilities*. London: Routledge.

Forman, F.J. (ed.) (1989) *Taking our Time: Feminist Perspectives on Temporality*. Oxford: Pergamon Press.

Fowlkes, M. (1980) *Behind Every Successful Man: Wives of Medicine and Academe*. New York: Colombia University Press.

Fox, M. (1989) 'Unreliable Allies: Subjective and Objective Time in Childbirth' in F.J. Forman (ed.) *Taking our Time*. Oxford: Pergamon Press.

Hantrais, L. (1993) 'The Gender of Time in Professional Occupations', *Time and Society*, 2, 2, 139–57.

Hochschild, A. (1990) *The Second Shift: Working Parents and the Revolution at Home*. London: Piatkus.

McRae, S. (1990) *Keeping Women In: Strategies to Facilitate the Continuing Employment of Women in Higher Level Occupations*. London: Policy Studies Institute.

Martin, J. and Roberts, C. (1984) *Women and Employment: a Lifetime Perspective*. London: HMSO.

Moore, W. (1963) *Man, Time and Society*. London: John Wiley and Sons.

Morris, L. (1995) *Social Divisions: Economic Decline and Social Structural Change*. London : UCL Press.

Phoenix, A. and Woollett, A. (1991) 'Motherhood: Social Construction, Politics and Psychology' in Phoenix, A., Woollett, A. and Lloyd, E. (eds) *Motherhood: Meanings, Practices and Ideologies*. London: Sage.

Reinharz, S. (1992) *Feminist Methods in Social Research.* Oxford: Oxford University Press.

Richardson, D. (1993) *Women, Motherhood and Childrearing.* Basingstoke: Macmillan.

Rue, R. (1975) *Organisation and Service Problems.* Proceedings of a Conference on Women in Medicine. London: HMSO.

Stephens, J. (1996) 'From "Honorary Chap" to Mother: Combining Work in the Professions with Motherhood' in Pilcher, J. and Coffey, A. (eds) *Gender and Qualitative Research.* Aldershot: Avebury.

Walby, S. (1986) *Patriarchy at Work: Patriarchal and Capitalist Relations in Employment.* Cambridge: Polity Press.

Walby, S. (1990) *Theorizing Patriarchy.* Oxford: Basil Blackwell.

Witz, A. (1992) *Professions and Patriarchy.* London: Routledge.

7 Negotiating the Home and the School: Low Income, Lone Mothering and Unpaid Schoolwork

Kay Standing

INTRODUCTION

At the same time as the number of lone-mother families living on low incomes has increased (Department of Social Security, 1993), schools and education policy in the UK has demanded the greater involvement of parents in their children's schooling (Department of Education, 1994). Parental involvement, however, is presented as an ungendered concept – ungendered on paper but not in practice. It is primarily mothers who are involved in the day-to-day work of their children's schooling, regardless of their marital situation (Lareau, 1989; Reay, 1995; David *et al.*, 1996) – it is maternal, rather than parental involvement – and performed under differing material conditions.

The implications of this for women's household work has not been considered adequately in previous feminist debates on the household. This chapter begins to explore the relationships between mothers and their children's schooling, examining the ways in which the demands of the school dictate the organization of the household and the particular implications this has for low-income lone-mother families.

The co-ordination of the household and school day is an activity that seems so obvious, so banal, that it merits little consideration in literature on household work or education. It is seen as part of the everyday lives of women. However, as Gillian Rose (1993: 17) argues:

> For feminists, the everyday routines traced by women are never unimportant, because the seemingly banal and trivial events of the everyday are bound into the power structures which limit and confine women. The limits on women's everyday activities are structured by what society expects women to be, and therefore to do.

The acts of parental involvement, preparing children for school, taking them to school and helping with homework are all seen as part of the work of mothering (Smith, 1988; Enders-Dragesser, 1991; Reay, 1995). Yet these tasks are time consuming, and require planning, forethought and effort by mothers to ensure the daily routine of the school and the home run smoothly. In this way, such work constitutes part of the invisible, everyday household work of mothers. Normative expectations also define what is 'proper' mothering (Smart, 1996), and exclude groups of women who fall outside of 'normal' mothering, and threaten patriarchal control of the family and household:

> In the context of 'normalizing motherhood', working class unmar-ried mothers are perceived as most disruptive of the norms. They are presumed to be 'bad mothers' in opposition to the married 'good mother'.
>
> (Bortolaia Silva, 1996: 4)

Both ideologies of 'good mothering' and parental involvement are infused with a white, middle-class conception of mothering skills (Walkerdine and Lucey, 1989; Walkerdine, 1990). Current ideals of mothering contain a strong pedagogical element, conceptualizing mothering in terms of its edu-cational functions. Mothers are expected to teach children, and teach them in a way which co-ordinates with the school. Implicit in this is the assump-tion that certain 'types' of mothers (lone mothers, poor mothers, black mothers) cannot mother 'properly' (Edwards, 1995).

This chapter aims to raise issues around the unpaid schoolwork of mothers by highlighting the gendered nature of parental involvement (that it is mothers, not fathers who are involved in their children's schooling) and the hidden work in the home and the school that mothers perform in support of their children's schooling. For low-income lone-mother fami-lies this unpaid schoolwork takes place within structural, economic and ideological constraints which this chapter discusses using the voices of lone mothers themselves. The chapter begins by explaining what is meant by parental involvement, and what the unpaid schoolwork of mothers involves. It then outlines the position of lone mothers in the UK, and how they are placed in a particular, negative relationship to the schools through the construction of low-income lone mothers as 'feckless' and a 'social threat'. Using data from a research project, I then give examples of how the school impacts on lone mothers' household work, and how this rein-forces gender inequalities.

MATERNAL INVOLVEMENT IN EDUCATION

It is true that discipline begins at home. Children learn a great deal in their earliest years ... When your child starts at school you can play your part in many ways. By law you are responsible for making sure that he or she goes to school regularly, and on time. But you can do more than that. For instance, by supporting the schools policy on behaviour you can help the school run efficiently and to develop pupils full potential. If your child is an older pupil, he or she may need a quiet space to work at home.

You might also volunteer to share your skills and interests with pupils and teachers, and attend meetings and other events at the school. Such support can have a very positive effect on the life of the school, and on your own child's performance.

(The updated Parents Charter, DoE, 1994, p. 25–6)

Parents' undertakings:
To ensure my child is at school on time with all the things she needs (uniform, PE kit, pencil case, swimming kit etc).
To encourage my child to complete all work set and give her all the support I can, making sure she gets a good night's sleep every night.
To encourage my child to complete her homework and provide, to the best of my ability, suitable conditions for her to do this.

(Example of a School Contract)

The consensus amongst educationalists in Britain is that there should be a 'partnership' between the home and the school in which parental involvement is central, (see for example Wolfendale, 1989; Atkin *et al.*, 1991). As the above examples from the 'Parents Charter' and home/school contract from one of the schools in the research study show, parents are expected to be available both at home and in the school to work with and support their children's learning.

Parental involvement as defined by educational policy and the schools involves a range of pedagogical and educational tasks which articulate to the school. These include the provision of a 'positive learning environment', and the organization of routine household tasks to fit the school day. Parental involvement means helping with homework, helping in the classroom as classroom assistants, reading with your child, taking part in activities and outings, and doing 'extra curricula activities'. It entails providing time, space and equipment (books, computers etc.) for children to work at home, and supporting the school in various ways – attending meetings and school events as well as supporting the philosophy of the school. Parental involvement presupposes the availability of time, material resources and knowledge of the education system. Whilst this is an issue for all mothers, it has different implications for lone-mother households.

Much of the work done in the home by mothers supports the smooth running of the school organization, in terms both of preparing children for school and supporting children's schooling on a daily basis. In the pre-school years mothers are expected to prepare their children for entry into school (New and David, 1985). Children are expected to be able to recognize numbers, colours, letters of the alphabet, be prepared for the school day and be able to sit quietly and work. On entering school, mothers have a range of tasks to do with their children. Whilst there are differences in how mothers understand their support and involvement in their children's schooling, mothers all share participation in a range of household tasks that involve the practical maintenance, emotional and educational work in support of their children's schooling on a daily basis. These are not only the educational tasks that I describe above, but also the routine household tasks such as washing and dressing children (Walkerdine and Lucey, 1989). Children must be dressed to a certain standard (possibly in uniform), have to arrive at school at a specified time, have all the equipment they need for the school day, be provided with food (such as breakfast and potentially lunch) at times which co-ordinate with the school timetable, be collected from school at a specified time with a responsible adult at home; time and space must be provided for homework, and children must be put to bed in order to get adequate rest to prepare them for the following school day.

As children move through the school system and take on some responsibility for their everyday participation in the classroom themselves, the schoolwork required of the mother changes from physical to emotional support, and the material costs of schooling rise. All mothers share this emotional labour, and constraints on their activities and the shape of the day (Tivers, 1985), but there are particular implications for women mothering alone on low incomes.

Dorothy Smith and Alison Griffith (1990) argue that parental involvement schemes implicitly depend on the existence of the nuclear, two-parent family, with breadwinner father and stay-at-home wife and mother. This family model releases the mother for household and schoolwork, and serves to problematize other ways of living and different family forms. Yet family structures are changing, and at the same time as schools have been demanding the greater involvement of mothers, the number of lone-mother families in the UK has been increasing, and the number of nuclear families declining (Burghes, 1996), thus undermining this model of parental involvement. The implications of this for both education and for the unpaid household work of mothers have not, on the whole, been considered in educational and social policy or feminist writing on the household.

Feminist debates around household work, childcare and power in the 1970s and 1980s (such as Oakley, 1974) largely ignored the role played by mothers in the school and in unpaid schoolwork at home. It often assumed that entry to schooling brings 'liberation' from the drudgery of domestic and childcare work (Gavron, 1963) allowing mothers to (re)enter the paid labour market. However, as I will show in this chapter, childcare and domestic responsibilities may change as children enter school, from physical to emotional work, but the responsibility for providing 'good enough schooling' falls on to mothers, whose lives are organized around school hours and holidays. The particular implications that this has for lone-mothers on low incomes are the concerns of the rest of the chapter.

LOW INCOME, LONE MOTHERS AND MATERNAL INVOLVEMENT IN SCHOOLING

Lone mothers currently make up 19 per cent of all families with children in the UK (Millar, 1992). Lone-mother families are increasingly characterized by poverty and dependence on state benefits. Two-thirds of lone-mother families are in poverty. Over 60 per cent have incomes below half the national average, and 70 per cent rely on state benefits (Roll, 1992). Whilst not all lone mothers are on low incomes, and lone mother-hood is not the prerogative of those who are in poverty, lone motherhood has important repercussions for those dependent on benefits (Bradshaw and Millar, 1991), and different implications for educational choices and involvement in schooling (Standing, 1997a). Research in Germany has shown that for some lone mothers being on benefit can been seen as a positive opportunity at certain stages of their lives (Madge and Neususs, 1994). Certainly in relation to the school day whose hours and holidays do not co-ordinate with the paid employment market, combined with a lack of affordable childcare, for many lone mothers being on benefit is the only way they can negotiate their household schedule with the school day.

There is an inherent contradiction between parental involvement and British (and North American) policy and rhetoric on lone-mother families. The current emphasis on getting lone mothers back into the paid work-force (Brown, 1989; Bradshaw and Millar, 1991) in order to cut welfare dependency is at odds with the stress on parental involvement in schooling which relies on mothers being at home to work with their child and help in the school. At best, ideologies of motherhood are ambivalent about mothers of young children working outside the home, emphasizing the mother's primary responsibility for children (Brannen and Moss, 1991). It also reinforces the notion of women's 'double burden' or 'second shift', as mothers who are in paid employment combine this with childcare duties and school involvement. Policies are similarly contradictory, reflecting the historical ambiguity over the status of lone mothers (Lewis, 1992) and failing to provide the means (in terms of affordable childcare) to facilitate lone mothers' entry to the paid workforce. Moreover, localized family and community beliefs on the compatibility of motherhood and work may encourage mothers to stay at home with their children (Edwards and Duncan, 1996). Whilst neither lone-mother nor working-mother families fit this model of good mothering, low-income lone mothers are particularly disadvantaged by the negative representation of them in the media, and in government policy and rhetoric.

A contradiction also remains between the view of parental involvement schemes and of lone-mother families. Parental involvement is presented as a universal panacea for society's ills – with positive parental support children from all social backgrounds can do well (Smith and Tomlison, 1989) and can prevent juvenile delinquency and crime (see Utting *et al.*, 1993). However, lone-mother families are seen by the New Right as part of the 'underclass' (Murray, 1990, 1994; Davies, 1993), and the source of the breakdown of the moral order, thus allegedly creating the very social conditions that parental involvement is seen to resolve:

> On the evidence available, such children tend to ... do less well at school ... to suffer more unemployment, to be more prone to deviance and crime and, finally, to repeat the cycle of unstable parenting from which they themselves have suffered.
>
> (Dennis and Erdos, 1992: xii)

In this way, the discourses of parental involvement and those around lone motherhood are inherently contradictory.

In the reminder of the chapter I will focus on the gendered work of parental involvement by looking at the 'micro-details' (Lareau, 1989) of lone mothers' unpaid schoolwork – the everyday household tasks that are negotiated around the school – and the structural and ideological constraints placed on low income lone mothers.

THE RESEARCH

> [W]e had all this thing about single parents were like the root of all
> evil ... I mean all the pressure we was getting like the government say-
> ing we're doing this, that and the other, and people believed it.
>
> (Michelle, 26, white working-class lone mother,
> income support, 2 children)

My research began in the summer of 1993, in the midst of the demoniza-
tion of lone mothers, as expressed by Michelle, above. The research project
is both the product, and the contestation of these negative representations.

The data for this chapter is drawn from in-depth interviews with
28 low-income lone mothers living on a large inner city council estate in
North London, participant observation in four local primary schools, and
interviews with eight teachers – the head teacher and one class teacher in
each school (Standing, 1998). It is an area with high levels of (male)
unemployment, and a large percentage of lone-mother families and ethnic
minority groups. The schools have a strong emphasis on parental involvement schemes and home-school links, and also have high levels of children receiving free school meals, and of pupils for whom English is a
second language. In reporting the data the names used are pseudonyms.

The women were contacted through snowballing techniques, beginning
with my own social network on the estate. Although a small sample, the
women reflect the varied ethnic make-up of the area. They have diverse
ethnic and class backgrounds, and range in age from 22 to 48. The women
became lone mothers through various routes, (single motherhood, divorce
and separation), and live in a variety of family situations, including living
with parents or with a new partner who does not share parenting responsibilities, as well as in lone mother and children households. All of the
women were on low incomes (below the national average) and claiming a
variety of state welfare benefits (including income support, family credit
and housing benefit). Four of the women were in full-time employment,
six in part-time work, and the remainder reliant on income support.

At the beginning of the research, issues of difference were at the forefront. I was not a lone mother, nor did I share the class and ethnic positioning of many of the women. As such I was aware of the dangers inherent in
the research of reinforcing negative stereotypes of lone mothers (especially
in the final stages of the research process, analysis and writing up, see
Standing, 1997b), but I wished to represent the diverse experiences of low-
income lone mothers in terms of how they understood their involvement in
their children's schooling, and how they were viewed by the schools.

My research is primarily concerned with how lone mothers negotiate their relationships with the schools in the context of the current negative representations of lone mothers as a 'social problem' (see the work of Murray, 1990; 1994 and the underclass debates). It is not primarily concerned with issues of power in the household. The interviews were (largely) unstructured, exploring the women's understandings of their situation as lone mothers, and their day-to-day involvement in their children's schooling. However, as the interviews progressed I became aware that the running of the household was to a large extent dictated by the school, and much of the women's household work was done in relation to the school. I am aware that the emphasis the women placed on the importance of the school timetable in the organization of the household could have been influenced by the framing of interviews in terms of their parental involvement in schooling. However, mothering and children's schooling seem so intertwined in the ideologies on good mothering and parental involvement that it seems to be impossible to talk to mothers about their children without reference to schooling. The running of the household and day-to-day lives of the women appeared to be, to a large extent, dictated by the demands of the school.

MANAGING THE SCHOOL DAY

> [E]verything is organised around Joanna and the school.
> > (Claire, 41, white working-class lone mother,
> > income support, 2 children)

The centrality of the school day was common in all the women's interviews. Central to the organization of the day and household routine is the 'school run'. The taking and collecting of children to and from school is a low-status yet essential task that commands little respect or consideration either amongst educationalists or (most) feminist theorists. Yet it is one factor that dictates the everyday lives of mothers of school-age children. Mothers' days are organized around taking and collecting children to and from school, nursery or playgroup, or, if the mothers are in paid employment, the responsibility for arranging 'school run' provision falls on their shoulders. The routine domestic and household tasks such as shopping, cooking and cleaning become more time consuming for mothers working under greater material constraints. Framing all this is the school, as the household is organized around the needs of the children, and thus around the school day/year. Karen illustrates how the daily routine revolves around taking and collecting children from school and nursery, leaving little time or opportunity for anything else:

> up at quarter to seven, get Conor's uniform ready, wake him up, come down here, get his breakfast, he gets dressed... make sure he's got his bag with all he needs in it... Pack him off at quarter past seven, get myself ready, get the girls up, come down, give them breakfast, take them back up, get them ready, get them to school, I take Kylie first then take Sky to nursery 'cos she doesn't have to be there 'til quarter to ten... Get home, tidy up, maybe do some shopping... Then I go and pick Sky up at quarter to three, pick her up, then go and get Kylie... Walk down to the station, pick Conor up, go home... Do the dinner, they colour and play while I'm doing the dinner, and then, um, we have our dinner, they watch telly, or play a game. I check Conor's homework, have a bath, get their 'jamas on... they go to bed and I'm in bed by half past nine, and it's the same thing every day, day in, day out.
>
> (Karen, 32, white working-class lone mother,
> income support, 3 children)

For some of the women, such as Karen, schooldays seemed to be marked by a tiring, monotonous routine. This is not to say that they did not enjoy and find great pleasure and satisfaction in mothering and their children – they did, and the quality of the relationship with their children was seen as one of the best factors in their images of themselves as lone mothers. Rather the work of co-ordinating the mother day (mother's everyday routines) and the school day under conditions of sole supporting, low-income mothering was presented to me as 'hard work', as tiring and time consuming, and above all, as unacknowledged, invisible work:

> I mean, bringing up children on your own is very difficult, people forget you've got them 24 hours, seven days a week, and it is very stressful.
>
> (Michelle, 26, white working-class lone mother,
> income support, 2 children)

Family and female kinship ties played a crucial role in negotiating between the home and the school for lone mothers. For the women whose family lived nearby, and who provided practical and emotional support, the organization of the mother day was easier to co-ordinate, as family took over the maternal involvement in school. Again it was women – sisters, grandmothers, aunts – whose time and energy was directed into the school. The involvement of men – absent fathers, or new partners – was noticeable by its absence:

> He [the father] never did anything anyway. He wasn't involved in their schooling, he didn't take an interest.
>
> (Karen, 32, white working-class lone mother, income support, 3 children)

Family provided both economic, physical and emotional support. The availability of family help and support was a central factor in the women's understandings of the organization of the mother day, and the ways in which they co-ordinated it with the demands of the school. Family-provided childcare enabled many of the women to supplement their income with some form of paid work, and provided time for the women away from the children.

> He's off with my mum ... She'll take him to school. He stays for school dinners, but that's from choice, he's got the choice. She'll then go and pick him up as well ... She has him till about six o'clock. She gives him his dinner, 'cos she like, she cooks for my dad anyway, so it's like a family meal. So when I get home, everything's really done ... My mum is, she's very involved, she does two days a week [in the school] she's always helped with the kids outings, they all know her.
>
> (Carol, 29, white working-class lone mother, full-time work, 1 son)

The involvement of female kin allowed the women to co-ordinate the household and the school day in a way which was satisfactory to the mothers.

The women without family nearby experienced the organization of the mother day differently, often speaking of feeling under pressure, both from the time demands of the school, and the emotional and mental demands of unsupported lone mothering. The absence of another adult meant less time was available; the women had no-one to take pressure from them, so that they could organize time for themselves. The process of everyday living on a low income is in itself time consuming, and leaves women with little or no energy for anything else, once the demands of the school day have been met:

> the worst thing is ... having no-one there to sort of support in a practical way. If I'm exhausted I still have to make sure Joanne's had a bath and done her reading, and Wayne's got his work finished. It'd be nice to take a day off occasionally. It's just, I don't feel I can spend much time relaxing, and money, money's a big problem.
>
> (Claire, 41, white working-class lone mother, income support, 2 children)

Lone mothering brought with it further contradictions in the organization of the mother day and the power relations within the household. The
women often, but not always, had only themselves and their children
around whom to organize their time. This gave the women both power
over their (limited) resources, leaving them with more income for themselves and their children (see also Bradshaw and Millar, 1991; Graham,
1993), and power in decision making for their family, as Carol illustrates:

> I can decide for Daniel what I think is best without interference from
> anybody else.
>
> (Carol, 29, white working-class lone mother, full-time work, 1 son)

The absence of a partner also brought with it autonomy in the organization
of their time, freedom from having to organize around the demands of a
partner, and often a lessening of household work as Michelle describes:

> No-one to clean up after, no dirty socks stinking out the wash basket, I
> don't have to cook if I don't want to.
>
> (Michelle, 26, white working-class lone mother,
> income support, 2 children)

However, this was balanced by the lack of support from a partner, as
Claire above has illustrated.

There is a disjuncture too, between the paid-work schedule and the
school schedule (Griffith and Smith, 1990) which Karen, below highlights:

> If I worked say, what am I going to do in the six weeks holiday? In all
> the holidays? It could be a week, it could be three weeks, it could be six
> weeks. Then I've got three different kids of three different ages at three
> different schools, then what do you do? No one's going to want to look
> after three kids. So at the moment there's no chance of me going back
> to work.
>
> (Karen, 32, white working-class lone mother,
> income support, 3 children)

This meant the mothers who were in paid work chose jobs (typically part-
time, low-paid and low-status) to fit around the school hours, in order to
co-ordinate the school run:

> It's perfect because, erm, it's what I dreamed of getting. I mean the
> work sucks, point blank, but the job is noon to three, Monday to Friday,
> term time only.
>
> (Susan, 38, black lone mother, part-time work, 2 daughters)

The experience of Susan (above) is typical of many lone mothers. Susan works part-time as a catering assistant in the local secondary school. Highly qualified in the United States of America, her 'dream job' is a low-paid, low-status post, chosen simply because it fits in with the school timetable, hours and holidays, and is a steady and reliable source of income.

HOMEWORK IN THE SCHOOL AND SCHOOLWORK IN THE HOME

Parental involvement also assumes that women are available to help in the classroom, and in the home after school – the assumption that women's time and energy is endlessly available to be called on by the school rests on a particular view of women's roles in the family, as the quote below illustrates:

> Schools are always looking for people to help, so I suppose if they think a single parent can't go out to work 'cos of the kids, well, they'll tap that resource as quickly as possible.
>
> (Claire, 41, white working-class lone mother, income support, 2 children)

The women experienced this help in contradictory ways, for example:

> When I wasn't working it was lovely, because I was able to get myself involved in there, in the primary school, and I used to do that by way of taking, going swimming with them, in the water, doing some cookery classes for the infants, I used to go in on a certain day every week, so I did have a big commitment.
>
> (Maria, 42, white working-class lone mother, full-time work, 3 daughters)

However, for Karen this classroom help was experienced as an unwelcome expectation of the school, a feeling of being 'forced' to contribute her limited time and energy:

> I've been in [the school] and you have to, you're not made to, not made to help, but like they want parents to help more now, and so she's only there a week and I had to clean, wash all the towels for the whole nursery.
>
> (Karen, 32, white working-class lone mother, income support, 3 children)

Most of the women interviewed had at some stage helped in the classroom. The unpaid work that the mothers did in school was an extension of the household work done in the home – 'read with them, tell them stories, cook with them … just help out' (Michelle). It was taking the domestic and childcare skills of women – cooking, cleaning, reading to children – out of the home, and into the school with little acknowledgement of these skills.

The expectation of schools that mothers' time is always available extends to the out-of-school hours. The demands of homework provide a way of the school monitoring the running of the household, as well as dictating its schedule. It breaks down the public-private divide by bringing the work of the school into the home, with little acknowledgement of its impact on the household:

> I have to be at home, I have to supervise the children, I have to clean the house, I have to cook, I have to make sure my household is running smoothly, and er, I have to work, I have to go home, I have to make sure I'm there because, er, I have to be there to make sure their homework is done, that I am around, as a kind of support unit for them.
>
> (Desmie, 45, black Afro-Caribbean lone mother,
> full-time work, 3 children)

All of the women read to their children at home, helped with homework, or did some kind of schoolwork, the majority every night:

> She's always had a homework every evening … she reads every evening, she has to review the book and draw a picture from [it], and that's every evening and sometimes there's extras like some English and spelling she has, so we have to work on it every day.
>
> (Claire, 41, white working-class lone mother, 2 children)

Most of the women couched their school work in terms of the parental involvement discourse and their 'mothering' role, seeing it as work done not for the school, but for their children:

> It's part of my job as a mother, I'm responsible for them, it's always part of my job to see that they get a good education, and if that means by me helping them when they come home, then that's fine.
>
> (Grainne, 28, white Irish working-class lone mother,
> income support, 2 daughters)

Not all of the mothers however, saw their schoolwork with children at home as 'part of the mothering role'. Several had distinct boundaries between school and home, believing for example that:

> school is for learning, when he comes home he should be playing, doing other things, not learning, learning all the time.
>
> (Maya, 22, black working-class lone mother, 1 son, income support)

These were boundaries which homework blurred. This lack of acknowledgement of the work mothers do inside and outside the schools, and the differential circumstances of lone-mother families, leads to the reinforcement of gender, class and race discrimination.

LONE MOTHERS, HOUSEHOLD WORK AND SCHOOLING

There were differences in the ways the women organized and negotiated the household and the school day. However, the responsibility for involvement in children's schooling was always the mother's. In this way mothers' involvement in their children's schooling can be conceptualized as a form of unpaid household labour which brings the work of the school into the home and brings into question where the boundaries of household work lie. Uta Enders-Draggesser (1987) argues that the hours of unpaid hidden women's labour involved both in work as volunteers in the school, and in homework is both exploitation and a misogynistic practice. Through women's unpaid schoolwork, the school exercises control and ideological influence over mothers and children by a patriarchal double standard in which (often) female teachers work, whilst mothers, who are doing identical work, 'help' their children out of love and obligation. In this way, she argues, maternal help amounts to lessons taking place outside of the school organization, and the privatization of education. It takes the responsibility from the school into the home with no recognition of the differing backgrounds and resources available to mothers, and with no recognition of the role played by other providers of childcare, such as grandmothers, relatives or paid carers. In addition there is a further contradiction, as increasingly teachers have a low status and wage level in comparison to other professions requiring similar levels of training.

The ways in which the women negotiated their timetables around the demands of the school, whether in paid employment or not, were influenced by the quality and quantity of help and support from family, friends and, to a much lesser extent, partners and absent fathers. It was this family support, or lack of it, that was crucial in the co-ordination of paid work and the school timetable. For those mothers not in paid employment, family support, both materially and in kind – by way of childcare – was crucial to the organization of the mother day, in particular to the amount of time the women perceived they had for themselves, or for paid employment opportunities. However, the women did share certain material and ideological constraints on their involvement in their children's schooling.

For low-income lone mothers, the co-ordination of the school day and the mother day is inherently contradictory. For lone mothers on benefit, available both to be involved in the classroom and organize their day around the school, inequalities of access to resources, both of time (through support of other adults) and materially (finances, adequate housing, access to transport etc.), linked with the negative representation of lone mothers on benefit, mean they are both discursively and structurally disadvantaged in relation to the schools. Those lone mothers who were in paid employment had to co-ordinate their working day with the school timetable, or provide satisfactory childcare for the out of school hours.

By not recognizing their differential situation, schools conceptualize lone mothers as 'failing' to give their children enough support because of their different family structure and economic situation:

> If you're a lone parent with not much money then you can't afford the things that would help with your child's education, computers etc. ... reports, I know she would get better marks if she could word process 'em.
>
> (Jane, white working-class lone mother, income support, 1 daughter)

Maria illustrates the difficulty of meeting the school's expectations on mothers' roles:

> I got the impression that if she wasn't doing well it was my fault ... well that really got up my nose, because you know, she's there for 7 hours, or God knows how long, and if she's at home ... you know the hours before they go to bed, you want to be doing other things ... I do resign myself to 15 minutes, half an hour a night on each of them, but I did take umbrage at the fact that they, it was like my fault if they weren't getting on ... because I'm a single parent ... I was in a position where I was less likely to give my time to them, now if two parents had been there, it would've been easier for them, in theory ... I'm not saying the dad's around all the time, but in theory I felt um, a bit put out and angered by the fact that it was on me, it was my fault if they weren't doing well, 'cos I had to resign myself to doing this every night, and yeah, most of the time you could, but if you didn't you were made to feel guilty.
>
> (Maria, 42, white working-class lone mother,
> full-time work, 3 daughters)

Maria points to both the structural and ideological constraints facing lone mothers. The absence of a father figure throws up contradictions. There may be 'freedom' from having to organize time around another adult, as discussed above, but it may also mean that there is less time available to devote to involvement in children's schoolwork. Implicit in this is the view that children would do better if the father was present.

In this way, the unpaid schoolwork of mothers becomes invisible twice over, invisible as household labour, as work which requires thought, planning and time, and invisible as work which, through homework and the child's behaviour in school, disappears into the child and emerges as the child's performance in school (Griffith and Smith, 1991). As the example from Maria shows, this invisible household work is only acknowledged when the child does not fit the classroom order, is not doing well, or is a 'problem'. Then the schoolwork of mothers is scrutinized for what is wrong (Griffith and Smith, 1991), and in lone-mother families, what emerges as 'wrong' is the family structure. Whilst there is no single experience of 'being' a lone mother (Smith, 1988), and there are contested and contradictory discourses around lone motherhood (Phoenix, 1996) the negative ideas around lone motherhood organize lone mothers into a particular, negative relationship with the schools. This is a relationship in which a child's performance at school becomes problematized through her home background, and the mother's household work is mediated and judged by her child's performance and behaviour at school. The lone mother family is placed in a deficit relationship to the school – she is seen as 'lacking' and lone mothers' involvement in their children's schooling also becomes apparently deficient, with children's educational 'problems' being blamed on family structure.

Within the deficit view of lone-mother families, the work that lone mothers do with their children is seen to be 'inadequate'. Annette Lareau's (1989) research in the USA shows that although lone mothers participate more in their children's schooling, their work is seen to be 'deficient'. The evidence from my research appears to support this view, that lone mothers' parental involvement becomes conceptualized by the schools as inadequate.

The boundaries of parental involvement are set by the school, and there is a fine line between mothers' work being supportive of the school, or being conceptualized as 'over involved' and 'pushy mothers'. For the schools in the research, all with a high percentage of lone-mother families, despite rhetoric to the contrary, the negative discourses around lone motherhood informed the general ethos of the school, making implicit judgements of lone mothers, for example:

I don't see any difference with lone parents, but having said that, most of the difficult parents, the ones we have problems with are lone

parents … lone mothers, because they live alone and don't have the social support, tend to live their lives through their children.
(Mr Clayton, headteacher, Blue Coat Church of England voluntary aided primary school)

In this way, lone mothers' identities are constructed by the school through their children, and they are thus judged through their children's behaviour and performance in the classroom.

Although all the women felt they were 'doing the best' for their children, the schools interpreted their involvement as deficient. This feeling was reflected on by the mothers, that they had, through their family situation, somehow 'neglected' their children:

I mean I've neglected my kids basically, with their learning, trying to work and keeping the family together, being a single mum.
(Lorraine, 30, black Afro-Caribbean working-class lone mother, part-time work, 2 children)

This has a class and race element as well as a gender one. Living in racist and patriarchal society imposes both structural and moral constraints on black lone mothers. The black women in the research were more likely to have challenged the schools over their children and their own involvement, but were also more likely to have been viewed as 'problem' mothers by the schools – as having unrealistic expectations for their children, for example:

There was one teacher who was just so racist … she said I should not expect my children to achieve, she could never bring herself to say his work was excellent.
(Desmie, 45, black African lone mother, full-time work, 3 children)

The experiences of the school's low expectations are linked to the women's social positioning as black, low-income lone mothers:

I think expectations are quite low, and I think it feeds into all that other stuff about sort of having a view of these kids as somehow, you know, deprived. So yes, they're black, they're from single parent families, they live in the inner city, so therefore we don't have to expect very much of them.
(Helen, black lone mother, income support, 2 sons)

Within parental involvement lone mothers' work in the household for the school is both invisible and deficient. The lack of awareness shown in the demands of parental involvement of the differential social position of lone mothers, as well as of race and class inequalities, means that the school-work of low-income lone mothers becomes constructed as inadequate and wrong.

CONCLUSIONS

This chapter has begun to explore how the school schedule dictates the everyday lives of lone mothers, in terms both of school hours and holidays, the unpaid monitoring of children's schoolwork at home and the expectation of mothers' unpaid help in the classroom. In this way I argue that the work of the home is brought into the school, and that of the school into the home, and the boundaries of the public and private, and the location where household work takes place are brought into question. The school becomes part of wider power relations which structure the domestic sphere and women's position and responsibility within it.

The requirements of parental involvement place the responsibility for academic 'success' on parents. Whilst lone mothers on low incomes are held to blame for economic disadvantage, crime and delinquency (Murray, 1990) disadvantage or privilege are seen to occur in the domestic sphere, separate from the school and other structural factors. The differential educational, financial and social circumstance of lone mothers are ignored. This chapter has shown how lone mothers, by being a family form that does not provide a type of mothering work which co-ordinates with the work organization of the school (Smith, 1988), are seen to 'fail' to give their children enough support.

The lack of acknowledgement that parental involvement takes place under differing circumstances – those of family structure, social class, ethnic origin, economic situation – serves to reproduce class, race and gender inequalities. The negotiations between the home and the school take place for lone mothers under material and ideological constraints – whilst these negotiations may be eased by the availability of family help and other factors, the work of negotiating the home and the school is difficult to do under the conditions of low-income lone mothering. The denial of the gendered nature of this involvement works to obscure and hide the work that mothers do in relation to their children's schooling. By accepting parental involvement as an ungendered concept, free from class and cultural associations, the unpaid schoolwork that mothers do inside the home as well as in school, is rendered invisible. This gender neutrality favours fathers (even where the father may not be present, let alone involved in children's schooling) by removing the work that women do for their children and their children's schooling and constructing it as 'nurture' and 'natural' (Smith, 1988; Smart, 1989). The unpaid schoolwork that lone mothers do to create opportunities for their children, and the power relations implicit in it, is part of the invisible, gendered work of women in the household and an issue which needs further debate in feminist theorizing on the household.

REFERENCES

Atkin, J., Bastiani, J. and Goode, J. (1991) *Listening to Parents: an approach to the Improvement of Home-School Relations*. London: Croom Helm.

Bradshaw, J. and Millar, J. (1991) *Lone Parent Families in the UK*. London: HMSO.

Brannen, J. and Moss, P. (1991) *Managing Mothers*. London: Unwin.

Brown, J. (1989) *Why Don't They Go to Work?* London: HMSO.

Bortolaia Silva, E. (ed.) (1996) *Good Enough Mothering: Feminist Perspectives on Lone Motherhood*. London: Routledge.

Burghes, L. (1996) 'Debates on Disruption: What Happens to the Children of Lone Parents' in E. Bortolaia Silva (ed.) *Good Enough Mothering: Feminist Perspectives on Lone Motherhood*. London: Routledge.

David, M., Davies, J., Edwards, R., Reay, D. and Standing, K. (1996) 'Mothering and Education: Reflexivity and Feminist Methodology' in L. Morley and V. Walsh (eds) *Breaking Boundaries: Women in Higher Education*. London: Taylor and Francis.

Davies, J. (1993) *The Family: Is it Just Another Lifestyle Choice?* London: IEA Health and Welfare Unit.

Dennis, N. and Erdos, G. (1993) *Families without Fatherhood*. London: Institute of Economic Affairs.

Department of Education (1994) *The Updated Parents Charter*. London: HMSO.

Department of Social Security (1993) *Social Security Statistics 1992*. London: HMSO.

Edwards, J. (1995) ' "Parenting Skills": Views of Community Health and Social Service Providers about the Needs of their "Clients" ', *Journal of Social Policy*, 24, 2, 345–41.

Edwards, R. and Duncan, S. (1996) 'Rational Economic Man or Lone Mothers in Context? The Uptake of Paid Work' in E. Bortolaia Silva (ed.) *Good Enough Mothering: Feminist Perspectives on Lone Motherhood*. London: Routledge.

Enders-Dragasser, U. (1987) 'Mothers' Unpaid Schoolwork in West Germany' in P.A. Schmuck (ed.) *Women Educators, Employees of Schools in Western Countries*. Albany: State of New York Press.

Enders-Dragasser, U. (1991) 'Child Care: Love, Work and Exploitation', *Women's Studies International Forum*, 14, 6, 551–56.

Gavron, H. (1963) *The Captive Wife: Conflicts of Housebound Mothers*. London: Routledge and Kegan Paul.

Graham, H. (1993) *Hardship and Health in Women's Lives*. London: Harvester Wheatsheaf.

Griffith, A.I. and Smith, D.E. (1990) 'What Did you do in School Today? Mothering, Schooling and Social Class', *Perspectives on Social Problems*, 2, 1–24.

Lareau, A. (1989) *Home Advantage: Social class and Parental Involvement in Elementary Education*. London: Falmer.

Lewis, J. (1992) *Women in Britain Since 1945*. London: Blackwell.

Madje, E. and Neususs, C. (1994) 'Lone Mothers in Berlin: Disadvantaged Citizens or Women Escaping Patriarchy? The Diverse Worlds of European Patriarchy', *Environment and Planning*, 26a, 9, 1419–33.

Millar, J. (1996) 'Poor Mothers and Absent Fathers: Support for Lone Parents in Comparative Perspective' in H. Jones and J. Millar (eds) *The Politics of the Family*. Aldershot: Avebury.

Murray, C. (1990) *The Emerging British Underclass*. London: IEA Health & Welfare Unit.

Murray, C. (1994) *Underclass: the Crisis Deepens*. London: IEA Health and Welfare Unit.

New, C. and David, M.E. (1985) *For the Children's Sake: Making Child-care More than Women's Business*. Penguin: London.

Oakley, A. (1974) *The Sociology of Housework*. Oxford: Marlin Robertson.

Phoenix, A. (1996) 'Social Constructions of Lone Motherhood: a Case of Competing Discourses' in E. Bortolaia Silva (ed.) *Good Enough Mothering: Feminist Perspectives on Lone Motherhood*. London: Routledge.

Reay, D. (1995) 'A Silent Majority? Mothers in Parental Involvement', *Women's Studies International Forum*, 18, 3, 337–48.

Rose, G. (1993) *Feminism and Geography: the Limits of Geographical Knowledge*. London: Polity.

Smart, C. (1989) *Feminism and the Power of Law*. London: Routledge.

Smart, C. (1996) 'Deconstructing Motherhood' in E. Bortolaia Silva (ed.) *Good Enough Mothering: Feminist Perspectives on Lone Motherhood*. London: Routledge.

Smith, D.E. (1988) *The Everyday World as Problematic: a Feminist Sociology*. Milton Keynes: Open University Press.

Smith, D.E. and Griffith, A.I. (1990) 'Co-ordinating the Uncoordinated: Mothering, Schooling and the Family Wage', *Perspectives on Social Problems*, 2, 25–43.

Smith, D.J. and Tomlinson, S. (1989) *The School Effect: a study of Multi-Racial Comprehensives*. London: Policy Studies Institute.

Standing, K. (1997a) 'Scrimping, Saving and Schooling: Lone mothers and 'Choice' in Education', *Critical Social Policy*, 17, 2, 79–99.

Standing, K. (1997b) 'Writing the Voices of the Less Powerful: Research on Lone Mothers' in J. Ribbens and R. Edwards (eds) *Feminist Dilemmas of Qualitative Research: Public Knowledge and Private Lives*. London: Sage.

Standing, K. (1998) *Lone Mothers' Involvement in their Children's Schooling: Inside and Outside the Discourse*. PhD dissertation, London: South Bank University.

Tivers, J. (1985) *Women Attached: Daily Lives of Women with Young Children*. London: Croom Helm.

Utting, D., Bright, J. and Henricson, C. (1993) *Crime and the Family: Improving Child-Rearing and Preventing Delinquency*. London: Family Policy Studies Centre.

Walkerdine, V. (1990) *Schoolgirl Fictions*. London: Verso.

Walkerdine, V. and Lucey, H. (1989) *Democracy in the Kitchen: Regulating Mothers and Socialising Daughters*. London: Virago.

Wolfendale, S. (1989) *Parental Involvement: Developing Networks Between School, Home and Community*. London: Cassell.

8 'Oh Please, Mum. Oh Please, Dad': Negotiating Children's Spatial Boundaries

Gill Valentine

INTRODUCTION

How to manage children's use of space is one of the biggest headaches for most parents. They are torn between wanting to protect their children from public dangers (in particular abduction, murder, traffic and accidents, see for example Cahill, 1990; Hillman *et al.*, 1990; Hillman and Adams, 1992; Blakely, 1994; Katz, 1995; Valentine, 1996a, 1996b), while also wanting them to be free to develop their independence by negotiating public space alone. In turn children want autonomy from their parents and are also subject to peer group pressure to 'play' outside the home further, longer and later. Children's spatial ranges (the distance and time children are allowed outside the home unsupervised by an adult) are therefore a source of constant negotiation in households between parents and their children, and between siblings.

There is a significant body of work within geography as an academic discipline (which overlaps with environmental psychology) on children's environments which has focused on children's access to and use of space and their perceptions of and attachment to place (see for example Anderson and Tindal, 1972; Blaut and Stea, 1974; Bunge and Bordessa, 1975; G. Moore, 1976; Hart, 1979; Downs, 1985; R. Moore, 1986; Ward, 1990; Katz, 1991, 1993, 1994). This work (which is summarized in Matthews, 1992 and Aitken, 1994) suggests that as children grow up they are allowed more spatial autonomy (Matthews, 1992). The age of ten appears to be a particularly significant watershed, beyond which children are deemed competent enough to handle roads and traffic alone and therefore are granted more spatial freedoms (Hart, 1979), although girls, according to a number of studies, are more restricted than boys (Saegert and Hart, 1978; Hart, 1979; Moore, 1986). This gendered nature of children's access to public space has been attributed to the fact that parents are more worried about girls' vulnerability to sexual assault by strangers than they are about boys; and to the fact that girls have traditionally had more domestic responsibilities than boys.

These studies however paid little attention to the processes through which children's spatial autonomy was negotiated, focusing largely on observing children, rather than on the discussions within households through which the children's competence was defined. This chapter therefore uses material from research conducted in Cheshire, Derbyshire, Greater Manchester and Yorkshire to explore the interactive processes within households through which children's spatial boundaries are determined. Particular consideration is given to the way parents construct gendered notions of their children's competence to negotiate public space safely, and to the way that children understand and exploit power dynamics in the household between their mothers and fathers. Attention is also paid to the way children in reconstituted and lone-parent households manipulate their 'biological' and 'social'[1] parents (and siblings), playing one household off against another to maximize their spatial autonomy.

In this chapter I emphasize two theoretical concepts: 'competence' and 'performance'. Competence has become a key concept in sociological work on children in the 1990s. A number of writers have pointed out that within both academic and contemporary popular understandings of childhood, children are commonly understood not to be different from adults, but to be less than adults (Waksler, 1986; Alanen, 1990; Blitzer, 1991). As a result they claim there has been a tendency to ignore children's own experiences and own understandings of the world (Waksler, 1986). Qvortrup (1994: 4) for example argues that 'the adult world does not recognize children's praxis, because competence is defined merely in relation to adults' praxis.' This critique has prompted the development of a body of sociological work which has sought to acknowledge children's competence by demonstrating the sophistication they exhibit in managing their own space, time and social relations and by exposing some of the ways children resist the definitions of childhood which are imposed on them by adults (Alanen, 1990; Prout and James, 1990).

The concept of performance is derived from the work of Judith Butler. In *Gender Trouble* (1990: 33) she argues that 'gender is the repeated stylization of the body, a set of repeated acts within a highly rigid regulatory framework that congeal over time to produce the appearance of substance, of a natural order of being'. In the same way, age like gender, is also understood in this paper to be a performative act that is naturalized through repetition.

The findings of this chapter are based on a two-year study funded by the ESRC which used multi-methods to explore parental concerns about children's use of public space. The research canvassed the opinions and experiences of parents with a child aged between eight and 11 years old. This age group was selected as this is the stage when children begin to venture beyond the immediate vicinity of the home environment and thus independent neighbourhood play becomes a reality. The study consisted of two stages.

1. A self-completion questionnaire with cover letter and return envelope was distributed to parents through primary schools. This asked 75 questions divided into seven sections which explored the parents' attitudes to the local area, the child's play, the child's travel to school, the child's play through time, and their concerns for their child, and asked for biographical information about all the household members. Parents were asked to give answers only in relation to the child who had been given the questionnaire at school and not to include other children in the household. Nearly four hundred questionnaires were completed and returned.

2. On the basis of the responses to the questionnaire, 70 households were selected to take part in semi-structured in-depth interviews involving adults and children. Where there were two adults taking a parenting role in the household (some of which were 'social' rather than 'biological' parents) every effort was made to interview both of them, although this was not possible in every case. The in-depth interviews were used to develop issues explored in the survey, to cover additional themes of (often local) importance that were not addressed in the questionnaire; and to explore the complexities and contradictions in parents' attitudes and behaviour. The interviews considered not only parental attitudes towards the child given the questionnaire at school but also other children (older and younger) in the household and hence also explored how parents' attitudes to children's play varies according to a child's gender, age and position in the 'family'. The interviews were taped, transcribed and analysed using conventional social science techniques for handling qualitative data. Both methods were successfully piloted before being implemented in the research proper. In addition, focus groups were conducted with children in order to explore how they resist and contest parental restrictions.

NEGOTIATING CHILDREN'S COMPETENCE: AGE AND GENDER

The evidence of this research is that children's spatial boundaries are the product of complex negotiations within households between children and adults which take place within the broader framework of local and national discourses about what it means to be a 'good parent' and where it is appropriate for a child to be allowed to go unaccompanied by an adult at a given age. Rather than children's spatial boundaries being rigidly fixed by adults according to a child's biological age, 'age', appears to be a performative identity, which is highly contested within households and which is sometimes simultaneously defined in contradictory ways. As Solberg (1990) has argued, children do not passively adhere to adult's definitions of what they are capable of doing at specific biological ages but play an active part in negotiating the meanings ascribed to their 'age' within their households. By performing or demonstrating competence in one aspect of their lives children use this evidence of their 'maturity' to try to negotiate more independence in other situations (Valentine, 1996a, 1997a). In particular, children use performative strategies in the private sphere of the home, such as cleaning their bedroom or helping in the kitchen, as levers to win more autonomy from their parents in public space.

> Richard's eight and he's not responsible enough to go to the shops on his own, so no he can't. If in six months' time he suddenly becomes responsible at home, then OK, fair enough. So it's not exact, an age, it's the actual child themselves.
>
> (Father, 'middle class', urban non-metropolitan borough)

While sometimes this strategy may be successful, on other occasions parents do not let the definition of a child's competence in one space spill over into another space. Rather, understandings of children's maturity in public and private can stand in awkward contradiction to each other. For example, this mother explains how she trusts her son sufficiently to allow him to take on responsibilities in the kitchen in an environment full of domestic hazards but does not let him walk to school alone.

> He knows it's about trust and about being honest, about – he'll only get those freedoms as he shows me he's capable of accepting those responsibilities. You start them within the home, giving him responsibilities, and building them up. I mean he makes toast and the next thing I want him to start learning is how to use the rings, the hobs, you know. Then when I know he can accept responsibility I'll actually start allowing him to go to school and back on his own.
>
> (Lone parent, 'working class', urban non-metropolitan area)

In the majority of cases – although there were a few exceptions – parents employed tougher and stricter measures of their children's competence in public space before they allowed their offspring a semblance of independence, than they adopted in private space, emphasizing the extent to which contemporary parents consider traffic accidents and stranger-dangers to be more important than domestic threats to their children's safety. Indeed, parents sometimes used 'stranger-danger' warnings to restrict their children's use of space, despite the fact that their children were deemed more 'grown up' in other situations – not because they were necessarily anxious about their children's 'streetwise' skills but rather because of anxieties that their offspring would get in with the wrong social crowd or become involved in drugs (Valentine, 1996a). Thus definitions of competence were also shaped by parental perceptions of their own locality – both in terms of the social make-up of their own neighbourhood (in relation to 'class' and 'race' tensions, drugs, crime, vandalism, gang violence and so on) and the physical characteristics of the environment (such as proximity to parks, alleys or places where their children may get into 'social' trouble as well as physical dangers). These evaluations in turn are influenced by the time of day (night-time is considered more dangerous because the people who dominate public space changes and therefore so too does the nature of space (Valentine, 1989)) and time of year (children have more freedom in the summer when daylight hours are longer; and in the vacation when their parents may be at work most of the day).

Often parents tested out children's newly negotiated spatial competence by using covert surveillance to ensure that they could handle their new found independence as this woman describes:

> [when her daughter started walking to school with friends] I used to hide around the corner like a Japanese sniper [sic] and I used to go, I used to watch them ... and then run. I used to have to run like the clappers before she came strolling down otherwise you see that would cause a row. But just for a couple of weeks I watched her do that.
>
> (Mother, 'middle class', urban metropolitan borough)

Children who broke the rules or behaved irresponsibly with their new found freedom would then find themselves returned to their previous status of 'less adult'; whereas those who demonstrated their maturity could be rewarded by being granted more independence. 'Conceptually therefore, children may "grow" or "shrink" in age as negotiations take place' (Solberg, 1990: 120). One consequence of this is that it encourages children to conceal 'dangerous' experiences from their parents because of a fear that informing them about these incidents might lead to a renegotiation of their spatial freedoms. Indeed children often described their parents' evaluations of local risks as irrational or naive, because they argued adults spend less time in the local area and so have less local knowledge on which to base risk assessments than the children themselves (Valentine, 1997a).

Children's performances of competence are also highly gendered. Although previous studies have suggested that parents perceive girls to be more vulnerable than boys, girls in this study seem to be more adept at negotiating responsibility. While girls were repeatedly identified by their parents (particularly their mothers) as sensible, logical and rational, and therefore as able to identify dangerous strangers – who are gendered as male (Valentine, 1996a) – in public space and to take appropriate action to avoid a threatening situation, boys were commonly described as 'immature', slow, irrational, and easily led by peers (as the quote below explains). Boys' lack of selfawareness in public space was also related to parents' perceptions of gender differences in sexual maturity. Mothers argued that their daughters were more body conscious at an early age and thus they found it easier to initiate conversations with their daughters about 'inappropriate touch' and sexual dangers than with their sons. Girls therefore receive more education about how to manage themselves in public space than boys. As a result girls were considered to be more 'streetwise' than their 'innocent' brothers.

> My son's a bit dizzy [laughter]. He is, he's sometimes not, sometimes he's on another planet, you know, he, he, he's not very responsible at all really, he's [pause] I mean you do say to him 'Don't get into strangers' cars or whatever' but I could see him doing it, I could. She's more level headed. She would come 'No', it would come straightaway. She's more sensible. She's quite a dominant person ... she can take care of herself [laughter].
>
> (Mother, 'middle class', rural village, Derbyshire)

This narrative of gender performance – 'the sensible girl' and the 'dizzy boy' – reinforces other gendered narratives, for example educational research which suggests that girls are now out-performing boys at all ages at school and linguistic research which demonstrates that girls are more skilled at using language than boys (Maltz and Borker, 1982); but it also contradicts popular assumptions about the gendered nature of public space, namely that girls/women are more at risk in public space than boys/ men (Stanko, 1987; Valentine, 1989, 1992). Indeed, parents frequently drew on well publicized cases of child sex murders and paedophile rings to argue that boys are equally at risk from sexual abuse as girls; and they articulated a further concern about boys' vulnerability to interpersonal and gang violence, especially in their teens. In particular, south Asian parents were concerned that their sons' vulnerability to racially motivated violence will increase as they grow up. These fears are supported by the findings of a number of studies (Hesse *et al.*, 1992; Keith, 1995; Toon and Qureshi, 1995), including the work of Watt and Stenson (1998) in which they demonstrate that white youths actively use violence to exclude other ethnic groups from their neighbourhoods.

Previous research (for example Hart, 1979; Bigner, 1974) has suggested that eldest children, especially girls, are commonly expected to help out in the household by looking after younger siblings in public space. It is argued that this burden of responsibility restricts the eldest child's spatial ranges but allows the younger children to enjoy more extended spatial ranges than an only or 'first born' child. Furthermore several studies have suggested that boys with sisters are more protected than those with brothers (because traditionally girls have been more protected than boys), while girls with brothers enjoy more freedom than those with sisters (because they range further under the protection of Big Brother). However the evidence of this research is that position in the family has only a minor effect on parents' attitudes to children's safety because parents are increasingly unwilling to place the burden of responsibility for younger children's well-being on older children's shoulders. This reflects both the seriousness with which parents regard potential public dangers and the extent to which parents idealize childhood as a time when children should be free from responsibility. Where elder children are expected to take care of younger siblings it appears that having a sister increases the independent opportunities for boys because of girls' perceived greater maturity, rather than the other way round (Valentine, 1997b).

HOUSEHOLD DYNAMICS: GENDER AND PARENTING

Historically different understandings have been established through the law but also through popular norms about what it means to be a parent, what it means to be a child and the relationship between parents and children (Jamieson and Toynbee, 1989). Contemporary research suggests that the authoritarian role which was traditionally adopted by parents is breaking down, and that today's parents are closer to their own children than they were as children to their own parents, with the consequence that the distinction between adults and children is becoming increasingly blurred (Modell and Goodman, 1990; Ambert, 1994). In particular, contemporary parents allow their children a greater voice to articulate their own preferences and agendas in household decision-making processes (Jamieson and Toynbee, 1989). As a result Ambert (1994: 536) claims: 'Daily life offers evidence to the effect that adolescents have become less tolerant of parental supervision and that this is leading to more conflict between adults and children within the household.' As Solberg (1990: 119) has argued, 'although in many ways children's position is a weak one they do not passively adapt themselves to what their parents say and do' (Solberg, 1990: 119). Indeed a number of studies have demonstrated how children are agents in their own lives and resist adults' definitions of their lives in different social contexts – in public space, at school and at home (Woods, 1985; Katz, 1991; Sibley, 1995). This is particularly evident in relation to the negotiation of spatial boundaries.

Research suggests that mothers and fathers often take on different parenting roles and have different ways of treating their children (Tein *et al.*, 1994) – although they will often try to present a united front to the children so that the latter believe they share a more common view on parenting than they actually do (Acock and Bengtson, 1980). Children in two-parent families exhibited a sophisticated knowledge of this gender division of parenting and the power dynamics in households, playing their mothers and fathers off against each other (Valentine, 1997b).

It is mothers who do the lion's share of everyday parenting work in most households. Consequently, they have the most daily contact with their children and come under the most pressure from their offspring to relax spatial restrictions. In the face of this domestic and emotional stress mothers tend to be less consistent than fathers in their parenting strategies, sometimes giving into their offspring's persistent demands to be allowed to go out unsupervised. Paradoxically therefore while mothers were often described (and indeed labelled themselves) as the most 'fussy' and the most 'anxious' parent, they were also commonly considered the 'softest' parent. Despite all the media attention granted to the 'new man' which has suggested that the role of the father in the home is changing, dads still appear to adopt a quite autocratic or traditional position in the household (Valentine, 1997b). Men's ability to maintain 'ideal' restrictions on their children's use of space (as agreed with their partners) is facilitated by the fact that fathers are often more distanced from their children's daily lives. When they then come home and discover that the children have been given more freedom to go out by their mothers than the father had previously agreed to, this can lead to domestic tension. Although of course there were some households where the fact that the father worried less than the mother meant that he was also prepared to grant his children greater licence to explore public space independently. Some of these opinions are reflected in these quotations from parents and a teenage girl.

Mother: I'm at work sometimes at night, you're [to her partner] in charge, aren't you?
Social Father: She's very soft with them sometimes though, let's them get away with murder, don't you?

Mother: You [to him] have to be quiet, don't you, have to keep your mouth shut sometimes, don't you, duck?

Social Father: Have to bite my lip.

Mother: I am soft, I don't know what... my Dad was same, my Mum was soft and Dad were very strict.

(Mother and 'Social Father', 'working class', rural village, Derbyshire)

Father: I don't like Sally going out by herself.

Mother: He doesn't like Sally going out full-stop.

Int.: Is that because she is the youngest or because she is a girl?

Father: No, I was exactly the same with Paul when he first started. I didn't like it when Phillip first started to go by himself.

Mother: But they went by themselves at a much earlier age.

Father: Well I didn't like it even then. I told her [to interviewer] I never liked it then. That wasn't with my approval they went. It was just something you [to wife] did.

(Mother and Father, 'middle class', rural village, Derbyshire)

I just keep on asking me Mum 'cos I know me Dad'll say 'no'... when I ask my Mum and sometimes she says 'yes', sometimes she says 'no', so then I wait until she's gone to sleep and then I go out.

(Girl, 'working class', urban metropolitan area)

Children living in lone-parent households and 'reconstituted families' with a 'biological' parent and a 'social' parent, while also maintaining contact with their other 'biological' parent who is living in a different household, have particular scope to manipulate their multiple kinship relations because children's welfare is often a major source of tensions between women and their ex-partners and new partners. These women describe some of the problems of negotiating children's spatial ranges when the children spend time in different households with adults who have different understandings of their competence.

He's [her ex-partner, the children's father] totally irresponsible ... Totally useless ... when I talk about abduction it frightens me, it's wrong to slag him off but he's not, he's not got mothers' instincts ... But he takes them to Fun Fairs on Sundays, you know, Camelot, that type of thing and I know he goes on rides with Joe [their son] and Lauren's [their daughter] sat on the bottom waiting, that frightens me. Um – anybody could just walk off with her... he's quite irresponsible ... you're on edge all the time thinking will they come home, will he get them back alive? I'm more worried about him [the father] than the stranger.

(Lone mother, 'middle class', urban metropolitan borough, Greater Manchester)

Well he ['Social Father'] thinks I'm overprotective, which I am, I think. I mean I agree with him, I am overprotective but he's, he's only lived in the country all his life and I mean I don't think he realises what dangers are out there you know, whereas I do. I mean he's only their step-dad and I mean he's never had children before ... so he just thinks of it like it was when he was little where you were allowed to go anywhere as long as your Mum knew where you were, but no, I know I'm overprotective. I mean it was only him really that Debbie's got as much freedom as she has, you know, because he keeps saying 'Oh you know, other kids 'll torment her', so I give in and she goes out.

(Mother, 'working class', rural town, Derbyshire)

Household negotiations which determine children's spatial boundaries are framed in relation to popular discourses within the law, childcare professionals, media and so on, about what it is appropriate for children to do at different ages; and in relation to discussions with other parents about how they treat their offspring. Isabel Dyck (1990) has argued that women's 'street relationships' with other women are built on trust and reciprocity and formed within a negotiation of understanding about keeping children safe and secure' (page 473). She argues that social interactions between mothers at children's sports clubs, the school gates and so on play an important role in the way women discuss and interpret professional and popular discourses about how they should bring up their children (Dyck, 1989, 1990).

In particular, neighbourhood social networks appear to perform a regulatory function. Wyness argues that parents' 'emotional investment in their children becomes so all-encompassing that parents' social and moral identities are bound up with their parenting roles' (Wyness, 1994: 194–5). As a result women who do not adopt what is defined locally as 'good practice' are labelled 'bad mothers'. Thus some women either restrict their children's use of space in a way they do not consider necessary, or give them greater licence than they would ideally like to, in order not to step out of line with local common-sense constructions of what it means to be a 'good mother'. Lone parents in particular, feel under pressure to adopt the same practices as two-parent households despite being more limited in terms of financial, time and personal resources, because they are conscious of the way lone-parent households are stigmatized in the popular media, and professional and social discourses (Valentine, 1997b). These women describe their experiences:

> I mean we all get together, we all – I think we all do the same and I think sometimes when we hear that some parents have allowed their children to go various places, you know, eyebrows are raised.
>
> (Mother, 'middle class', commuter village, Cheshire)

> I think I'd worry about the neighbours being a single Mum when I was [she now has a partner]. You've got to be so careful, you know, if they think you're not bringing them up right – and they're soon there to pull you down a bit.
>
> (Mother, 'working class', rural village)

This is something that children can turn to their own advantage. In the quotes below a girl describes how she and her friends play their mothers off against each other by manipulating their anxieties about local parenting 'norms'.

> I want her knock on for me and then if she's no around I ask Rianna to knock on for me and then when me Mum and Dad says 'yeah' [because Rianna's parents have allowed her out] and then I'm allowed out, then I go and knock on for her and then she'll be allowed out [because the speaker's parents have let her out] and then we just go.
>
> (Girl, 'working class', British South Asian, urban metropolitan area)

When these subversive tactics fail, teenagers often flout parental restrictions outright, for example, by sneaking out of the house unobserved or by claiming that their watches stopped while they were out. Indeed, while parents described children as vulnerable or incompetent; teenagers were often equally quick to represent adults – who fall for these tricks – as gullible, naive and incompetent (Valentine, 1997a).

> I ask me Mum and if she says 'no', then I ask my Dad, if he says 'no' I'll go up to me bedroom window, climb out of the window onto the extension roof, onto the wall and then I go.
>
> (Boy, 'working class', urban metropolitan)

When kids get caught dodging parental restrictions it is apparent that the traditional warning 'Wait till your father gets home' is still a potent threat. In line with other studies, this research identified a clear gender division in household disciplinary styles, fathers tending to adopt a more authoritarian role, using physical punishments, shouting and threats, while mothers were more inclined towards verbal reasoning and social punishments, such as grounding (Hart and Robinson, 1984; Siegel, 1987). Here too mothers were also described as 'inconsistent' and 'soft' in terms of enforcing punishments, whereas fathers were represented as stricter and more likely to carry out their disciplinary threats. Again, this gender difference was attributed to the fact that mothers spend more time with their children on a daily basis and so are more likely to succumb to children's pleas for leniency as a result of tiredness and frustration; whereas fathers are more distanced from their offspring and so are less vulnerable to manipulation by them. These two fathers describe their roles:

> And the girls know that if they do wrong they'll get smacked for it, even Sarah at 12 years of age you know. They know that they've got that little bit of leeway with Kath [his wife] and Kath says to me sometimes that they've been doing this, that and the other, I said 'why don't you do something about it?' and it's always left to me. I always remember when me Dad – I could twirl me Mum a bit but whenever me Dad came into the house that was it then. It was a little bit of fear as well but it always brought me up in good stead you know, I've always believed in what he did was right, although sometimes I was a bit scared. And the girls have admitted to me sometimes that they've been a bit scared of me. I've never bruised them or anything like that but I'll always give them a good slap if they've done wrong.
>
> (Father, 'middle class', non-metropolitan area, Cheshire)

> I'm not here very much so I have the advantage of being able to walk in, sort of look cleanly at a situation without having any emotional involvement in the situation, sorting it all out – I tend to be probably stricter on them. I also have a lot shorter temper so they know if they push it with me they're really asking for it.
>
> (Father, rural village, 'middle class', Derbyshire)

Paradoxically, the one form of household where this pattern was less evident was in traditional two-parent households where the father was in full-time paid employment and the mother was a full-time homemaker. In this context, mothers commonly assumed responsibility for all aspects of their children's lives including their punishments.

One way that parents sidestep children's resistance to spatial boundaries is by disguising their attempts to restrict their children's access to independent use of public space. This is done by subtly structuring their children's leisure time, so limiting their opportunities for independent activities. Two-thirds of the parents surveyed claimed that their children participate in some form of organized play activities. One-fifth of the respondents stated that their child is a member of at least three different groups. As a result children's leisure time is increasingly being spatially contained within child-adult segregated 'private' spaces, such as institutional play schemes, or children's sports clubs (Valentine and McKendrick, 1997) – spaces to which children are largely ferried in the safety of parental cars. Hillman *et al.* (1990) estimate for example that in 1990 British adults spent 900 million hours ferrying their children around.

As a consequence David Sibley (1995: 16) argues that:

> For children in the most highly developed societies, the house is increasingly becoming a haven. At the same time the outside becomes more threatening, populated by potential monsters and abductors so the boundary between the home (safe) and the locality (threatening) is more strongly drawn.

Thus children's spare time is becoming more centred on the home and its immediate environment (40 per cent of the parents surveyed stated that their offspring spend most of their outdoor leisure time in private gardens) or institutional activities (Valentine and McKendrick, 1997). As a result parental fears are robbing children of the opportunity for independent environmental exploration, a loss lamented by the tabloid and broadsheet newspapers in headlines such as 'The Death of Childhood' (Ellis, 1995) and 'Poor Children Prisoners of Fearful Parents' (Cooper, 1995).

CONCLUSIONS

Children's spatial boundaries are often referred to in geographical work on children's use of space as if they were fixed by adults according to a child's biological age. This chapter has shown however that the setting of children's spatial boundaries within households, rather than being defined by parental decree, is an interactional process. Where boundaries are established and who has most power in their determination is dependent on how 'children' and 'adults' perform their identities as 'competent in public space' and as 'competent authority' respectively, and how these performances are read by each other.

Both children's and parents' performances of competence are highly gendered. The 'sensible girl' and 'dizzy boy' narrative reinforces other contemporary gender narratives which suggest that girls are more skilled than boys in a range of contexts. In contrast 'the soft mum' and the 'strict dad' narrative harks back to more traditional understandings of gender roles and gender divisions of labour within the household.

While parents' superior age, size and life experiences means that their power over their children is literally embodied; this is not to imply that children's position is necessarily a weak or passive one. Rather, children actively challenge parental performances of authority. Often where parents' performances are weak and children's are strong, children can resist parental restrictions on their use of space and indeed often have a significant voice in household decisions. In particular children often exploit their superior local knowledge and familiarity with the neighbourhood to argue that their parents' risk assessments are naive. Thus power in the household is mutually constituted through the interaction of its members.

Households in turn are nested within neighbourhoods, communities, nations and so on (Aitken, 1994). Thus individual household negotiations about children's use of space are framed with reference to local and national discourses about the performance of gender and age – specifically what it means to be a 'good' mother and also what it is appropriate for children to do at particular stages of their physical development. In order to understand more about gender and power within the household, there is therefore a need for more research to explore how parents and children talk about and understand these discourses and the contextual processes by which these understandings are used in the negotiation of their own identities.

A strong element in this research has been fluidity in the way identities are performed and read. For example, while constructions of children's competence in one space, for example 'the home', may influence the way their competence is defined in another space, such as the street, sometimes children's identities are simultaneously defined in contradictory ways in different spaces. This suggests that there is a need for researchers to pay more attention to the way negotiations in a household context both shape, and are shaped by, social relations in other geographical spaces. In particular, most parents employed stricter measures of their children's competence in public space before they allowed their offspring independence than they adopted in private space. This suggests that children are being increasingly construed as 'vulnerable' and 'incompetent' in public space, despite the fact that statistically they are more at risk in private space from people that they know (Cream, 1993), and from domestic accidents (Roberts *et al.*, 1992). Thus while stranger-danger education is intended to keep children safe, for some it may have the consequence of putting them in situations where they are more, not less, at risk of abuse and violence. Indeed because 'private space' is supposed to be safe space it also encourages young people to deny or remain silent about their experiences. The research therefore also demonstrates that there is a need for more research to consider the way children are taught about and conceptualize 'public' and 'private space'.

NOTE

1. The term social parent is used to describe those adults who are not a biological parent of children in the household but who nonetheless take on a parenting role. In other words they are usually the partner of the children's 'natural' parent.

REFERENCES

Acock, A. and Bengston, V. (1980) 'Socialization and Attribution Processes: Actual Versus Perceived Similarity Among Parents and Youth'. *Journal of Marriage and the Family*, 43, 501–18.
Aitken, S. (1994) *Children's Geographies*. Washington DC: Association of American Geographers.
Alanen, L. (1990) 'Rethinking Socialization, the Family and Childhood'. *Sociological Studies of Child Development*, 3, 13–28.
Ambert, A.M. (1994) 'An International Perspective on Parenting: Social Change and Social Constructs'. *Journal of Marriage and the Family*, 56, 529–43.
Anderson, J. and Tindal, M. (1972) 'The concept of Home Range: New Data for the Study of Territorial Behaviour' in W. Mitchell (ed.) *Environmental Design: Research and Practice*. Los Angeles: University of California Press.
Bigner, J. (1974) 'Second Borns' Discrimination of Sibling Role Concepts'. *Developmental Psychology*, 10, 564–73.
Blakeley, K. (1994) 'Parents' Conceptions of Social Dangers to Children in the Urban Environment'. *Children's Environments*, 11, 16–25.
Blaut, J. and Stea, D. (1974) 'Mapping at the Age of Three'. *Journal of Geography*, 73, 5–9.
Blitzer, S. (1991) 'They are Only Children, What do They Know? A Look at Current Ideologies of Childhood'. *Sociological Studies of Child Development*, 4, 11–25.
Buchner, P. (1990) 'Growing up in the Eighties: Changes in the Social Biography of Childhood' in the FRG in L. Chisholm, P. Buchner, H. Kruger and P. Brown (eds) *Childhood, Youth and Social Change: a Comparative Perspective*. London: Falmer Press.
Bunge, W. and Bordessa, R. (1975) *The Canadian Alternative: Survival, Expeditions and Urban Change*. Geographical Monographs No.2. Toronto: York University.
Butler, J. (1990) *Gender Trouble: Feminism and the Subversion of Identity*. London: Routledge.
Cahill, S. (1990) 'Childhood and Public Life: Reaffirming Biographical Divisions'. *Social Problems*, 37, 390–402.
Cooper, S. (1986) 'Confronting a Near and Present Danger: How to Teach Children to Resist Assault' in D. Haden (ed.) *Out of Harm's Way: Readings on Child Sexual Abuse, Its Prevention and Treatment*. Phoenix: Oryx Press.
Cream, J. (1993) 'Child Abuse and the Symbolic Geographies of Cleveland'. *Environment and Planning D: Society & Space*, 11, 231–46.

Downs, R. (1985) 'The Representation of Space: its Development in Children and in Cartography' in R. Cohen (ed.) *The Development of Spatial Cognition*. New Jersey: Hillsdale.

Dyck, I. (1989) 'Integrating Home and Wage Workplace: Women's Daily Lives in a Canadian Suburb'. *The Canadian Geographer*, 33, 329–41.

Dyck, I. (1990) 'Space, Time and Renegotiating Motherhood: an Exploration of the Domestic Workplace'. *Environment & Planning D: Society & Space*, 8, 459–83.

Ellis, W. (1995) 'The Death of Childhood'. *The Times*, 1 August: 13.

Hart, R. (1979) *Children's Experience of Place*. New York: Irvington.

Hart, C. and Robinson, C. (1994) 'Comparative Study of Maternal and Paternal Disciplinary Strategies'. *Psychological Reports*, 74, 495–98.

Hesse, B., Rai, D., Bennett, C. and McGilchrist, P. (1992) *Beneath the Surface: Racial Harassment*. Aldershot: Avebury.

Hillman, M. and Adams, J. (1992) 'Children's Freedom and Safety'. *Children's Environments*, 9, 10–22.

Hillman, M., Adams, J. and Whitelegg, J. (1990) *One False Move: a Study of Children's Independent Mobility*. London: Policy Studies Institute.

Hood Williams, J. (1990) 'Patriarchy for Children: on the Stability of Power Relations in Children's Lives' in L. Chisholm, P. Buchner, H. Herman Kruger and P. Brown (eds) *Childhood, Youth and Social Change: A Comparative Perspective*. Basingstoke: Falmer Press.

James, S. (1990) 'Is there a "Place" for Children in Geography?' *Area*, 22, 3, 278–83.

James, A. and Jenks, C. (1996) 'Public Perceptions of Childhood Criminality'. *British Journal of Sociology*, 47(2), 315–31.

Jamieson, L. and Toynbee, C. (1989) 'Shifting Patterns of Parental Authority, 1900–1980' in C. Corr and L. Jamieson (eds) *The Politics of Everyday Life*, 86–113. London: Macmillan.

Katz, C. (1991) 'Sow What you Know: the Struggle for Social Reproduction in Rural Sudan'. *Annals of the Association of American Geographers*, 8, 488–514.

Katz, C. (1993) 'Growing Girls/Closing Circles: Limits on the Spaces of Knowing in Rural Sudan and US Cities, in C. Katz and J. Monk (eds) *Full Circles: Geographies of Women Over the Life Course*. London: Routledge.

Katz, C. (1994) 'Textures of Global Change: Eroding Ecologies of Childhood in New York and Sudan'. *Childhood*, 2, 103–10.

Katz, C. (1995) 'Power, Space and Terror: Social Reproduction and the Public Environment'. Paper presented at Landscape Architecture, Social Ideology and the Politics of Place Conference, Harvard University, Cambridge, Massachusetts. Available from the author.

Keith, M. (1995) 'Making the Street Visible: Placing Racial Violence in Context'. *New Community*, 21, 551–65.

McNeish, O. and Roberts, H. (1994) *The Facts of Life: the Changing Face of Childhood*. Barnardos: London.

Maltz, D. and Borker, R. (1982) 'A Cultural Approach to Male-Female Miscommunication' in J. Gumperz (ed.) *Language and Social Identity*. Cambridge: Cambridge University Press.

Matthews, M.H. (1992) *Making Sense of Place: Children's Understandings of Large-Scale Environments*. Hemel Hempstead: Harvester Wheatsheaf.

Modell, J. and Goodman, M. (1990) 'Historical Perspectives' in J. Feldman and M. Elliot (eds) *At the Threshold: the Developing Adolescent*. Cambridge: Harvard University Press.

Moore, G.T. (1976) 'Theory and Research on the Development of Environmental Knowing' in G.T. Moore and R.G. Golledge (eds) *Environmental Knowing*. London: Stroudsberg, Dowden, Hutchinson and Ross.

Moore, R. (1986) *Childhood's Domain: Play and Place Development*. London: Croom Helm.

Perez, C. and R. Hart (1980) 'Beyond Playgrounds: Planning for Children's Access to the Environment' in P. Wilkinson (ed.) *Innovations in Play Environments*. London: Croom Helm.

Prout, A. and James, A. (1990) 'A New Paradigm for the Sociology of Childhood? Provenance, Promise and Problems' in A. James and A. Prout (eds) *Constructing and Reconstructing Childhood: Contemporary Issues in the Sociological Study of Childhood*. Basingstoke: Falmer Press.

Qvortrup, J. (1994) 'Childhood Matters: an Introduction' in J. Qvortrup, M. Bardy, G. Sgritta and H. Wintersberger (eds) *Childhood Matters: Social Theory, Practices and Politics*. Aldershot: Avebury Press.

Roberts, H., Smith, S. and Lloyd, M. (1992) 'Safety as a Social Value: a Community Approach' in S. Scott, G. Williams, S. Platt and H. Thomas (eds) *Private Risks and Public Dangers*. Aldershot: Avebury Press.

Saegert, S. and Hart, R. (1978) 'The Development of Environmental Competence in Girls and Boys' in M. Salter (ed.) *Play: Anthropological Perspectives*. Cornwall, NY: Leisure Press.

Sibley, D. (1995) 'Families and Domestic Routines: Constructing the Boundaries of Childhood' in S. Pile and N. Thrift (eds) *Mapping the Subject*. London: Routledge.

Siegel, M. (1987) 'Are Sons and Daughters Treated more Differently by Fathers than by Mothers?' *Developmental Review*, 7, 183–209.

Solberg, A. (1990) Negotiating Childhood: 'Changing Constructions of Age for Norwegian Children' in A. James and A. Prout (eds) *Constructing and Reconstructing Childhood: Contemporary Issues in the Sociological Study of Childhood*. Basingstoke: Falmer Press.

Stanko, E. (1987) 'Typical Violence, Normal Precaution: Men, Women and Interpersonal Violence in England, Wales, Scotland and the USA' in J. Hanmer and M. Maynard (eds) *Women, Violence and Social Control*. Basingstoke: Macmillan.

Tein, J.Y., Roosa, M. and Michaels, M. (1994) 'Agreement between Parent and Child Reports on Parental Behaviour'. *Journal of Marriage and the Family*, 56, 341–55.

Thompson, L. and Walker, A. (1989) 'Gender in Families: Women and Men in Marriage, Work and Parenthood'. *Journal of Marriage and the Family*, 56, 341–55.

Toon, I. and Qureshi, T. (1995) 'The Contestation over Residential and Urban Space in the Isle of Dogs'. Paper presented at the British Sociological Association Annual Conference, University of Leicester, April.

Valentine, G. (1989) 'The Geography of Women's Fear'. *Area*, 21, 385–90.

Valentine, G. (1992) 'Images of Danger: Women's Sources of Information about the Spatial Distribution of Male Violence'. *Area*, 24, 22–9.

Valentine, G. (1996a) 'Children Should be seen and not Heard?: the Production and Transgression of Adults' Public Space'. *Urban Geography*, 17, 2, 205–20.

Valentine, G. (1996b) 'Angels and Devils: Moral Landscapes of Childhood'. *Environment and Planning D: Society and Space*, 14, 581–99.

Valentine, G. (1997a) ' "Oh yes I can". "oh no you can't.": Children and Parents' Understandings of Kids' Competence to Negotiate Public Space Safely'. *Antipode*, 29, 1, 65–89.

Valentine, G. (1997b) ' "My son's a bit dizzy". "My wife's a bit soft". Gender, Children and Cultures of Parenting'. *Gender, Place and Culture: a Journal of Feminist Geography*, 4, 1, 37–62.

Valentine, G. and McKendrick, J. (1997) 'Children's Outdoor Play: Exploring Public Concerns'. *Geoforum*, 28, 2, 219–35.

Waksler, F.C. (1986) 'Studying Children: Phenomenological Insights'. *Human Studies*, 8, 171–82.

Ward, C. (1990) *The Child in the Country*. London: Bedford Square Press.

Watt, P. and Stenson, K. (1998) 'Going Out and About: Youth and Space in a Southern English Town' in T. Skelton and G. Valentine (eds) *Cool Places: Geographies of Youth Cultures*. London: Routledge.

Woods, D. (1985) 'Nothing Doing'. *Children's Environments Quarterly*, 7, 2–14.

Wyness, M. (1994) 'Keeping Tabs on an Uncivil Society: Positive Parental Control'. *Sociology*, 28, 193–209.

9 Intra-household Power Relations and their Impact on Women's Leisure

Sarah Gilroy

INTRODUCTION

This chapter examines the place of intra-household power relations in the understanding of women's access to, and experience of, leisure. In so doing it draws upon analyses in two growing fields of study: women's leisure and the household. Thus the key questions that are raised in this chapter centre around the nature of power relations within households and how these impact on women's leisure.

This focus stems from recently completed research (Gilroy, 1996; 1997) which explored the relationship between women's involvement in physical activity and empowerment. In the process of interviewing 28 women about their physical activity, data concerning other leisure activities and intra-household relations were gathered. It is important however to acknowledge that the household data formed a subsidiary part of the research rather than the main focus. Thus the data I refer to in this chapter emerged whilst developing a broader understanding of the social context of each woman's leisure.

In-depth interviews were conducted with a sample of 24 women during 1988. The women interviewed came from a group of 51 who, at the end of a general questionnaire about their leisure (completed by 172 women), said that they would be interested in discussing further some of the issues raised in the questionnaire. The women who were not interviewed either lived some way outside the town of Upton, or could not be contacted, or had changed their minds about being involved in the research. The 24 women grew to 28 after one of the women I had interviewed suggested I meet with four other women she knew through her involvement at a Health and Fitness club. All the interviews were tape-recorded and on average lasted an hour and a half. Most of the interviews took place in the women's homes, although one woman found it more convenient to come to my house. An interview guide was used, although the pattern of the interviews varied in accordance with the varied responses from the women.

Following full transcription of the interviews the data were analysed by a process of sifting, identifying and refining categories that emerged from the data. At the same time connections between the categories were explored and emerging patterns and incongruities were identified (Gilroy, 1996).

The women interviewed, whilst being diverse in terms of their age (see Table 9.1), marital status and parenthood (see Table 9.2), occupation (see Table 9.3), and income (see Table 9.4) were similar in terms of ethnic background with only one being anything other than a white European. As far as I was aware all were heterosexual, although the women were never asked to describe their sexuality. Although a fairly wide variety of women

Table 9.1　Age of the Women Interviewed

Age	No.
16–25	0
26–35	9
36–45	5 + 1*
46–55	3 + 2*
56–65	4 + 1*
66 +	3
No response	1
Total	28

*Age based on comments made at group interview (these women had not completed the leisure questionnaire).

Table 9.2　Personal Circumstances of the Women Interviewed

Personal circumstances	No.
Single (no child)	1
Single (with child)	3
Married (no child)	8
Married (child at home)	8
Married (child left home)	2
Widowed/Divorced	2
Total	24*

*Not including the 4 women who had not completed the questionnaire.

Table 9.3   Occupation of the Women Interviewed

Occupational status	No.
Student	3
Housewife	6
Part-time	7
Full-time	2
Retired	5
Casual	1
Unemployed	0
Other	0
Total	24*

*Not including the 4 women who had not completed the questionnaire.

Table 9.4   Income of the Women Interviewed

Income level	Personal income no.	Household income no.
None	8	1
up to £2,499	6	*
£2,500–£4,999	3	2
£5,000–£7,999	4	0
£8,000–£10,999	1	2
£11,000–£13,999	0	2
£14,000–£16,999	0	1
£17,000–£19,999	0	3
£20,000–£22,999	0	1
£23,000–£25,999	0	1
£26,000 +	0	1
Not Known	0	1
No Response	2	9
Total	24	24

*For Household Income the starting point was given as 'up to £4,999'.

were represented in the research a small exploratory study of this nature cannot make general claims for all women. However, it can make a valuable contribution to theoretical debate around gender, power and leisure, not least by supporting claims made by other studies.

Firstly, it is worth commenting on women's leisure and the household. Most research on household relationships has paid little attention to leisure or to the impact of the employment of household members on leisure, with the notable exceptions of Deem (1986) and Green *et al.* (1987). Indeed the edited collection by Anderson *et al.* (1994), whilst containing some publications from the Social Change and Economic Life Initiative (SCELI) research programme, fails largely to discuss households and leisure. This is particularly disappointing given that the second part of the SCELI programme, the Household and Community Survey, involved interviewing respondents about their leisure activities. Similarly, it is disappointing that leisure researchers have for the most part failed to draw sufficiently upon the work of 'household' researchers such as Vogler (1994) and Pahl (1991) who have done much to unravel the relationship between household finances and power relations. This study demonstrates the links that can be made between these academic areas.

Before proceeding further it is important to consider what is meant by the 'household' for, as Morgan (1996) comments, the use of the term is potentially problematic. Not only is it at times used synonymously with 'family' but it is also seen as an: 'undifferentiated whole, a black box, which ignores or smoothes over differences within it' (Morgan, 1996: 25). For example the use of the term 'household strategies' implies a shared and agreed view of how the household deals with particular situations, but it may also mask any contestation within the household. In this chapter 'households' are seen as being relatively dynamic, changing domestic contexts rather than stable, unchanging 'institutions'. As people join and leave the household, or as their status within it changes through, for example, the process of becoming adult, so relationships between household members and others change, and so the dynamics of the household will be (re)constructed. Such a view of the dynamic (re)construction of the household facilitates a way of understanding the impact of household members moving through the life cycle (Rapoport and Rapoport, 1975). Equally 'external' factors, such as changes within the labour market, will also have a dynamic and ongoing impact on household relations (Vogler and Pahl, 1993). The household, therefore, is not seen as a separate entity operating within the 'private' sphere, but as a 'space' where individuals work out their daily lives.

Through examining the day-to-day lives of the women I interviewed and the workings of their households, the processes of contestation, accommodation, resistance and negotiation come to the surface in the women's accounts of how they live their lives. As Crompton and Mann (1986) argued, by focusing on the day-to-day aspects of people's lives it is possible to avoid depersonalizing the agent. The accounts that are drawn upon here also point to particular constructions and reconstructions of the identities of the subjects as women, as housewives, and as mothers, and bring to the fore the sometimes contradictory nature of how they lead their lives.

Whilst clearly the nature of employment (for both women and their partners) has a major impact on women's leisure, it is not, I will argue (along with Le Feuvre, 1994, and Gregson and Lowe, 1993), the only or main explanatory tool for understanding women's experience of leisure. This research seeks, therefore, to move beyond previous research (Smith *et al.*, 1973; Glyptis, 1989) on women's (and men's) leisure which has tended to use employment status as one of the starting-points for analysis, thereby neglecting intra-household power relations.

The primary concern of this chapter is to explore the negotiation and playing out of household dynamics in daily life, and how that affects women's leisure and what this can tell us about women's agency. This is not to deny the importance of employment status as a key factor when considering access to leisure, for as Morris (1990: 3) has argued: '[t]he organization of, and participation in, paid work necessarily plays a major part in the internal dynamic of the household', in addition to which, as will be illustrated, it affects household members' access to the key resources of money and time.

The following discussion begins with the broader issues of women's involvement in the labour force and then moves to consider aspects of women's structural positions within the household, and, in particular, systems of financial control and the division of domestic labour. Having set the broader context of their lives, the discussion then shifts to analyse the negotiations around leisure that the women engage in and how they operate within discourses of 'woman', 'housewife' and 'motherhood'. In so doing the chapter seeks to draw the fields of leisure and household studies closer together by focusing on the nature of negotiation within households and how this affects women's leisure. Central to this analysis is an exploration of the construction and reconstruction of intra-household power relations.

EMPLOYMENT, DOMESTIC LABOUR AND THE HOUSEHOLD

Paid employment and unpaid labour (particularly in the home), by both men and women, play a major part in the dynamics of the household. Whether the work of household members is paid or unpaid, done outside or inside the home, it gives a structure to the day and week. The structure itself can enable or constrain members' leisure, with those in greater control of their work pattern being more able to make it consonant with their leisure patterns (Green *et al.*, 1987; Horrell *et al.*, 1994). However care must be taken not to slip into a position of assuming that this greater degree of control means that such women have freedom to construct their leisure as they want.

These women's stories support the view that women's involvement in paid or unpaid labour is subject to a range of influences. No one factor seems to be any more influential than another in the decision-making process, although for those women with children, the social and emotional needs of the household often took precedence over purely financial considerations. Such cases seem to represent an extension of Bourdieu's (1992) notion of the women sacrificing her needs to the needs of others, particularly children and male partners. On the other hand it could be argued that placing the concerns of others before themselves demonstrates the extent to which their identities as mothers and housewives operated within the dominant discourses of the 'good' mother and the 'good' housewife (see Bartky, 1990; Ballaster *et al.*, 1991). For some households, traditional views about women's roles seemed to prevail, for example the husband of one of the women felt very strongly about wanting to 'save' his wife having to do paid work as his mother had. Decisions about women's involvement in paid work were generally not ones taken solely by the woman herself but came out of discussion with her partner. Whether this process was the same for the decisions about the involvement of the male partner in paid labour was not something that the research explored.

A key area of interest in terms of employment and the household has been the impact that changes in the composition of the labour force have had on the internal workings of the household. Increasing economic activity of women and a rise in male unemployment has led to speculation that there would be changes in the division of domestic labour with women doing less and men doing more. The work of Morris (1990) on households with an unemployed male, and Gregson and Lowe (1993, 1994) on dual-career households suggests that employment is not as influential in leading to renegotiation of the division of household labour as others (for example Wheelock cited in Gregson and Lowe, 1993) have argued. Building on Morris's (1990) work which suggests that social networks may be more influential, Gregson and Lowe (1993) stress the importance of gender identities in the way in which men and women come to define themselves in terms of gender and therefore their roles within households. Furthermore, the relationship between income generation and power within the household has come under scrutiny as the increasing economic activity of women raises the question of whether women are gaining more power within households (Burgoyne, 1990).

My focus shifts now to consider the nature of power within households, or within heterosexual marriages or relationships. Attention in the literature is drawn to the question of not only how the resources of money and time are allocated, but by whom, and on what grounds (Vogler, 1994). Research suggests that even though women are often responsible for managing finances this does not necessarily mean that they have control over them, nor is their access to money equal to that of their male partners (see Burgoyne, 1990; Pahl, 1991; Vogler and Pahl, 1993). Morris (1993: 534) claims that '...access to psm [personal spending money] is considerably higher among men than women, and particularly so when the woman is not employed'.

As Bartky (1990) points out, women are not forced at gun-point to operate within dominant discourses of femininity (and I would add, motherhood), so it is important to understand the benefits women can gain from doing so. This appreciation of the benefits and pleasures women experience in their domestic lives (which is reminiscent of Giddens' (1993) argument for a more positive view of power) is something which Radner (1995) also supports.

FINDING TIME FOR LEISURE

Time is a crucial commodity so far as leisure is concerned but, as Deem (1986, 1996) and others (Le Feuvre, 1994) have shown, it is particularly so for women. Through discussing the accounts of the women I interviewed, this section explores how the women found time for their leisure. Pseudonyms are used throughout. The two key issues which were put in the foreground by the women in discussions about their leisure concern the impact of labour (both paid and unpaid), and the impact of other household members on their leisure.

The Organization of Labour

Being in paid employment in many ways enables leisure, not just in so far as it may increase the amount of money that can be spent on leisure, but paradoxically because it may create more time for leisure. Deem (1986) found that women in employment seem more able to compartmentalize their time than women in unpaid work. This was echoed by Wendy who reported:

> ... I know it sounds stupid, but now that I'm working I find that I have got more time, because you make sure you keep up, like doing the housework for example. If you're not working you say 'oh, well I'll do it tomorrow' ...

That the structuring of time due to paid employment should facilitate, at least for some, access to leisure time is even more remarkable given that as Morris (1990) and Gregson and Lowe (1993) have illustrated, being in paid employment did not necessarily reduce the woman's domestic work.

One explanation of this comes from Deem (1996) who, building on the work of Adam (1995) suggests that the 'produced time' which results from being in paid employment marks off time which may under certain circumstances become their 'own time'. Those not in paid employment have no direct access to produced time and therefore might find it more problematic to find their 'own time'.

The degree of control that the women in my research had over the structuring of the working day, seemed on the surface to bear a direct relationship to their access to leisure time. Linda, for example, worked as a data entry operator during set hours which fitted in with the times her children were at school. She had very little flexibility over her hours, so her other tasks of caring for the children and the household and having some leisure had to be fitted in to the remaining hours in the day. Ruth, on the other hand, appeared to have been able to exert a degree of control over her work and, in consequence over her leisure, following her promotion to a level where she was able to take her days off when she wanted. As with Le Feuvre's (1994) research, use of time for the women in this research was closely linked to being a 'good wife and mother,' with women often spending their 'free time' caring for their children and/or partner. However, focusing on what the woman does can lead to a partial picture emerging, as Gill's account demonstrates. Gill's position in relation to balancing being a full-time student with being a mother was facilitated by her partner's desire to redistribute the division of domestic labour, so that he did more and she did less. She initially resisted these attempts which suggests that she was somewhat reluctant to change her role as wife and mother. This supports Gregson and Lowe's (1993) conclusion that gender identities are important in understanding why people act as they do. Her partner's gender identity was not challenged by his taking on more chores within the household, whilst her reluctance to let him do more suggests that her gender identity was connected to her role as housewife and mother.

DEMANDS/NEEDS OF OTHER HOUSEHOLD MEMBERS

When analysing the women's accounts it was tempting to start from the assumption that women's occupational attainment and thus their control over their paid work would be the most significant factor in explaining their control over their leisure. This would lead to prioritizing work relations and social class in analysis of their leisure behaviour. Close analysis, however, suggested that other factors may be more significant than social class or work relations. Jenny's account of why she structured her working day and her leisure in the way she did, points to the influence of her partner:

> … that's why I go [to the gym] in the daytime, because of Howard saying he doesn't like sitting at home, em while I go out. And I, but I don't tend to ask, I tend to go and say I'm going to so and so, but not 'Is it all right, do you mind if I go?', and so he sits at home and does his paperwork and things, and sometimes gets quite resentful.

Whilst Jenny's work flexibility made such an arrangement possible, she was aware that she would have problems accommodating her husband's wishes if she had had less flexibility.

> … if I changed jobs and I had a strict nine to five, it would be very difficult because I wouldn't know what to do really, whether I should go in the evenings, because I'd be loath to give up going, and if you compromise and sort of go once a week or something, it's really not worth you doing it I don't think.

Jenny's commitment to her marriage was such that she was prepared to arrange her leisure in order to spend time with her husband, but her comments revealed a tension in how she wanted to divide her time. At the time I interviewed Jenny the flexibility of her work had saved her having to make harder decisions.

Such an investment of time into a marriage or partnership was relatively common for the women who were in relationships and in paid employment. Other accounts however, revealed less of a sense of accommodating to a partner's expressed wishes (particularly when they ran contrary to the woman's) and conveyed more of a sense of a mutually convenient arrangement. Ruth, for example said that:

> … if I want to do anything in particular, I'll do it during the day, so that we can do something together in the evening. Purely because, I mean of the hours that I work, em it's much more flexible. Most of my exercise is taken during the day when he's not here.

Ruth's partner similarly seemed to try and arrange his leisure time around her work, so if she was working on a Saturday, he would try and arrange his golf for then. This kind of reciprocity seemed to be centred around a shared desire to spend their leisure time together rather than separately (see also Morgan, 1996). Finding time to spend leisure together was regarded by some as being a necessity, as opposed to just being preferable. Jo, for example, felt that:

> ... you've got to be very careful within a marriage if you're both doing a job which takes a hell of a lot out of you, there must you know be a lot of problems, there's got to be give and take.

Part of this 'give and take', as far as Jo was concerned, meant that she gave up her full-time job and got a part-time one. Betty was similarly aware of the dangers of not spending enough time with her husband:

> I do think you do need a certain amount of time together, because if you've got very different interests all the time then, em, you grow apart, you don't stay as close together. So I think it's very important, and particularly now both our girls are away from home. The pattern of life changes.

It is significant, I feel, that these comments come from the two women, Betty and Jo, who had reached stages in their lives (in their late forties/ early fifties) when their children had either left, or were about to leave home. For them, leisure time having been gained, was not easily given away. Betty was fortunate in so far as she was in a position where she did not have to go back to full-time work for financial reasons, and in fact chose not to because, as she put it: '... I value my free time, and I don't think I could, I wouldn't want to work full-time again, I think life would be much too hectic ...'

Central to this discussion is the question of whether spending time with their partner was for these women about pleasure or the exercise of power, or both. It would be too hasty to interpret Jenny's story as if she was powerless and subsuming her interests to those of her husband, and not getting any pleasure from her leisure. A more appropriate interpretation may be that her accommodation to his wishes at that time was one small part of the working through of gender power relations within the household. Leisure is just one of a number of social contexts within which gender power relations may be worked out: others including sexual relations, the use of space and employment. As Jenny herself said, she did not ask him if he minded her going out at other times, and in addition to going to the gym three times a week she also went to evening classes three nights a week and had piano lessons. So acceding to his wishes over her attendance at the gym could be seen as a small concession to make given the other times she is out enjoying her leisure.

FITTING IN WITH THE HOUSEHOLD – LIVING WITH CONTRADICTIONS

The demands of others (partners, children, dependants) in the household has a major impact on the patterns of the woman's day (see Talbot, 1996). The employment status of adults, the presence and age of children will also impact on daily life in the household and on member's access to leisure. As both Wimbush (1986) and Deem (1986) have shown, many women, particularly those with children, have their day structured by the 'timetables of others'. Such timetables can make it difficult for women to find time for leisure, purely because they can end up with little time left for themselves. The working 'day' for mothers, particularly for those with pre-school age children, can mean being 'on call' for 24 hours (Wimbush, 1986; Green *et al.*, 1987).

As Wimbush (1986: 139) found with the mothers she interviewed: 'Most of their time was controlled and consumed by the family, domestic work and other obligations.' Weekends and holidays led to work intensifying as opposed to lessening (see Deem, 1996). The main problem reported was that of the need to compartmentalize time between work and leisure, in order to enjoy some leisure. As Wimbush (1986), Deem (1986) and Green *et al.* (1990) have illustrated, often the boundaries between work and leisure are blurred, for example, women ironing whilst watching television, or child-minding combined with going swimming. In this sense it was hard for some of the women to identify what actually was leisure for them as opposed to facilitating someone else's leisure. Opportunities for personal leisure invariably centred around times when the children were either out of the house, preoccupied or asleep (Wimbush, 1986). Wendy found that even with her children at school she did not have any time to do what she wanted and at times this got her down.

… I never have any time to myself at all, which I do really because I go to the Adult Learning Centre and things like that, but because it's in the daytime, and my husband's at work and the kids are at school, you don't think it's time for yourself, where it is really, but you think because it is in the daytime, em I can't really explain I think you understand what I mean. You know it is time for myself, but because its in the daytime and they're, they're not at home anyway, I don't class it as being time for myself. Whereas if they were at home, and I was doing something then I'd class it as time for myself.

Whilst it appears as if Wendy had time to herself, that was not how she felt. The cooking class and the gardening class that she went to enabled her to produce low-budget meals and save money on plants by raising cuttings and swapping them with others at the classes. They appear to enable her to function more effectively as a wife who was able to eke out a limited household income. The irony of Wendy's position is that whilst she felt her leisure was not really her own when the rest of the family are out, she also said that she would feel guilty if she went out when her husband and the children were at home. At the same time she thought people would have happier marriages if they made time for themselves. Her experiences bear similarities with those of the women in Deem's (1996) research who experienced holidays away from home as not producing the time for themselves that they thought they might have had because their time was subject to the time hierarchies and demands of others.

Linda's story reveals how her husband's leisure patterns also added to her unpaid work in terms of childcare and housekeeping, which further constrained her leisure. It was not just his employment that created problems for her, but his leisure patterns as well. More than this, it was the right to leisure that he assumed that he had at the expense of spending time with the family that aggravated her. When the children were younger, she saw herself as having no option but to look after the children when he went off to play golf. She saw the problem as lessening as the children got older.

> It doesn't aggravate me now, I think it doesn't aggravate me because the children are bigger and I feel freer and I can now do what I want to do. Whereas ... but say you're standing there with a little toddler that's swinging round your legs going 'Mum, Mum, Mum' and the other one is in your arms and you've got your husband going 'I'm off then I'll see you in five hours', with his golf, it does tend to aggravate you slightly, but now they're older and they're doing what they want to do, and I'm doing what I want to do.

Linda's account is somewhat contradictory, for a few moments later she spoke of the frustrations of seeing her husband as having access to leisure, whilst she did not.

> I mean last weekend I wanted to go in my garden and do the gardening, and by the time that I'd done everything that everyone else wanted me to do, the weekend was over, and I got so aggravated about it. I said,

'it's all right for you, you come home from work', I said 'you go off Saturday and play golf, you go off Sunday, come home from work Sunday and play golf', I said 'I want to do what I want to do'. And then Richard said: 'leave the hoovering, leave it, leave it, leave the washing up and go into the gardening', and I said, 'Oh, I can see you'd be highly delighted coming home from your golf and taking the hoover round the house, and you just don't, do you'.

The contradictions seem to operate on different levels, for at one moment Linda was complaining about the way in which Richard could go off and play his golf, but at another she is saying that she could not sit down and watch him doing housework whilst she did 'nothing'. She (and her mother) also balanced her frustrations with him going off and playing golf with the way he helped out when she was having the children. They described how once when the children were ill and she developed pneumonia he was 'very good', and it seems that these past actions absolved him from more recent 'misdemeanours'. It is important to recognize that the expression 'very good' is a gendered one. The dominant discourse of being a 'good' wife as reflected in Sue's account seems to contain the expectation that a woman would do what was needed when her partner fell ill, and that as such she would gain little extra recognition for it. For a man to help his female partner in such a way, however, earns him extra kudos, and enhances his reputation as a 'good' partner.

The multi-layering of contradictions is not surprising given that for both partners it can be seen that there are both gains and losses. During Linda's interview her mother was there for some of the time and occasionally she interjected comments reminding Linda that whilst she might have her frustrations with Richard and married life, it was not all that bad. For example, in support of Richard she said to Linda that: 'You've got a good husband... You couldn't expect a man to do that lot with a job like he's got.' They both agreed that in an emergency Richard would do things like the ironing, and hoovering, and indeed had done them when Linda was in hospital giving birth. There are some similarities between Linda (and her mother's) perceptions that she was lucky that Richard was good in emergencies, and Goodnow and Bowes' (1994) discussion of women who were seen to be lucky because they had a partner who shared household tasks. The comments from both Linda and her mother imply that Linda is lucky to have Richard as a husband – even though she might moan about his absence from the household. Their comments, as Goodnow and Bowes (1994) suggest, violate an assumption of equality; Linda's involvement in the household is taken for granted, but Richard's is regarded as a bonus.

The tensions between Linda's identity as a mother and a wife, and her identity as an individual with her own leisure rights and needs, reflect the extent to which it can be argued she was struggling against dominant ideologies about motherhood and domesticity. In practical terms her actions, such as her choice of working hours to fit in with the children, bear testament to her 'acceptance' of her role as a mother. Her comments, however, about how she felt when her husband went out and played golf, suggested that she saw his role as a father and husband in slightly different ways than he did.

Like Linda, Hazel wanted to be able to get up and go with the freedom that her husband seemed to have. However, she knew, from experience, that the cost of doing so was high in terms of the preparation before and clearing up after the event which she felt rendered the going out almost worthless in terms of what it offered as leisure. Just as Linda reported that her husband never stopped her doing what she wanted, so Hazel's husband told her to 'do what you want'. This strategy of saying that their wives could do what they wanted, whilst not facilitating it in practice, in effect shifted the problem away from the husband. What emerged from the data was the husband's affirmation of his wife's freedom to 'do what she wanted', but what was not evident was any practical support to enable her leisure, as she enabled his. The lack of support was not something neutral: it was in effect constraining.

Such were the contradictions that many of the women lived with, trying to reconcile their desire for leisure with the time available and with their own subjectivities as mothers and partners. For example, a lack of time for herself was not perceived by Sue to be particularly problematic, because she felt that she still managed to find time for herself in some senses:

> ... I'm not a person who really rushes round from A to B, I mean sometimes the timetables, and when I say timetables I mean ... the swimming lesson tends to put a structure on your day that wouldn't otherwise be there, but I do tend to chat and converse a lot ...

As with many of the women in Le Feuvre's (1994) study, much of Sue's life centred around the children:

> ... my life is probably family-centred a great deal of it I would have thought you know, because there are swimming lessons for the children as well, but you know I'm quite happy doing these things and I do the sewing class, but that has a practical base as well I'm making clothes for my daughter ...

When asked about her leisure, Sue was not sure whether the sewing class, the music, and the swimming was leisure or work, because she saw it as being part of child rearing. In fact all of her out-of-home leisure activities had some connection with her children's development and welfare. Although middle-class herself, Sue's experiences relate closely to Le Feuvre's (1994: 171) findings about working-class women who: '... found it difficult to imagine something they would like to do [on a totally free day] that was not in some way linked to the domestic/family sphere.' Even though most of Sue's leisure was constructed around her role as a mother and a housewife, she did not convey any sense of frustration at this: on the contrary she seemed quite content to subsume her needs to those of the family, and gained pleasure out of doing so. This offers some support for Coward (1987) and Pringle (1988) who argue that it is possible, even when women might objectively be seen to be in a relatively powerless position, that they may be gaining some pleasure.

CONCLUSIONS

The data discussed in this chapter suggest that a central element to making sense of women's leisure is the need to understand their identities as partners, wives, and/or mothers. How a woman operated within the discourses of motherhood and being a 'good' housewife defined her leisure experience. These discourses, whilst often being closely related, need not necessarily be so (Gilroy, 1996). Whilst employment (or the lack of it) was an important factor, I would support Le Feuvre (1994) in arguing that it is not the key variable on which to base analyses. Whilst Le Feuvre (1994) sees class and gender identities as being of equal importance to employment, there is only partial evidence from this research to support her focus on class.

By exploring the workings of the household it has been possible to reveal the ways in which women live their gendered identities and how these interact with other household members. Through this examination of intra-household relations it is possible to identify the way in which women's leisure is for some constructed to fit in with the time schedules of others, whilst for others it takes precedence over their role as housewife, mother or partner. As with Gregson and Lowe's (1993, 1994) research, changes in the employment status of women rarely led to a change in the amount of domestic labour performed, although there were, in my research, examples of male partners initiating changes in the division of household labour.

Invariably, the actions of household members have implications for other members' leisure, whether it concerns how much money is spent on leisure and whose leisure it is spent on, or whether it is about the time that is spent on leisure. Questions regarding women's identities and women's access to leisure, what they do, with whom, when and where and at what expense can only be answered through examining the household context. The data generated by this research suggest that these women can be seen as having agency, though it is not unlimited. Gender identities and conceptualizations of the role of a 'good' housewife and mother are struggled over and need to be seen in the dynamic context of intra-household power relations.

REFERENCES

Adam, B. (1995) *Timewatch: the Social Analysis of Time.* Cambridge: Polity Press.

Anderson, M., Bechhofer, F. and Gershuny, J. (eds) (1994) *The Social and Political Economy of the Household.* Oxford: Oxford University Press.

Ballaster, R., Beetham, M., Frazer, E. and Hebron, S. (1991) *Women's Worlds: Ideology, Femininity and the Woman's Magazine.* Basingstoke: Macmillan.

Bartky, S.L. (1990) *Femininity and Domination: Studies in the Phenomenology of Oppression.* London: Routledge.

Bourdieu, P. (1992) *Distinction: a Social Critique of the Judgement of Taste.* London: Routledge.

Burgoyne, C.B. (1990) 'Money in Marriage: How Patterns of Allocation both Reflect and Conceal Power'. *The Sociological Review*, 38, 4, 634–65.

Coward, R. (1987) *Female Desire: Women's Sexuality Today.* London: Paladin.

Crompton, R. and Mann, M. (eds) (1986) *Gender and Stratification.* Cambridge: Polity Press.

Deem, R. (1986) *All Work and No Play.* Milton Keynes: Open University Press.

Deem, R. (1996) 'No Time for a Rest? an Exploration of Women's Work, Engendered Leisure and Holidays'. *Time and Society*, 5, 1, 5–25.

Giddens, A. (1993) *The Constitution of Society: Outline of the Theory of Structuration.* Cambridge: Polity Press.

Gilroy, S. (1996) 'The Embody-ment of Power? – Women and Physical Activity'. Unpublished PhD dissertation. Milton Keynes: The Open University.

Gilroy, S. (1997) 'Links Between Physical Activity and Social Power' in G. Clarke and B. Humberstone (eds) *Researching Women and Sport.* London: Macmillan.

Glyptis, S. (1989) *Leisure and Unemployment.* Milton Keynes: Open University Press.

Goodnow, J.J. and Bowes, J.M. (1994) *Men, Women and Household Work.* Oxford: Oxford University Press.

Green, E., Hebron, S. and Woodward, D. (1987) *Leisure and Gender: a Study of Sheffield Women's Leisure Experiences.* London: Sports Council and ESRC.

Green, E., Hebron, S. and Woodward, D. (1990) *Women's Leisure, What Leisure?* London: Macmillan.

Gregson, N. and Lowe, M. (1993) 'Renegotiating the Domestic Division of Labour? a Study of Dual Career Households in North East and South East England'. *The Sociological Review*, 41, 3, 475–505.

Gregson, N. and Lowe, M. (1994) 'Waged Domestic Labour and the Renegotiation of the Domestic Division of Labour within Dual Career Households'. *Sociology*, 28, 1, 55–78.

Horrell, S., Rubery, J. and Burchell, B. (1994) 'Working-time Patterns, Constraints and Preferences' in M. Anderson, F. Bechhofer and J. Gershuny (eds) *The Social and Political Economy of the Household*. Oxford: Oxford University Press.

Le Feuvre, N. (1994) 'Leisure, Work and Gender: a Sociological Study of Women's Time in France'. *Time and Society*, 3, 2, 151–78.

Morgan, D. (1996) *Family Connections: an Introduction to Family Studies*. Cambridge: Polity Press.

Morris, L. (1990) *The Workings of the Household*. London: Polity Press.

Morris, L. (1993) 'Household Finance Management and the Labour Market: a Case Study in Hartlepool'. *The Sociological Review*, 41, 3, 506–36.

Pahl, J. (1991) 'Money and Power in Marriage' in P. Abbott and C. Wallace (eds) *Gender, Power and Sexuality*. London: Macmillan.

Pringle, R. (1988) *Secretaries Talk*. London: Verso.

Radner, H. (1995) *Shopping Around: Feminine Culture and the Pursuit of Pleasure*. London: Routledge.

Rapoport, R. and Rapoport, R.N. (1975) *Leisure and the Family Life Cycle*. London: Routledge.

Smith, M., Parker, S. and Smith, C. (1973) *Leisure and Society in Britain*. London: Allen Lane.

Talbot, M. (1996) 'Time and Context in Women's Sport and Leisure' in G. Clarke and B. Humberstone (eds) *Researching Women and Sport*. London: Macmillan.

Vogler, C. (1994) 'Money in the Household' in M. Anderson, F. Bechhofer and J. Gershuny (eds) *The Social and Political Economy of the Household*. Oxford: Oxford University Press.

Vogler, C. and Pahl, J. (1993) 'Social and Economic Change and the Organisation of Money within Marriage'. *Work, Employment and Society*, 7, 1, 71–95.

Wimbush, E. (1986) *Women, Leisure and Well-Being*. Edinburgh: Centre for Leisure Research, University of Edinburgh.

Part IV
Gendered Work, Income and Power

10 Unequal Partners: Inequality in Earnings and Independent Income within Marriage

Sara Arber

INTRODUCTION

This chapter argues that gender inequality in the earnings and independent income of partners forms the basis of fundamental inequalities in economic power between husbands and wives. Despite women's increased participation in paid employment, gender inequality in incomes within marriage is resilient and varies little according to a woman's labour market participation, her age or whether she has children. Gender inequality in earnings in the private sphere of the household is a critical factor in maintaining women's disadvantaged position in society.

There is a contradiction in contemporary society between the general acceptance of equality of opportunity and of pay for women (Witherspoon and Prior, 1991), and the normative structure of the domestic domain in which husbands are still generally accepted as the 'main breadwinner' and financial dominance in the family is equated with masculinity. Failure to contest this normative structure is a major factor in the perpetuation of women's disadvantaged position in British society. Western societies have achieved some progress towards gender equality in the labour market in terms of equality of occupational achievement between men and women who work full-time, although substantial gender inequalities in earnings remain (Arber and Ginn, 1995a). Gender inequality in economic roles in the household may be more resistant to change. Women's disadvantaged position in British society can only be understood by considering the relationship between women's role in the public sphere of the labour market and their economic position in the private sphere of the home (Arber and Ginn, 1995a; Brannen *et al.*, 1994).

Women increasingly have some economic independence through participation in paid work, with nearly two-thirds of married women employed. However, most of the post-war growth in women's employment has been in part-time employment (Hakim, 1993a, 1995; Elias and Gregory, 1994). Modest increases in the proportions working full-time did not occur until the late-1980s. A major change has been the growth in the proportion of women with pre-school children who are in paid employment (Elias and Hogarth, 1994), but among such mothers full-time employment is concentrated in professional and managerial occupations (Glover and Arber, 1995). This will produce greater class polarization among women and couples. Gregson and Lowe (1993) suggest that women in professional and managerial occupations with young children are mainly buying services outside the household, such as domestic help and childcare, rather than sharing work more equally within the household.

Occupational segregation, whereby women are concentrated in certain occupations, especially clerical, secretarial and personal service work remains pronounced, and some commentators suggest has increased over recent years (Hakim, 1993b). However, women have made major inroads into the professions and now form half the entrants to law, medicine, accountancy and pharmacy. Despite the 'glass ceiling', which hinders women's promotion to the highest levels of many professions and management, women are increasingly found at the higher reaches of many occupations. Thus, although women are still in a disadvantaged position in the labour market, there are signs that this disadvantage has diminished (Crompton and Sanderson, 1990; Siltanen, 1995). Hakim (1991, 1995) argues that women's low occupational attainment mainly reflects their own 'choice' to give their families priority over their paid employment. However, because both their husbands and society generally place the responsibility for childcare and other domestic work upon women, their choices are heavily constrained in a way that men's are not (Ginn *et al.*, 1996). It is likely that if women could choose to have a family without sacrificing their employment opportunities (as men are able to do when they become fathers) their commitment to employment and occupational attainment would be higher.

Women's earnings still lag behind those of men. There has been a narrowing of the gender earnings differential in full-time pay since the mid-1980s from women earning 75 per cent of men's hourly earnings in 1987 to 81 per cent of men's earnings in 1993. The gender differential in weekly earnings is greater, because men work longer hours on average than women; women increased their weekly earnings as a percentage of men's from 67 per cent in 1987 to 73 per cent in 1993 (Department of Employment, 1993; Dale and Joshi, 1992). Gender inequalities in earnings are mainly due to the gender-segregated structure of the labour market, and the ways in which women's jobs are often defined as less skilled than similar jobs undertaken by men. However, figures on gender differences in earnings understate gender inequality in remuneration from employment, since men are more likely than women to receive a range of employment benefits, such as company cars, generous employer-paid pension schemes, paid time off and private health care (SCELI 1989). Women value earnings as a source of financial independence during their working life (Joshi, 1984), and earnings are the key factor influencing women's financial well-being in later life through occupational pension acquisition (Arber and Ginn, 1991; Ginn and Arber, 1991, 1994).

The position of women in the public world of paid employment and the private domain of the family is inextricably linked. Gender inequalities within the family are greater than those in the labour market and seem more resistant to change. As argued in Arber and Ginn (1995a), a vicious circle is created which connects women's lack of economic power within marriage and their disadvantaged position in the labour market. Women's employment opportunities, and hence earnings, are constrained by having to shoulder the bulk of responsibility for domestic work. Where women earn less than their husband this will tend to perpetuate their relative powerlessness in marriage; the ideology that women's labour market contribution is less valuable and more easily dispensable than that of their husband is reinforced. This in turn leads to the expectation that women will perform the bulk of domestic labour, constraining their opportunities in the labour market.

ECONOMIC INDEPENDENCE VERSUS ECONOMIC POWER WITHIN MARRIAGE

The majority of married women are in paid work and therefore have some economic independence in the family, but this does not mean that they have economic power *vis-à-vis* their partner. If a woman contributes substantially less financial resources than her partner, it is likely that her employment will continue to be seen as subsidiary to his, and she will have less influence over decision making within the family.

In much writing there is an implicit assumption that women's increased labour-force participation, especially in full-time work, will increase women's economic power in the home. For example, Dale and Foster (1986: 124–5) write:

> The Marxist tradition ... has always emphasized the progressive implications of women's participation in waged work. Engels ... argued that

women's liberation depended on taking all women out of the home and into public industry ...

Most socialist feminists today are rather critical of Engels' naive assumption that once women were absorbed into factory work, the sexual division of labour in the home would disappear and men's patriarchal attitudes and behaviour would wither away ...

[However], it remains true that the main thrust of socialist feminist thinking on women's economic position tends to be around the issue of how women can improve their labour market position. It is assumed that women want to work outside the home, that this is progressive and that the key problem is how to introduce changes both in the workplace and the home which will enable women to do so.

Although women's complete economic dependency within marriage is now a minority experience, most women working part-time are not earning enough to achieve 'genuine economic independence in terms of the balance of economic power within households and of equality in household financial arrangements' (Lister, 1992: 20). Lister argues that lack of an independent income is linked to inequality in decision-making, and that 'women's increased participation in the labour market has opened up only very limited avenues to economic independence' (1992: 10), because of women's low pay, part-time work and lack of access to occupational welfare and its accompanying fiscal advantages.

Women's employment may be a prerequisite for economic power in the household but is clearly not sufficient. The key determinant of economic power in the household is the relative size of each partner's income rather than the absolute amount of a woman's independent income. This chapter follows Duncan *et al.* (1994: 1) in defining 'independent income to represent money that is paid directly to women, whether from earnings, social security, investments or maintenance payments'.

Recent years have seen a burgeoning of research on inequalities in resources within the household, demonstrating that women may experience poverty within the household, even though the whole household would not be classified as in poverty (Arber, 1993). Women often lack money they can regard as their own, and have less personal spending money than men. Pahl's influential work (1989, 1990) has documented the nature of financial allocation mechanisms within households, showing that wives are more likely to be responsible for budgeting decisions and less likely to have overall control of how money is spent. Pahl (1989) found that where both partners are employed, overall control of financial resources and decision making reflects the relative earning power and economic contribution of each partner. Vogler and Pahl comment that 'there is now a considerable body of research which suggests ... the partner with the larger income is likely to play a more dominant part in decision-making' (1994: 263–4). Brannen and Wilson (1987) also document the implications of the distribution of resources within the household for the power and status of different household members. The current chapter builds on this work, but focuses explicitly on the relative earnings and independent income of each partner in married and cohabiting couples.

EARNINGS AND INDEPENDENT INCOME AMONG MARRIED COUPLES

There has been little British research on the relative level of earnings and independent income of marital partners. Dale and Joshi (1992) report analyses of the Family Expenditure Survey which show that wives only earned 23 per cent of couples' total earnings in 1986. Among two-earner couples, wives earned 30 per cent, compared with 26 per cent in 1968. Data published by the Central Statistical Office showed that married women on average contributed 17 per cent to household income in 1989 (CSO 1989: Table 21). Where both partners were employed, women contributed 27 per cent of the couple's income in households with dependent children and 33 per cent of the couple's income where there were no dependent children in the household.

Webb (1993) produces somewhat higher figures for women's independent income as a proportion of all income within private households, rising from a quarter in 1971 to a third in 1991, but this figure includes all households, and partly reflects the increasing proportion of lone-mother households and widows living in separate households. It does not necessarily reflect greater equality in income receipt between men and women in couple households. All these figures present data as the average percentage of income or earnings contributed by women. They provide no information about the relative earnings or income of partners, and give no clues as to the proportion of women with higher earnings or income than their partner.

Brannen and Moss's (1987, 1991) study of women who returned to work full-time after their first birth found that only a quarter of the mothers earned as much as their husband, and they contributed 44 per cent of the total household resources. They showed that women with higher earnings than their husband were more likely to return to work than other women.

WIVES WITH HIGHER EARNINGS THAN THEIR PARTNER

Qualitative research provides some insights into the ways in which greater earning power of women is often played down by women themselves. Wilson (1987) found that the few women earning more than their husband, often saw this as a source of embarrassment to themselves and their partners. Among women who earned more than their husband there was greater emphasis on the stated importance of sharing resources.

A major stumbling block to women's equality in the domestic sphere is the influence of the cultural ideology as to the proper roles of husbands and wives within marriage. Carling (1992) argues that couples in which women earn more do not simply follow 'economic rationality' in the domestic division of labour, because they are influenced by cultural norms. McRae (1986) conducted qualitative interviews with 30 'cross-class' married couples; defined as women with a supervisory non-manual or professional/ managerial job married to a man with a manual job or who was self-employed on his own account. Although all the wives had an occupationally superior position in terms of the Registrar General's social classes, only half earned more than their husband. McRae did not explicitly separate these two groups in her analysis. She found that some occupationally dominant women maintained traditional domestic and childcare roles to reinforce their image of themselves as good wives and mothers and to give the impression that their husband was dominant in the household. Brannen (1991) and Brannen and Moss (1991) found that most mothers working full-time with young children fully embraced the ideology of the 'proper mother' and believed that their own jobs were less important than their husbands'. Studies of unemployed men (such as McKee, 1987; Morris, 1990) have found that their wives were concerned to maintain conventional gender roles rather than their husband taking on equal amounts of domestic work and childcare.

Despite the continuing power of the domestic gender ideology, McRae (1986) found that for some higher-earning wives there had been a change in attitudes and behaviour consequent upon their greater relative earning power than their husbands. She reports evidence of a more equal division of domestic labour and increased female power within some cross-class households.

Until women have higher earnings than their partners, it is unlikely that cultural expectations about appropriate gender roles relating to the domestic division of labour will be challenged. The extent to which economic rationality modifies conventional attitudes and behaviour is a moot point, but the lack of evidence of role reversal and equal sharing of domestic and childcare tasks in Britain suggests that the persistence of income inequality within marriage and the prevailing gendered norms are both important and are likely to influence each other. It is unlikely that major progress towards equality in the home will occur without greater equality of the economic contributions of both partners within marriage.

AIMS AND METHODS

This chapter aims first to explore the extent of earnings inequality between partners among couples in the mid-1990s, and whether there are differences in earnings inequality at various stages of the life-course. Second, the chapter examines inequality in independent income (from all sources) among working-age couples, and across the life-course, including in later life. Finally, the chapter assesses to what extent earnings and income inequality is less among women who have never had children and women in higher middle-class occupations.

Combined data from three years of the General Household Survey (GHS), 1992/3 to 1994/5 is analysed (OPCS 1992–94). The GHS is a national representative survey which interviews all adults aged 16 and over in about 10,000 households each year in Great Britain. The response rate averaged 81 per cent in 1992–94 (Bennett *et al.*, 1996). Combining data from three years provides a larger sample for analysis and therefore more reliable estimates for the British population.

The analysis of income inequality between partners uses data based on the total gross income of each partner. Questions on earnings and personal income in the GHS are subject to a non-response of about 10 per cent. Income data is available on 11,800 couples where the wife is aged 20–59 and about 3,000 couples where the wife is 60 or over. The analysis of earnings inequality focuses on women aged 20–59 where both partners are employed, about 6,800 couples. Earnings are based on usual gross amounts per week, and include regular overtime. Independent income includes gross income from all sources, including earnings, child benefit, income support, maintenance payments, and income from investments and savings received by an individual.

Ten per cent of couples were cohabiting in 1994, defined as unmarried adults of the opposite sex who considered themselves to be living together as a couple (Bennett *et al.*, 1996). The terms 'married' are used to include those who are cohabiting, and 'husband' and 'wife' to include cohabiting male and female partners respectively. Part-time employment is defined as employment for 30 hours or less each week. The measure of class is a regrouping of the OPCS Socio-Economic Groups (SEGs).

In 1992–5, 34 per cent of wives aged 20–59 worked full-time, 36 per cent worked part-time and 30 per cent were not in paid employment. Only 7 per cent of wives are employed when their husbands were not in paid work, with slightly more working part-time than full-time.

EARNINGS INEQUALITY BETWEEN DUAL-EMPLOYED MARITAL PARTNERS

The inequality of women's economic position in the family is analysed first by comparing the relative earnings of partners for the two-thirds of couples who are dual-earners. Earnings dominance of men over their wives may be a major factor used by men to justify their own occupation as the more important and their own role as that of 'main breadwinner', as well as to justify men's unequal participation in domestic tasks and child-care. This section focuses on couples where the wife is aged 20–59.

'Equal earnings' is defined as a situation where the wife earns between 45 and 55 per cent of the total gross earnings of the couple. According to this definition, 16 per cent of dual-earner couples have equal earnings, and the wife earns more than her husband in 9 per cent of couples (see Table 10.1). Thus, in three-quarters of dual-earner couples, the wife earns under 45 per cent of the couples' total earnings. This is the case for 57 per cent of couples where the wife works full-time, but over 90 per cent where she

Table 10.1   Equality of Earnings among Dual-Employed Couples, Wife Aged 20–59

Employment status of wife	Wife's earnings as a % of couple's total earnings					Row %	No.
	<25%	25<45%	45<55% Equal	55<75%	75+%		
Wife works full-time	9	48	28	12	3	100	3229
Wife works part-time	63	28	5	3	1	100	3545
All dual-employed couples	38	37	16	7	2	100	6774

Source: General Household Survey, 1992/93, 1993/94, 1994/95 (author's analysis).

works part-time. Women working part-time earn a very small amount compared with their husband, over 60 per cent earning under a quarter of the couple's total earnings. Nearly three-fifths of women working full-time earn less than their husband and only 15 per cent earn more than their husband. Thus, equality of earnings is unusual, and the norm in Britain is for husbands to earn substantially more than their working wives.

Inequality of earnings among dual-earner couples is not restricted to particular stages of the life-course. Less than 10 per cent of wives earn more than their husband in each five year age group, except for women in their late fifties, where this rises to 13 per cent. A somewhat higher proportion of younger couples, where wives are in their twenties, have equal earnings, mainly because few have children at this age, but even among dual earner couples where the wife is aged 20–4, two-thirds earn less than their husband. Thus, a woman's age has little effect on her likelihood of having equal or higher earnings than her husband.

In over 90 per cent of dual-earner households, the wife's earnings do not exceed those of her partner, so that the husband's employment is likely to take precedence. In such households, wives' own careers may be defined as secondary because in terms of earnings they *are* secondary, thus perpetuating the vicious cycle referred to above.

With cross-sectional data such as the GHS, we do not know whether the small percentage of full-time working women who earn more than their husbands do so throughout their working life, or whether it is only for a temporary phase. However, earnings dominance seems to vary little across the age range. Longitudinal data would be needed to identify women who were earnings-dominant over a long period, unlike women whose economic dominance was too short term to have a significant effect on their domestic relationships.

INEQUALITY IN INDEPENDENT INCOME BETWEEN PARTNERS

The previous section showed that working wives are rarely economically dominant and that gender inequalities in earnings in dual-earner couples are very substantial. This section analyses inequality in independent income between partners among couples of all ages. The relative level of income of partners is measured by the wife's gross income as a proportion of the couple's gross income from all sources, including earnings, state benefits, child benefit, maintenance payments, income from savings, etc. Income inequality is first considered for couples where the wife is aged 20–59.

A fifth of wives are not in employment while their partners are employed, and here our assumption is that the wife will virtually always have a lower independent income than her husband. In 7 per cent of couples, the wife is in employment while her husband is not, and we assume that these wives will all have a higher independent income than their partners. This section also examines the 10 per cent of couples where neither partner was in paid employment to see whether earnings inequality between dual employed couples is replicated in terms of income inequality where neither partner is employed. Table 10.2 shows to what extent these assumptions are borne out.

Table 10.2   Equality of Independent Income of Partners by Couple's Employment Status, Wife Aged 20–59

Couple's employment status	Wife's income as % of couple's total income						
	<25%	25<45%	45<55% Equal	55<75%	75+%	Row%	No.
Husband employed							
Wife works full-time	10	47	27	13	3	100	3578
Wife works part-time	56	34	5	4	1	100	3854
Wife not employed	89	8	1	1	1	100	2409
All employed husbands	47	32	12	6	2	100	9841
Husband not employed							
Wife works full-time	4	9	9	31	47	100	378
Wife works part-time	21	30	14	19	16	100	418
Wife not employed	70	13	6	6	6	101	1217
All not-employed husbands	48	16	8	13	15	100	2013
All couples	47	30	12	7	4	100	11854

Source: General Household Survey, 1992/93, 1993/94, 1994/95 (author's analysis).

Considering dual-earner couples where the wife works full-time, a quarter have equal incomes and in 16 per cent the wife has a higher gross income than her husband (Table 10.2); this is similar to the 15 per cent who earned more than their husband (Table 10.1). This very slight increase is probably because of the addition of child benefit to women's income. Among 'traditional' couples, where the husband but not the wife is employed, for 90 per cent the wife's independent income represents under a quarter of the total couple's income, as expected.

Among the small proportion of wives who work full-time while their husband is not employed, three-quarters have a higher income than their partner, 9 per cent have an equal income and 13 per cent have less income (Table 10.2). Although women generally have higher income in these cases, the relative income distribution is less unequal than the parallel case of wives who do not work while their husband is employed. The situation of women who work part-time while their husband is not employed is quite different; over half have a lower income than their husband, despite the fact that she is the only partner in the labour market. Thus, part-time work does little to redress the gender imbalance in economic power in these families.

Where neither partner is in employment, the wife has a higher independent income than her husband in only 12 per cent of couples, only 6 per cent have an equal income, and for 70 per cent the wife's independent income represents under a quarter of the total couple's income. Thus income inequality is very extreme among working-age couples where neither partner is in paid work. It largely reflects the benefit system in which eligibility for means-tested benefits is calculated on the combined income of a couple, but is usually paid to the man. Since income support is paid as a single sum to the claimant, by definition the other partner has no independent income, and may be very financially deprived within the couple.

Figure 10.1 shows very little variation in income inequality between partners across the life-course, except for the reduction in disparity for women above state pension age. Between age 30 and 60, almost half of married women have an independent income which is less than a quarter of that of their husband. This lack of independent economic resources is likely to be translated into a lack of power in the family.

Women above 65 are very unlikely to have a higher income than their partner – under 5 per cent. However, the gender differential in income is markedly less than at earlier stages of the life-course. The wife's income represents between 25 and 45 per cent of the couple's income among a higher proportion of older couples than couples where the wife is under 65. For most older couples, their greater equality in independent income reflects the levelling effect of state pension income. The national insurance

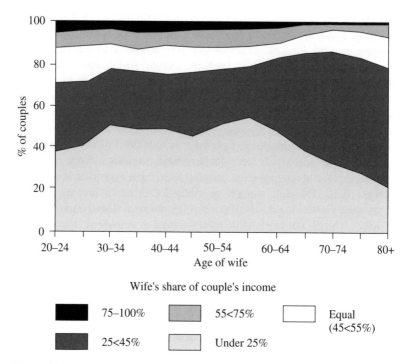

Figure 10.1   Wife's Independent Income as a Proportion of Couple's Gross Income by Age of Wife.

retirement pension provides most married women over 60 with a Category B pension, which amounts to 60 per cent of her husband's state pension, conventionally referred to as the 'married woman's allowance'. It is ironic, given the Marxist and feminist emphasis on participation in paid work as the means of emancipation for women, that inequality of income between partners is less among older people, because of the state pension, than in working life, when most married women have independent income from the labour market, but at a low level compared to their husband's level of earnings.

CHILDBEARING, SOCIAL CLASS AND ECONOMIC INEQUALITY BETWEEN PARTNERS

This section examines some of the factors expected to affect the degree of earnings inequality between dual-employed partners, namely childbearing history and the woman's own occupational class. It is expected that childless women are more likely than other women to have equal or higher earnings than their partner, since childbearing acts as a major constraint on married women's employment participation and occupational achievement in the labour market (Dex, 1987).

There is some variation according to parental status in the degree of earnings inequality, but the majority of women without children still have lower earnings than their husband. Only 14 per cent of childless women under 40 have higher earnings than their partner, 30 per cent are equal to their partner in this respect, and nearly half have earnings which represent 25–45 per cent of the couple's earnings. Among women under 40 with children, only 17 per cent, have earnings which are equal to or higher than their partner, while for the majority their earnings represent under a quarter of that for the couple. The pattern is repeated for women aged 40–59. Midlife women without children at home are somewhat more likely to have equal or higher earnings, 29 per cent, than women with children, but again the norm is to receive lower earnings.

A small proportion of employed married women, 8 per cent, work in higher professional and managerial occupations or as managers in large companies, and it might be expected that they would usually have earnings equality or higher earnings than their husband. Only a fifth of these married women are the higher earner, in nearly half the sample their husband earns more than they do. For women in lower professional occupations, such as teaching and social work, the earnings disparity is larger, with only 13 per cent of wives earning more then their husband, while the husband is the higher earner among two-thirds of these couples. Among women in clerical or manual occupations, there is little variation in the degree of earnings inequality according to the woman's occupational class; 80 per cent earn less than their partner.

Thus, even among the elite of women working in the highest occupational levels, few earn more than their husband. The factors responsible reflect both gender inequalities in the labour market which lead to lower occupational attainment and earnings of women, but also factors influencing choice of marriage partners and cultural ideology about the appropriateness of gender differences between marriage partners. There is a tendency towards social homogamy of marriage partners (Berent, 1954); people marry those with a similar educational level and occupational level (at the time of partnership formation). But in spite of this similarity in the characteristics of partners at the time of marriage, gender inequality occurs in each class, with men likely to have a somewhat higher occupational level than their wives (Arber and Ginn, 1995a) and a higher income than their wives. In addition, cultural values support the marriage age differential in which men are likely to be older than their wives, by two/three years on average.

CONCLUSIONS

In spite of the Equal Pay Act (1970) and the Sex Discrimination Act (1975), which have assisted women in entering the professions in increasing numbers, substantial gender inequality in earnings remains. Among dual-employed couples gender inequality in earnings is very great. Only 15 per cent of married women who work full-time earn more than their husband, compared with 57 per cent of couples where the husband earns more than his wife. As many as 91 per cent of women working part-time earn less than their husband. Thus, in Britain wives who are earnings-dominant are rare, despite nearly 30 years of equal pay legislation.

Married women who are not in paid employment rarely have a higher independent income than their husband. The small proportion of women who work full-time while their husband is not working are likely to have the higher income, but this is not the case for women who work part-time while their husband is not employed.

To the extent that women continue to earn less than their husband, they are likely to have less power to influence family financial decision making, and their lower earnings are likely to hamper attempts to equalize the domestic division of labour. Women who are not employed have very limited independent income compared with their husband, especially where neither partner is employed. These women are likely to have very little power in the domestic arena, as well as very little economic ability to establish a separate household should the marriage break down.

Despite the gains of full-time working wives in terms of occupational standing (Arber and Ginn, 1995a), achieving economic equality in the family is proving more intractable. Gender inequality in earnings and independent income is very pronounced between partners in the private sphere. The persistence of male economic advantage in the labour market is magnified in the family, reinforcing the ideology and practice of women's subordination. There is a reciprocal relation between the labour market and the family, with women's economic disadvantage in the labour market influencing their domestic role in the family, which in turn reduces women's ability to participate to their full potential in the public sphere.

The findings in this chapter suggest that *even* if women in the labour market had earnings equality with men, there would still be an earnings differential between marriage partners. Hence the extent to which earnings inequality in marriage exceeds earnings inequality in the working population may be seen as an indicator of patriarchy in the family and the persistence of cultural attitudes supporting the norm that women should not earn more than their partner. Sociological understanding of patriarchal practices of segregation and social control in the labour market needs to be complemented by studies of patriarchal relations in the family which perpetuate men's dominance in the home.

REFERENCES

Arber, S. (1993) 'Inequalities Within the Household' in L. Stanley and D. Morgan (eds) *Debates in Sociology, 1967–1992*. Manchester: Manchester University Press.

Arber, S. and Ginn, J. (1991) *Gender and Later Life: a Sociological Analysis of Resources and Constraints*. London: Sage.

Arber, S. and Ginn, J. (1995a) 'The Mirage of Gender Equality: Occupational Success in the Labour Market and Within Marriage'. *British Journal of Sociology*, 46, 1, 21–43.

Arber, S. and Ginn, J. (1995b) 'Choice and Constraint in the Retirement of Older Married Women' in S. Arber and J. Ginn (eds) *Connecting Gender and Ageing: a Sociological Approach*. Buckingham: Open University Press.

Bennett, N., Jarvis, L., Rowlands, O., Singleton, N. and Huselden, L. (1996) *Living in Britain: Results from the 1994 General Household Survey*. London: HMSO.

Berent, J. (1954) 'Social Mobility and Marriage: a Study of Trends in England and Wales' in D.V. Glass (ed.) *Social Mobility in Britain*. London: Routledge and Kegan Paul.

Brannen, J. (1991) 'Money, Marriage and Motherhood: Dual Earner Households after Maternity Leave' in S. Arber and N. Gilbert (eds) *Women and Working Lives: Divisions and Change*. London: Macmillan.

Brannen, J. and Moss, P. (1987) 'Dual Earner Households: Women's Financial Contributions After the Birth of the First Child' in J. Brannen and G. Wilson (eds) *Give and Take in Families: Studies in Resource Distribution*. London: Allen and Unwin.

Brannen, J. and Moss, P. (1991) *Managing Mothers*. London: Unwin Hyman.

Brannen, J., Meszaros, G., Moss, P. and Poland, G. (1994) *Employment and Family Life: a Review of Research in the UK (1980–1994)*. Employment Department Research Series No. 41. London: Department of Employment, HMSO.

Brannen, J. and Wilson, G. (eds) (1987) *Give and Take in Families: Studies in Resource Distribution*. London: Allen and Unwin.

Carling, A. (1992) 'Rational Choice and Household Division' in C. Marsh and S. Arber (eds) *Families and Households: Divisions and Change*. London: Macmillan.

Central Statistical Office (1989) *Family Expenditure Survey*. London: HMSO.

Crompton, R. and Sanderson, K. (1990) *Gendered Jobs and Social Change*. London: Unwin Hyman.

Dale, A. and Joshi, H. (1992) 'The Economic and Social Status of British Women'. *Acta Demographica*, 1, 27–46.

Dale, J. and Foster, P. (1986) *Feminists and State Welfare*. London: Routledge and Kegan Paul.

Department of Employment (1993) *New Earnings Survey 1993, Section A: Streamlined and Summary Analyses*. London: HMSO.

Dex, S. (1987) *Women's Occupational Mobility: a Lifetime Perspective*. London: Macmillan.

Duncan, A., Giles, C. and Webb, S. (1994) *Social Security Reform and Women's Independent Incomes*. Manchester: Equal Opportunities Commission.

Elias, P. and Gregory, M. (1994) *The Changing Structure of Occupations and Earnings in Great Britain, 1975–1990*. Employment Department Research Series No. 27. Sheffield: Employment Department.

Elias, P. and Hogarth, T. (1994) 'Families, Jobs and Unemployment: the Changing Pattern of Economic Dependency in Britain' in R. Lindsey (ed.) *Labour Market Structures and Prospects for Women*. Manchester: Equal Opportunities Commission.

Ginn, J. and Arber, S. (1991) 'Gender, Class and Income Inequalities in Later Life'. *British Journal of Sociology*, 42, 3, 369–96.

Ginn, J. and Arber, S. (1994) 'Heading for Hardship: How the British Pension System has Failed Women' in S. Baldwin and J. Falkingham (eds) *Social Security and Social Change*. Hemel Hempstead: Harvester Wheatsheaf.

Ginn, J., Arber, S., Brannen, J., Dale, A., Dex, S., Elias, P., Moss, P., Pahl, J., Roberts, C. and Rubery, J. (1996) 'Feminist Fallacies: a Reply to Hakim on Women's Employment'. *British Journal of Sociology*, 47, 1, 167–74.

Glover, J. and Arber, S. (1995) 'Polarization in Mothers' Employment'. *Gender, Work and Organization*, 2, 4, 165–79.

Gregson, N. and Lowe, M. (1993) 'Renegotiating the Domestic Division of Labour? A Study of Dual-Career Households in North East and South East England'. *The Sociological Review*, 41, 3, 475–504.

Hakim, C. (1979) *Occupational Sex Segregation*. Department of Employment Research Paper No. 9. London: HMSO.

Hakim, C. (1991) 'Grateful Slaves or Self-Made Women: Fact and Fantasy in Women's Work Orientations'. *European Sociological Review*, 7, 2, 101–21.

Hakim, C. (1993a) 'The Myth of Rising Female Employment'. *Work, Employment and Society*, 7, 97–120.

Hakim, C. (1993b) 'Segregated and Integrated Occupations: a New Approach to Analysing Social Change'. *European Sociological review*, 9, 289–314.

Hakim, C. (1995) 'Five Feminist Myths About Women's Employment'. *British Journal of Sociology*, 46, 3, 429–55.

Joshi, H. (1984) *Women's Participation in Paid Work: Further analysis of the Women and Employment Survey*. London: Department of Employment Research Paper No. 45.

Lister, R. (1992) *Women's Economic Dependency and Social Security*. Manchester: Equal Opportunities Commission.

McKee, L. (1987) 'Households Surviving Unemployment: the Resourcefulness of the Unemployed' in J. Brannen and G. Wilson (eds) *Give and Take in Families*. London: Allen and Unwin.

McRae, S. (1986) *Cross-Class Families: a Study of Women's Occupational Superiority*. Oxford: Clarendon Press.

Morris, L. (1990) *The Workings of the Household*. Cambridge: Polity Press.

Office of Population Censuses and Surveys (1988–90) *General Household Surveys 1988–1990* [Computer files. Colchester: ESRC Data Archive, 1990–2].

Office of Population Censuses and Surveys (1992) *General Household Survey, 1990*. London: HMSO.

Pahl, J. (1989) *Money and Marriage*. Basingstoke: Macmillan.

Pahl, J. (1990) 'Household Spending, Personal Spending and the Control of Money in Marriage'. *Sociology*, 24, 1, 118–38.

SCELI (1989) *Unequal Jobs, Unequal Pay*. Working Paper No. 6. Oxford: Social Change and Economic Life Initiative.

Siltanen, J. (1995) *Locating Gender: Occupational Segregation, Wages and Domestic Responsibilities*. London: UCL Press.

Vogler, C. and Pahl, J. (1994) 'Money, Power and Inequality Within Marriage'. *Sociological Review*, 42, 2, 263–88.

Webb, S. (1993) 'Women's Incomes; Past, Present and Prospects'. *Fiscal Studies*, 14, 4, 14–36.

Wilson, G. (1987) 'Money: Patterns of Responsibility and Irresponsibility in Marriage' in J. Brannen and G. Wilson (eds) *Give and Take in Families*. London: Allen and Unwin.

Witherspoon, S. and Prior, G. (1991) 'Working Mothers: Free to Choose?' in R. Jowell, L. Brook and B. Taylor (eds) *British Social Attitudes: the 8th Report*. Aldershot: SCPR.

11 Decision Making in Dual-Career Households

Irene Hardill, Anna C. Dudleston,
Anne E. Green and David W. Owen

INTRODUCTION

One of the most complex and controversial issues in the social sciences is the development and increased intensity of social polarization and exclusion. Two contrasting approaches have been employed in studying this phenomenon: one based on the 'global cities' thesis (Castells, 1989; Sassen, 1991; 1996), and the other, which is used in this chapter, focusing on the changing face of households (Pinch, 1993). While the household remains the basic social unit around which people conduct their lives (Pahl, 1984: 13), the structure, composition and organization of households is changing. One source of change is the growth in the number of women in paid employment. Throughout the 1980s and the 1990s, women have increased their share of employment in virtually all industries, occupations (including professional occupations) and areas in Great Britain (Green, 1994; McDowell and Court, 1994). McDowell and Court (1994) note that even in the better-paid professional occupations, short-term contract employment and practices such as incentive payments or bonuses are replacing secure, life-time salaried conditions that previously marked professional employment in the 'core' economy.

Generally speaking, men and women participate in the labour market on a very different basis, and the participation of women cannot be understood in isolation from their position in kinship and family structures, and their relationship to childbearing and reproduction (Horrell and Humphries, 1995). Their positions in paid and unpaid work are mutually determining (Bowlby, 1990; Sinclair, 1991). Moreover, households are being increasingly regarded as an arena of potential conflict (Morris, 1989), while the life chances of individual members of households are being affected by the way that economic restructuring affects other members of the household. Hanson and Pratt (1995: 141) have commented upon the fluidity and complexity of US families, and Stacey (1990: 269) coined the term 'postmodern family' to convey the sense of variable family strategies.

In Britain the Joseph Rowntree Foundation Inquiry into Income and Wealth highlighted a growing polarization between households containing non-working ('work poor') couples and those containing dual-earner ('work rich') couples. Increases in both of these categories of households, accompanied by an absolute and relative decline in households with one earner and a 'conventional' division of labour has been identified as a key factor in fuelling increasing inequality in British society (Hills, 1995; Hutton, 1995; Williams and Windebank, 1995). McDowell (1991: 415) describes the 'double pay cheque' families as the ones to have gained throughout the periods of recession, expansion and inflation that have accompanied economic restructuring.

There has also been much speculation about the effect women's formal labour-market participation has on the power balance within the household. Edgell (1980) found that in middle-class couples, routine housekeeping decisions were made by the wife, whilst career-related decisions were made by the husband. Therefore, residential location and labour market access/job search areas have tended to be a male decision. Edgell's results confirm the importance of the distinction between 'orchestration' power and 'implementation' power (Safilios-Rothschild, 1972). He demonstrates how marital decisions can be placed along a continuum with decisions which are perceived as important but infrequent at one end of the scale, and decisions which are perceived as unimportant but frequent at the other. Typically, the former are the responsibility of the male and the latter of the female (Edgell, 1980).

Recent work has also explored different strategies for intra-household co-operation and the interplay of production and reproduction, including work by Kiernan (1992). An attempt will be made to operationalize this categorization (see Figure 11.1) specifically through exploring career prioritization strategies in the dual-career households that we have interviewed. In a similar vein Gershuny *et al.* (1994) have also presented evidence of a gradual change in domestic practices concluding that there is evidence of some historical change towards greater equality within the household (see Figure 11.2 and Gershuny *et al.*, 1994: 183). However, Gregson and Lowe's (1993) study of dual-career households and the domestic division of labour found that the women surveyed were very likely to transfer the bulk of their domestic labour to a non-household individual (see also Hertz, 1987), and agreed with Morris' claim that 'women's employment does not provide a sufficient context for the renegotiation of the domestic division of labour' (Morris, 1990: 500).

While a large number of men, on average, are taking on a more active role in the domestic arena than in the past, this is often a 'helping' rather

Figure 11.1   Categorization of Household Types

Traditional home-maker/breadwinner type: a household in which the husband only works and the wife runs the home;

Middle type: a household in which the wife's work is less absorbing than the husband's, and in which she takes on more of the household tasks and looking after the children;

Egalitarian type: both male and female partners have equally absorbing work; household tasks and looking after the children are shared equally.

Source: Green (1995)

Figure 11.2   Gershuny's Categorization

Adaptive partnership – domestic division of labour reflects changes in the participation of household members in the formal economy. If the wife gets a paid job, the employed husband does a higher proportion of the household's domestic work than previously, to compensate for the wife's new work responsibilities outside the household.

Dependent labour – women's labour is secondary, and she is primarily responsible for the domestic inputs; thus the women's proportion of the couple's domestic labour is insensitive to change in her commitments outside the household.

Lagged adaption – the adjustment of work roles takes place not through a short term redistribution of responsibilities but through a process of household negotiation extending over a period of many years, and indeed across generations.

Source: Gershuny *et al*. (1994)

than a 'sharing' role. Hence, the reality is of many women going home from paid employment at the end of the working day to a 'second shift' of additional (non-market domestic) work. Thus, many women are left to occupy two roles (Pleck, 1985; Anderson *et al*., 1994): a situation which has been referred to as the 'superwoman syndrome' (see Newell, 1993) – with women attempting to excel in both paid work and domestic spheres. These two roles are to some extent incompatible, particularly for those women seeking career progression; hence many are frustrated in their ambitions (Dex, 1987; Green and Hardill, 1991; Rees, 1992). Research has shown that having a full-time uninterrupted working life, and being seen as promotable through having the ability and commitment (which often involves working long hours) to appear as a viable long-term prospect, are key factors influencing an individual's career progression (McDowell and Court, 1994; Rose and Fielder, 1988). High-status, well-paid jobs tend to be organized on a full-time basis, and therefore generally are incompatible with the successful managing of a home and unshared family responsibilities. An increasing number of professional and managerial posts are fixed term. This coupled with the need for migration to further careers could well delay or inhibit household formation, as well as be a cause of tension amongst couples forced to live apart as dual-location households.

The term 'career' implies some long-term progression within an occupation, or through a series of occupations, involving increasing levels of responsibility at each stage. Careers are characterized by a high degree of commitment, and so have an intrinsically demanding character (Rapoport and Rapoport, 1976). Recent analyses of work-history data from selected localities (Rose and Fielder, 1988; Anderson *et al.*, 1992) have revealed that approximately three-fifths of men and two-fifths of women in employment think of themselves as having a career. For the purposes of this research, dual-career households are defined as those in which both partners (that is, two heterosexual adults living as a couple in a two-person or larger household) are in occupations classified in major categories 1–3 of the Standard Occupational Classification (that is, managerial and administrative, professional and associated professional and technical occupations). Hence dual-career households are distinguished from dual-income households comprising all households in which two partners are in paid employment. Much previous research has concentrated on dual career 'families' rather than households (Fogarty *et al.*, 1971; Rapoport and Rapoport, 1976; Fogarty *et al.*, 1981), and has placed a particular emphasis on childcare strategies (Brannen and Moss, 1988). However, in the light of the declining number of 'nuclear' families (Duncan, 1991) and the rising number of childless couples with 'top jobs' (Elias and Hogarth, 1993), it seems appropriate to focus on 'households' rather than 'families'.

This chapter focuses on one sub-set of 'work rich' households – dual-career households – drawing on an empirical study in the East Midlands which was funded by the Leverhulme Trust. The main objective of the chapter is to examine empirically the degree to which the surveyed dual-career households are egalitarian in the way decisions and compromises are made in relation to career development and career prioritization. It could be hypothesized that within dual-career households, in which there is a high level of involvement in the paid economy, and where both partners have access to economic resources, egalitarian attitudes and practices towards career-related decisions/compromises could also be expected, especially amongst younger households.

RESEARCHING DUAL CAREER HOUSEHOLDS: METHODOLOGY

The empirical research strategy used three basic methods:

1. the assembly and analysis of data and information from secondary sources – including the 1991 Census of Population and the Labour Force Survey providing a quantitative background for the detailed case studies (see Green, 1995 for a review);
2. structured self-completion questionnaires covering 136 dual-career households – containing at least one partner who worked in 'Greater Nottingham' (see Hardill *et al.*, 1995 for a review);
3. semi-structured face-to-face interviews with thirty dual-career households, selected as far as possible to be representative of the age and occupational structure of dual-career households (as revealed by the analysis of secondary data sources and responses to the structured questionnaire). Pseudonyms were used to protect the identities of those interviewed.

In this chapter, a number of related issues addressed in the face-to-face interviews are analysed. The intention of the face-to-face interviews was not to collect detailed quantitative information, but rather to provide insights into the factors taken into account by dual-career households relating to careers. The focus is not on everyday discourse or ideology but on subjectivity, on the lived experience of human ties based on gender and the physical, economic and social context of that experience.

The personnel directors of five organizations based in Nottingham, including health-service and higher-education establishments, a major bank, and two large market-oriented private-sector manufacturing companies (one engaged in the food and drink industry and the other in pharmaceuticals), were approached to help in the identification of dual-career households. In this way the research team gained access to staff in a relatively comprehensive range of managerial, professional and associated occupations. Each of the participating organizations has a different organizational structure, and hence the internal labour-market conditions are somewhat different. In each of the dual-career households identified, at least one partner is employed at a Nottingham base by one of the five employers. The other partner could work for any employer (or indeed work in a self-employed capacity) at any location. It should be noted that the selection of Nottingham means that the study marks a 'break' from the London/South East focus which dominated in much previous research on dual-career families/households.

A PROFILE OF DUAL CAREER HOUSEHOLDS IN
GREAT BRITAIN

Analyses of data from the 1991 Census of Population household *Sample of Anonymised Records* (SAR) reveal that at the regional scale the incidence of dual-career households is greatest in the Rest of the South East (ROSE), Outer London and East Anglia. Indeed, a quarter of all dual-career households are resident in ROSE. Alongside ROSE, Outer London and East Anglia display an over-representation of dual-career households relative to all households, while in Inner London and the East Midlands the shares are similar to the national average. Clearly a 'southern' bias in proportions of dual-career households is evident.

Relative to other dual-earner households, dual-career households are more likely to:

- have both partners in full-time employment;
- travel longer distances to work;
- have two or more cars – two in three dual-career households have two or more cars, compared with two in five other dual-earner households and one in five of all households;
- be characterized by both partners travelling to work by car;
- live in the owner-occupied sector;
  (For further details regarding these characteristics see Green 1994, 1995.)

Clearly, in socio-economic terms, dual-career households form a privileged group. By supplementing quantitative analyses with qualitative analyses, a more complete picture of dual-career households may be achieved. The range of jobs held by the male and female partners in the 136 households span SOC Major Groups 1–3. Two-thirds held a first degree, and 60 per cent a professional qualification. The women partners held, in the main, stereotypical jobs in education (see Anne, Figure 11.6), nursing (Susan and Helen, Figures 11.3 and 11.4), while Samantha (senior analyst programmer, Figure 11.5) represents one of the minority of women in non-stereotypical managerial posts. As with the dual-career couples surveyed by Gregson and Lowe (1993), the Nottingham dual-career households relied heavily on non-household individuals, such as cleaners, childminders, nannies and au pairs, for help with non-market work. It tended to be the responsibility of the female partner to organize and pay for this help.

Figure 11.3   Susan and Rahul

Middle Type, Rahul has the lead career and decisions are made jointly.

Susan and Rahul are both in their early 30s, and although both have medical careers, they give priority to his career. He is a consultant pediatrician and she a nurse tutor. They have three school age sons. They have been together since 1983. Rahul trained at Guys Hospital (London), and is in paediatrics and intensive care work, which is highly specialized. He commented that, 'intensive care is not a particularly sought after field in paediatrics'. Susan said, 'he had an urge to work in a developing country'. Rahul set up a unit there. Susan said, 'the ... unit ... was running smoothly, doctors had been trained ... and he was beginning to feel he wanted a bit extra'. By this time Susan also had a job there that she loved in nurse education. But in 1993, they returned to Nottingham and Susan said, 'we tried to make a joint decision, but I'm sure in many relationships there is always a little bit more of one person in any decision than another'. Rahul found a challenging job before they returned to Britain but Susan, 'didn't know that I would have a job'. She was out of work for seven months, and then found work in the Education Department within the neo-natal service. She felt that she might well have progressed further in her career had she not gone abroad.

Figure 11.4   Pete and Helen

Middle Type, Pete has the lead career and takes the lead in decision making.

Pete and Helen are in their mid-forties, and have two grown-up children. Pete is a manager with a large manufacturing company, and Helen is a nurse, working part-time on permanent fixed night shifts. They met when they were students in the Midlands, and have been together since 1970. Helen said that for, 'both children [she] had a career break'. Since the birth of their first child Pete said that, 'Helen would work nights and I would work days. I don't know how we would have managed if she hadn't been [a nurse]. Although it is a right bind ... it's only because of [her work and salary] that we have been able to [afford to] move'. Pete's career has always had priority, he 'was trying to make a career for himself'. As a result he has worked for five different companies in four different regions. Helen commented, 'I've worked for five different Area Health Authorities ... because of his job'. When talking about the last three inter-regional moves – to the North West, to Humberside and then to the Midlands – Helen commented that each had been, 'traumatic for the children ... not popular'. When asked about Helen's career, Pete said, 'we decided that Helen's career would be on the back burner ... and it hasn't affected where we've looked at jobs ... where I work [was] more to the point'. With each inter-regional move they have been dual location for a short time. With regard to the future, Pete said that he, 'wouldn't move from here ... because we are now actually part of the community ... I've got a granddaughter just down the road', and Helen confirmed, 'we've put our roots down here ... Pete is planning early retirement'.

Figure 11.5   Simon and Samantha

Egalitarian, Samantha has the lead career. Decisions are made jointly.

Simon (a Sales Executive) and Samantha (a Senior Analyst Programmer) are in their early thirties, and work full time for the same manufacturing company. They have been together for just over a decade, and met at work when they were both, 'on a fast-track general management scheme'. Samantha commented, 'I had a very good start in my career because I was fast track and it gave me a lot of exposure to different functional areas'. Not long after getting together they were both posted to different regions, 'we didn't have any choice in the matter. We sort of did alternate weekends ... for eighteen months. It is always difficult on a Sunday night to tear yourself away'. After a spell back together in the north west, 'Simon was getting itchy feet ... [he got] an excellent job [in London] ... excellent training. It would open up some more doors'. At the same time she also left, 'basically I just got bored ... like a lot of people, I guess in Thatcher's generation, decided we don't want to wait ... we want to do it now'. She found a challenging position in the Midlands. So we did the weekend relationship bit again'. Simon said, 'we hated the fact that we weren't living together. It was probably more my fault than Samantha's because I said ... I wanted this particular job [in London]. I also wasn't keen on the job because I was working incredibly hard, about eighty hours a week'. Simon found a suitable post with Samantha's employer, 'right salary and exactly his profile'. Samantha is very committed to her job, 'I have a good awareness of the industry and I am quite hard-nosed'. Simon commented that, 'career is more important to Samantha than it is to me. [She] wants to have a specific career ... a progression in her career'. Samantha indicated that, 'we will probably try and have children next year. I will take maternity leave ... at the end of those six months, Simon will apply for a career break [5 years]. He can't wait – seriously – he cannot wait to give up work'. Relating to decision making Samantha said, 'everything we do ... is 50/50 down the line'. Commenting on their relationship Samantha said, 'I'm not where I am because I've got a supportive partner, but I'm still with Simon because I've got a supportive partner'.

DUAL CAREER HOUSEHOLDS AND DECISION MAKING

From the case study evidence (30 households) a variety of household characteristics and arrangements emerge. In half of the households both partners were aged over 40 (with a few aged in their late fifties), while in the other half ages of partners ranged from mid-twenties to late thirties. In two-thirds of households there were dependent children.

Each partner in the dual-career household was asked separately:

- how a specific decision was made – the selection of residential location and the actual choice of their present home;
- how major decisions (such as car purchase) were generally made, and who (if anyone) was most instrumental;

- if possible/appropriate, to designate one partner as 'leader' and one as 'follower' (that is in terms of first priority) in housing location and mobility decisions.

We did not seek to focus on the domestic division of labour but on decision-making processes relating to infrequent lifestyle decisions. As was noted above, each partner was interviewed separately, and following a comparison of their transcripts the couples were divided into:

- those who are joint decision makers;
- those in which the male leads; and
- those in which the female leads.

As may be expected from a sample of this nature, the majority of couples (23) said they made decisions jointly. For example, Ray (mid-forties school teacher) said, 'we decide everything together, we discuss everything together. We choose everything together'. Samantha (Figure 11.5)

Figure 11.6   Nigel and Anne

Egalitarian, Anne has the lead career. Decisions are made jointly.

Nigel (a part time lecturer with contracts with three employers) and Anne (a school teacher) are both in their early forties, and have been together for ten years. This is Anne's second marriage. Anne's two children from her first marriage live with them along with their eight-year-old daughter. Anne is a trained teacher, and Nigel originally qualified as a teacher, and after a decade in a secondary school switched to social work. Anne withdrew from the labour market for eight years during her first marriage, and cared for her two children, and did a little adult literacy work. They live in an Edwardian suburban terrace. When their daughter was born, Anne was prime carer for one year, 'When I was pregnant with Becky, it was Nigel's first child. He hated his job [social work] and I wanted to get back to work and it was an obvious solution. He really wanted to look after Becky'. Nigel said, 'we actually role reversed as they call it ... for me it was my first child, I felt that by going out to work I was missing out on something important'. He went on to say that, 'we don't particularly want both of us to be working full-time ... the pressures attendant on two full-time careers would be enormous'. So when Becky was one, Anne went back to full-time primary school teaching as, 'main wage earner' and, 'the whole style of teaching had changed.' Nigel said, 'when my daughter first started nursery school ... I started looking for opportunities to work myself. The first move I made was teaching night classes ... literature and creative writing'. He tends to teach part-time for, 'the same three or four employers'. He currently has three part-time teaching contracts which, 'is insecure ... my long term prospects are dim'. Anne said, 'we are quite egalitarian ... we have always been rebels in a way. My fifteen year old thinks we are freaks ... he still finds it difficult that we do things differently from the average house.

---

said, 'everything we do is 50/50 down the line'. Five couples said that the male partner had more influence. Adam, a chartered surveyor and Liz a senior social worker, are both in their late thirties, and Adam leads in decision making, while Liz often has to 'sort out' the aftermath of decisions, such things as paying bills. Adam said that 'Liz has the view that on all the important decisions then I usually take the lead and manipulate the way but she gets away with much more on less significant issues'. In two couples the female partner took the lead: for example, John (sales manager, late thirties) with May (a GP, late thirties), described himself as, 'the camp follower in this relationship'. It will not surprise the reader to discover that even in joint decisions there can be more of one partner than another: for example, Susan (nurse tutor with Rahul, consultant pediatrician, both in their early forties, Figure 11.3) commented that she was, 'sure [that] in many relationships there is always a little bit more of one person in any decision than another'.

For illustrative purposes the dual-career households were classified along the lines of: traditional, middle and egalitarian (Kiernan, 1992). Some researchers have used time budgets for analysing these issues, while others have drawn on questionnaires (Gershuny *et al.*, 1994). We have drawn on interview material using the following criteria:

- level of commitment of each partner to the labour market;
- occupation and hours worked of each partner;
- domestic responsibilities of each partner including childcare;
- 'lead' and 'follower' careers; and
- the attitudes and words of the informants.

Traditional

As you might expect from a sample of those working in SOC Major Groups 1–3, none of the couples when interviewed fell strictly into this category although several had reverted to this model when the children were young (see Susan and Rahul and Pete and Helen, Figures 11.3–11.4).

Middle

Seventeen households were classified as one where she takes on more of the household tasks and looking after the children, and his career is the lead career (see Susan and Rahul and Pete and Helen, Figures 11.3–11.4). Nine of these couples are over 40 and in six of them, the female partner currently holds a part-time professional post; and only two of the households are childless.

Egalitarian

Thirteen households displayed egalitarian tendencies (see Simon and Samantha and Nigel and Anne, Figures 11.5–11.6). Half of these couples have no children, and are aged under 40, with the female partner working full-time.

It would perhaps be more accurate to place the couples along a continuum ranging from traditional to egalitarian and to categorize the couples concerning the relative strength of their egalitarian tendencies. The households which exhibited the strongest egalitarian tendencies did tend to be younger (less than 40 years) than those in the middle category, perhaps providing some evidence of the longer-term gradual process of change in domestic practices (Gershuny *et al.*, 1994). Some of the older male respondents from the 'middle' households did indicate that if they and their partners were to have children now they might well consider different options (more egalitarian) than those that were 'open to them' at the time. For example, when asked what the ideal arrangement for domestic arrangements and childcare should be, Adam replied, '… it should be split equally between husband and wife, that's what society needs … I ought to be able to work shorter days but within the private sector [a suggestion of] that kind of arrangement is like banging your head against a wall.'

Rather than merely using the snapshot typology outlined above (Figures 11.1 and 11.2), an attempt has also been made to add a time dimension through the analyses of four household (and eight career) histories to illustrate the dynamics of career decision making and the related professional and personal dilemmas brought about by infrequent lifestyle decisions and events, such as relocation and birth of a child. Pete and Helen (Figure 11.4) and Susan and Rahul (Figure 11.3) have throughout their relationships prioritized 'his' career. Pete has followed a managerial career with several manufacturing companies, and as a result the family have moved four times to locations in northern and central England. Rahul has followed a very specific medical career in pediatrics, and the family has lived abroad as expatriates. Both Susan and Helen have nursing careers, which have been adversely affected by moves brought about by their partners' job, and by childbirth. Helen has held part-time posts since the birth of their first child, as well as having periods when she withdrew from the labour market. Susan has also had to withdraw from the labour market when abroad because of work permit problems, and then when she returned to Great

Britain it took her seven months to find a job. They have, therefore, moved between the middle and traditional categories of Kiernan (Figure 11.1).

The two other couples, Simon and Samantha (Figure 11.5) and Nigel and Anne (Figure 11.6) are currently egalitarian. Turning firstly to Simon and Samantha; they both have a strong commitment to the labour market, but Samantha's career is the most important. In pursuing their careers they have had periods when they were a 'dual location' household. Although they are currently childless, they would like children, and Simon is considering a career break. In the case of the second couple, since Anne's third child was one year old Nigel has been prime carer. Anne has the lead career (a full-time teaching post), while Nigel holds a series of part-time temporary lecturing contracts.

Finally, with regard to lead and follower careers, in the 30 households concerned the men and women were asked separately to identify the lead career in their household. In reply, respondents did indicate that career prioritization in their households had changed over time. Graham and Beth (mid-thirties), for example, have changed career priorities from his (university contract research) to hers (Scientific Officer) because Beth's job is more 'secure'. Nineteen of the 30 interviewed couples can be classified as the male currently having the lead career. For example, one male (university lecturer, early forties) said, 'I think Pat (early forties, librarian) always defers to my job ... this is partly economic and partly that she feels that my job is important to me'. Another male (Chartered Surveyor, late thirties) said, 'I suppose in a way that I have pursued my career pretty single-handedly, which dictates the way everything else flows'. The 'male lead career' couples tended to be over 40 years, with the female partner in a part-time professional post and with dependent children. Five couples were identified in which the woman had the lead career (for example, Simon and Samantha). Although, the female's career was identified as lead, in only three cases was residential location dictated by her job. These couples were childless, and aged under 40 years, with female partners working full time.

The remaining six of the couples indicated that currently their careers have equal weighting, although it may be more accurate to say that for some of the six at different points in time, one career has taken precedence. These partners are also under 40, and childless, with the female partner working full time. Moira (a University Administrator) and Bob (a Further Education lecturer), are almost 40 with no children, and have careers of equal weighting. In the past they have relocated for both their jobs, in turn. They also both indicated that future moves could be initiated by either career, and were dependent on how good the 'opportunity' was.

CONCLUSIONS

The evidence presented from this study of dual-career households reveals that in these 'work rich', highly educated households, significant gender differences emerge not with educational attainment, but with the effect of life cycle on the degree of labour-market attachment as well as labour-market disruptions caused by migration on the 'follower' career. It appears that attitudes and preferences are becoming more equitable: for example, in 23 (out of 30) households with whom in-depth interviews were conducted, both partners indicated they were joint decision makers concerning infrequent, lifestyle decisions but *not* career prioritization. Turning to an examination of lead careers, not surprisingly, in nearly two-thirds of households the male had the lead career; the remaining third were evenly split between those in which the woman led, and those where both careers roughly had equal weighting. Therefore, in what are arguably the most egalitarian of households, parity in terms of decision making and career development is not the norm.

It appears that egalitarianism in decision making is affected by factors other than the economic status of the female partner. These factors include age of partners, stage in life-cycle (that is, presence of children), type of job held (and labour-market and job search area) by each partner, and lastly whose career leads (in our study elder care did not emerge as a significant issue).

A number of the younger couples commented on the fact that labour-market changes – increase of short-term contracts and 'flexibility' – have had an effect on their relationship. Increasing insecurity of job tenure and the need for migration to further careers can delay or inhibit household formation. This is illustrated by the fact that 18 of the 30 sampled couples had had to live apart at some point during their relationship, and this can cause great tension and strain. What is not evident is how many couples did not fall within the remit of this research because they permanently have to live apart thereby delaying their household formation due to their respective careers.

REFERENCES

Anderson, M., Bechhofer, F. and Kendrick, S. (1992) 'Individual and Household Strategies: Some Empirical Evidence from the Social Change and Economic Life Initiative'. SCELI Working Paper, 24, University of Oxford.
Anderson, M., Bechhofer, F. and Kendrick, S. (1994) 'Individual and Household Strategies' in M. Anderson, F. Bechhofer and J. Gershuny (eds) *The Social and Political Economy of the Household.* Oxford: Oxford University Press.

Bowlby, S. (1990) 'Women, Work and the Family: Control and Constraints'. *Geography*, 76, 1, 17–26.

Brannen, J. and Moss, P. (1988) *New Mothers at Work: Employment and Childcare*. London: Unwin.

Castells, M. (1989) *The Informational City*. Oxford: Blackwell.

Dex, S. (1987) *Women's Occupational Mobility: a Lifetime Perspective*. Brighton: Harvester.

Duncan, S. (1991) 'The Geography of Gender Divisions of Labour in Britain'. *Institute of British Geographers Transactions*, 16, 420–39.

Edgell, S. (1980) *Middle Class Couples*. London: Allen and Unwin.

Elias, P. and Hogarth, T. (1993) 'Families, Jobs and Unemployment: the Changing Pattern of Economic Dependency in Britain'. Paper presented to a seminar on Labour Market Structures and Prospects for Women, University of Warwick.

Fogarty, M.P., Allen, I. and Walters, P. (1981) *Women in Top Jobs 1968–1979*. London: PEP.

Fogarty, M.P., Rapoport, R. and Rapoport, F. (1971) *Sex, Career and Family*. London: Allen and Unwin.

Gershuny, J., Godwin, M. and Jones, S. (1994) 'The Domestic Labour Revolution: a Process of Lagged Adaptation' in M. Anderson, F. Bechhofer and J. Gershuny (eds), *The Social and Political Economy of the Household*. Oxford: Oxford University Press.

Green, A.E. (1984) 'Geographical Perspectives on New Career Patterns: the Case of Dual Career Households'. Paper presented at the British-Swedish-Dutch Conference on Population Planning and Policies.

Green, A.E. (1995) 'The Geography of Dual Career Households: towards a Research Agenda'. *International Journal of Population Geography*, 1, 1, 37–52.

Green, A.E. and Hardill, I. (1991) 'Women Returners in Newcastle: a Comparison of Benwell and South Gosforth'. *Local Economy*, 6, 39–44.

Gregson, N. and Lowe, M. (1993) 'Renegotiating the Domestic Division of Labour? A Study of Dual Career Household in North East and South East England'. *Sociology* 28, 1, 55–78.

Hardill, I., Dudleston, A.C., Linacre, R., Green, A.E. and Owen, D.W. (1995) *The Location and Mobility Decisions of Dual Career Households in Great Britain: Research Methods*. Department of Economics and Public Administration Occasional Paper Series 95/3. Nottingham: Nottingham Trent University.

Hertz, R. (1987) *More Equal Than Others: Women and Men in Dual Career Marriages*. Berkeley: University of California Press.

Hills, J. (1985) *Inquiry into Income and Wealth – Volume 2*. York: Joseph Rowntree Foundation.

Horrell, S. and Humphries, J. (1995) 'Women's Labour Force Participation and the Transition to the Male Breadwinner Family: 1790–1865'. *Economic History Review* XLVIII, 1, 89–117.

Hutton, W. (1995) *The State We're In*. London: Cape.

Kiernan, K. (1992) 'The Roles of Men and Women in Tomorrow's Europe'. *Employment Gazette*, 100, 7, 491–99.

McDowell, L. (1991) 'Life without Father and Ford: the New Gender Order of Post-Fordism'. *Transactions of the Institute of British Geographers*, NS 16, 400–19.

McDowell, L. and Court, G. (1994) 'Gender Divisions of Labour in the Post-Fordist Economy: the Maintenance of Occupational Sex Segregation in the Financial Services Sector'. *Environment and Planning A*, 26, 9, 1397–418.

Morris, L. (1989) 'Household Strategies: the Individual, the Collectivity and the Labour Market – The Case of Married Couples'. *Work, Employment and Society*, 3, 4, 447–64.

Morris, L. (1990) *The Workings of the Household*. Oxford: Polity Press.

Newell, S. (1993) 'The Superwoman Syndrome: Gender Differences in Attitudes Towards Equal Opportunities at Work and Towards Domestic Responsibilities at Home'. *Work, Employment and Society*, 7, 2, 275–89.

Pahl, R. (1984) *Divisions of Labour*. Oxford: Blackwell.

Pinch, S. (1993) 'Social Polarization: a Comparison of Evidence from Britain and the United States'. *Environment and Planning A*, 25, 779–95.

Pleck, J.H. (1985) *Working Wives/Working Husbands*. Beverly Hills: Sage.

Rapoport, R. and Rapoport, R.N. (1976) *Dual Career Families Re-examined*. London: Martin Robertson.

Rees, T. (1992) *Women and the Labour Market*. London: Routledge.

Rose, M. and Fielder, S. (1988) 'The Principle of Equity and the Labour Market Behaviour of Dual Earner Couples'. SCELI Working Paper 3. Oxford: Nuffield College, University of Oxford.

Safilios-Rothschild, C. (ed.) (1972) *Towards a Sociology of Women*. Lexington, Mass: Xerox.

Sassen, S. (1991) *The Global City: New York, London, and Tokyo*. Princeton: Princeton University Press.

Sassen, S. (1996) 'Rebuilding the Global City: Economy, Ethnicity and Space' in A.D. King (ed.) *Re-presenting the City: Ethnicity, Capital and Culture in the 21st Century Metropolis*. Basingstoke: Macmillan.

Sinclair, M.T. (1991) 'Women, Work and Skill: Economic Theories and Feminist Perspectives' in N. Redclift and M.T. Sinclair (eds) *Working Women: International Perspectives on Labour and Gender Ideology*. London: Routledge.

Williams, C.C. and Windebank, J. (1995) 'Social Polarization of Households in Contemporary Britain: a 'Whole Economy' Perspective', *Regional Studies*, 29, 723–28.

12 Sexing the Enterprise: Gender, Work and Resource Allocation in Self-Employed Households
Anne Corden and Tony Eardley

INTRODUCTION

Growth in self-employment was a particularly striking feature of labour market change in Britain during the 1980s, and one significant aspect of such growth was the comparatively rapid expansion of this way of working among women. Data from the Labour Force Survey indicate that self-employment is still predominantly a male activity: in the winter of 1995/6 nearly 800,000 women were self-employed compared with just over 2.4 million men (Department of Employment, 1996). Nevertheless, between 1979 and 1990 the number of women recorded as working for themselves rose by more than 150 per cent, nearly twice the rate of increase for men (Department of Employment, 1993).

This chapter argues that survey data present only a partial view of the role of women in self-employment. As Arber and Gilbert (1992) have pointed out, certain forms of self-employment lie on a continuum of economic activity between waged work and unpaid domestic labour, which can blur women's relationship with the formal labour market. The work done by women in small business enterprises formally run by their domestic partners may also remain invisible. Much of men's self-employed work depends on a high level of participation and support from spouses. Such supportive activities can be represented in different ways for tax and social security purposes and in research surveys. Yet often none of the ways in which women's involvement is presented accurately reflects either actual working relationships or money transfers. The structure of work in households where the husband is self-employed may reinforce traditional gender divisions, yet detailed knowledge of business finances built up through tasks such as book-keeping can paradoxically give women considerable control over household finances.

Opportunities to explore these ambiguities and paradoxes came in a programme of research on low-income self-employed parents, commissioned by the Department of Social Security. The parents studied had all claimed Family Credit, an income-related social security benefit, available to families with children where a parent is in paid work for at least 16 hours per week. Family Credit acts as a supplement to low earnings and is designed to reinforce work incentives within the social security system. Full accounts of the research can be found elsewhere (Boden and Corden, 1994; Eardley and Corden, 1996a). The programme of work was carried out between 1991 and 1993, and central to the study were qualitative interviews involving adults in 73 families supported by earnings from self-employment.

First, we provide contextual background by describing the recent resurgence of self-employment, and some of the characteristics of those who are formally included among 'the self-employed'. We look at the picture of women's self-employment that emerges from survey data, and other recent small-scale research. The second part of the chapter looks at divisions of responsibility for the work undertaken in the self-employed families studied in depth in our own research. Analysis of the circumstances of the two-parent families threw further light on women's important role in couple households in which the man is formally self-employed, and enabled us to suggest a typology of gender/work relations in low-income self-employment. The third part of the chapter explores the managing strategies in these low-income families, where distinctions between business and household finance were not always clear. In two-parent families, however, it was generally women who had the major responsibility for household budgeting.

THE GROWTH IN SELF-EMPLOYMENT

As a form of economic activity, self-employment had been stagnant for several decades until the late 1970s, attracting little attention. A rapid resurgence in this form of work then occurred and by 1990 the number of people recorded as self-employed reached more than 3.4 million (Department of Employment, 1993). It has since fallen back slightly, but in the winter of 1995/6 some 12.5 per cent of all those in paid work were self-employed (Department of Employment, 1996).

The reasons for this resurgence are a matter of some debate (see Rees and Shah, 1986; Hakim, 1988; Steinmetz and Wright, 1989; Curran, 1990; Bögenhold and Staber, 1991; Campbell and Daly, 1992; Meager *et al.*, 1994). It is likely that a number of factors is involved. Other European and OECD countries have seen recent growth in self-employment, although none experienced the same levels of increase as the UK (Blackwell, 1994).

What appears to have happened, in Britain and other European countries, is a considerable increase in the number of people whose legal and contractual status is one of self-employment, but whose actual work situation is far from that of the small business owner, craftworker or professional worker – people traditionally grouped together as 'self-employed' (Dale, 1986). This new kind of self-employment, or 'quasi-self-employment', includes people engaged in homeworking, franchising and forms of freelancing and agency work for which self-employed status has become widespread, as well as the more familiar labour-only subcontracting in construction and agricultural work (Casey and Creigh, 1988; Hakim, 1988; Rainbird, 1991). A considerable growth in the numbers of dependent subcontractors has also been noted in both Australia (VandenHeuvel and Wooden, 1995) and the United States (Hulen *et al.*, 1993). For many engaged in this kind of work, their circumstances of employment may be more similar to those of employees.

The number of different definitions of self-employment in current use create further problems in understanding what has been happening recently. Different distinctions between employees and self-employed people are drawn according to the different requirements of legislation for taxation, social security, and health and safety protection (see Leighton, 1983; Casey and Creigh, 1988; McCarthy, 1993). This leads to a number of areas of uncertainty or ambiguity in defining people as self-employed in household surveys, with additional problems in determining the status of people who do only a few hours work each week (Boden and Corden, 1994).

WOMEN WHO ARE FORMALLY SELF-EMPLOYED

Even taking into account these ambiguities in definition and perception, the rapid expansion of formal self-employment among women in the UK during the 1980s has been striking. Net female self-employment rose by 151 per cent between 1979 and 1990, as against 82 per cent for men (Department of Employment, 1993). This was partly a reflection of women's growing labour market participation overall. Women still only make up a quarter of all people who are formally self-employed, and, over a working lifetime only about one-tenth of women experience self-employment at some time, compared with more than a quarter of men (Dex and McCulloch, 1995). However, self-employed women have some distinct characteristics. In the latter half of the 1980s, for example, women had a particularly high exit rate from self-employment even though their high rate of entry was sustained. One hypothesis is that women entering self-employment had difficulty surviving, through their relatively poorer access to financial and human capital, or their tendency to enter sectors with poorer business prospects (Meager, 1994).

Part-time work is important for women in self-employment, as is also true for women employees. By 1994, 51 per cent of self-employed women were working part-time (Dex and McCulloch, 1995), and women's full-time self-employment, unlike men's, decreased slightly between 1986 and 1994. Previous hypotheses to explain the disproportionate concentration of short working hours among self-employed women have included their need to combine work and responsibilities for children (Goffee and Scase, 1985) or care of relatives (Twigg and Atkin, 1991) and our own interviews provided some supporting evidence here (Eardley and Corden, 1996a).

Overall, women who are formally self-employed show a younger age profile than men: cross-sectional data show that peak ages for female self-employment in 1991 were 30–45 years, compared with 45–49 years for men. Self-employed women are also more likely to be married. In 1994, 74.4 per cent were married, compared with 50.3 per cent of women full-time permanent employees, and 72.1 per cent of self-employed men (Dex and McCulloch, 1995). Perhaps of greater interest is the economic activity of partners of self-employed people. For both sexes, there is a strong relationship between being self-employed and having a self-employed spouse (Daly, 1991) – an association found also in Australian data (Eardley and Bradbury, 1996). Some previous small-scale studies have found a relatively high proportion of separated and divorced women among the self-employed, leading to suggestions that self-employment may offer special opportunities for independence for women (Goffee and Scase, 1985). Quantitative data, however, do not support an association between divorce and self-employment (Curran and Burrows, 1989) and survey data on the working patterns of lone parents also suggest that self-employment is rare among this group (Bradshaw and Millar, 1991). Our own interviews showed that some lone parents, including men, do see opportunities in combining work and home responsibilities through self-employment, although it can be hard to maintain a viable business.

In terms of the kind of work carried out by self-employed people, there is a sharply gender-differentiated concentration in certain industries and occupations. In the winter of 1995/6, 31 per cent of self-employed men worked in construction, for example, as opposed to only 2 per cent of women. Women were concentrated in distribution and catering (26 per cent), where men were also well represented. Relatively high proportions of self-employed women worked in banking and finance (16 per cent), public administration, education and health (22 per cent) and 'other services'

(18 per cent), which include a range of personal and small-scale enter-prises such as hairdressing and cleaning. Overall, the great majority of self-employed women (85 per cent) work in the service sector, compared with just over half of self-employed men (Department of Employment, 1996). The regions with the highest rates of female self-employment are the South West, Inner London, East Anglia, Outer London, the South East and the West Midlands (apart from the West Midlands conurbation) according to Dex and McCulloch (1995).

One final characteristic of interest is the rate of participation in self-employment by people with health problems or disabilities. The Employment and Handicap Survey found that disabled people in work were slightly more likely to be self-employed than the general working population (Prescott-Clarke, 1990). Labour Force Survey data also found marginally higher rates of self-employment among respondents with health or disability problems which limited their opportunities for paid work (Daly, 1991). Studies of specific groups of self-employed people have found apparently high proportions of people who report disability or some serious health problem, for example men construction workers (Marsh *et al.*, 1981) and low-earning women homeworkers (Cragg and Dawson, 1981). The overall picture is unclear, however. A more recent study in six selected labour markets suggested that there was little differ-ence in perceptions of physical and mental health between employed and self-employed respondents (Rubery *et al.*, 1993). As we see later, in our study both men and women with health problems saw some opportunities for work in self-employment that would be hard to find as employees. People with additional caring responsibilities, in both couple and lone-parent households, also valued the flexibility of self-employment.

We conclude the first part of this chapter by considering the levels of incomes achieved through self-employed work. We have discussed else-where some of the technical and substantial difficulties in measuring incomes of self-employed people, and reviewed what is currently known about the earnings of this sector (Eardley and Corden, 1996a, 1996b). The most comprehensive recent study focusing specifically on the incomes of self-employed people is that of Meager *et al.* (1994), which supports the picture built up from previous quantitative work. While income data on self-employment has to be approached with some caution, the following patterns are clear. First, the distribution of labour income is more dis-persed for the self-employed as a whole than for employees. Secondly, at the bottom end of the income distribution the level of labour income is lower than for employees and it is higher at the upper end. Among the richest people, in the top income decile, mean self-employed earnings are one-third higher than those of employees, whereas among the poorest, in the bottom decile, mean self-employed earnings are only 70 per cent of those of employees. Income profiles differ substantially, however, by gender: self-employed women are much more likely than men in either decile, or employed women, to have very low incomes from work and less likely to have high labour incomes. This profile is associated both with women's greater propensity to carry out part-time self-employed work and with their relatively lower earnings if calculated on an hourly basis.

Over the period since self-employment began to grow, the increase in the lowest earning self-employed group has widened the already dispersed income distribution among self-employed people, and contributed to general income inequality (Jenkins, 1995). It is among this lower income group that the Family Credit population can be found.

This section has set the context by describing the characteristics and circumstances of people who are formally self-employed, looking specially at women's self-employment. The next section describes our findings from qualitative research with self-employed Family Credit recipients, which help us understand how such families combine work and family responsibilities.

SELF-EMPLOYED FAMILIES CLAIMING FAMILY CREDIT

In April 1991 there were 53,000 families in receipt of Family Credit whose main or only earner was self-employed, representing 15.5 per cent of all recipients (Department of Social Security, 1992). There was a large increase between 1983 and 1984 in numbers of self-employed recipients of Family Income Supplement, a similar benefit which was replaced by Family Credit, and in their share of the overall claimant population. This was during a period when self-employment generally was increasing most rapidly (Eardley and Corden, 1996a). Since 1988, when Family Credit was introduced, the proportion of self-employed families had remained more or less the same. Characteristics of these claimant families reflected those of the general population of self-employed people: male breadwinners were more likely to be self-employed than female breadwinners. Families receiving benefit on the basis of women's self-employed earnings represented only a small minority. Figure 12.1 shows the distribution of family types within the self-employed Family Credit population in April 1991.

In terms of occupational status, self-employed Family Credit recipients were concentrated in the catering, cleaning, hairdressing and other personal service occupations to a much higher degree than in the general

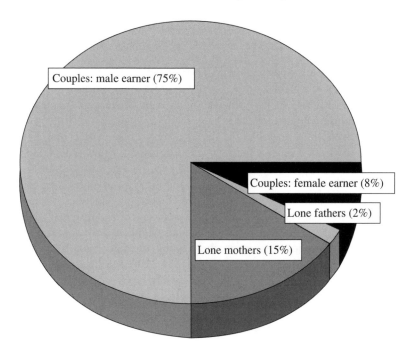

Figure 12.1 Self-Employed Family Credit Recipients, April 1991, by Family Type.
Source: Department of Social Security Statistics, 1991, Table A1.03 (rounded figures).

self-employed population, probably reflecting the relatively low earnings associated with this kind of work. Comparisons between employed and self-employed Family Credit recipients showed a striking difference in earnings. The authors' statistical analysis of Family Credit administrative statistics (Eardley and Corden, 1996a) showed that, in April 1991, self-employed families had average mean gross earnings from their main work of only 59 per cent of those of employees – £68.49 compared with £115.39 for employees. Families where a self-employed woman was the main earner (both couples and lone parents) had lower mean earnings than those with male earners, reflecting women's lower earning power. If calculated as an hourly rate, 58 per cent of all self-employed recipients had net hourly earnings, as assessed for benefit, of under £2, and among lone mothers, over a third had net hourly earnings of less than £1 per hour.

Such very low earnings among the self-employed families meant that more than 10 per cent, mostly couples with male main earners, had total incomes below what they could have received if they had been unemployed and claiming Income Support, (leaving aside housing costs). This raised fundamental questions about why people go on working on their own account, sometimes for long periods of time, when their endeavours bring such modest rewards. It was partly in order to pursue such questions that we conducted our in-depth interviews, and the rest of the chapter draws on this qualitative research.

There were three stages to the research programme. In the first wave of interviews the focus of interest was the nature of low-income self-employment and the way in which social security supports this form of working. Thirty-three families in which the main breadwinner was self-employed were interviewed during 1991. In selecting families, the aim was the representation of a range of occupation types and different stages of business development, and a range of family types and sizes. In the second wave, the focus was on families' living standards, and interviews were conducted with a further 30 families in 1992, selected to include a range of incomes among the three main family types – male-earner couples, female-earner couples and lone parents. In the third wave of 10 interviews in 1993, the aim was to look at a small number of businesses which apparently generated low profits but had relatively high turnovers (annual gross receipts of about £50,000 or more).

The families were selected from the Family Credit database, and lived in the northern English counties, North Wales, East Anglia, North London and the northern home counties. Interviews took place in respondents' homes, which were sometimes also their work premises. In two-parent families, both partners usually took part in the discussion, and in the 1992 wave, when the focus was on living standards, separate interviews were conducted with each partner. Full details of the research design and methods are available elsewhere (Eardley and Corden, 1996a).

Since our research was conducted the proportion of families claiming Family Credit whose main or only earner is self-employed has declined slightly, to 15 per cent in 1995 (Department of Social Security, 1996). There has also been some change in the ratio of gross earnings, comparing self-employed families with those headed by an employee. Nevertheless, in November 1995, average gross earnings of families with a self-employed head were only £82.46, compared with £113.58 for employees (Department of Social Security, 1996).

Fifty-seven of the families interviewed in our research contained two parents and it is the working lives of these 57 couples that form the focus for the rest of this chapter. All had applied recently for Family Credit and most were currently receiving benefit. The few who had been unsuccessful in their latest application had mostly received Family Credit during some previous period. The families who took part in the research were not statistically representative of the self-employed Family Credit population, but their characteristics suggest that they were not atypical. In any case, this is a fairly volatile population, and the circumstances of low-income self-employed families do not fit neatly into simple administrative categorisation.

ROUTES TO SELF-EMPLOYMENT

The overall picture of these 57 families was one of great heterogeneity in their family backgrounds, in their levels of skills and qualifications, and in the routes by which they had arrived in self-employment. The patterns of previous work histories suggested three main groups. The first were people who had been in the same area of work, usually as self-employed, for most of their working lives. These long-term self-employed people were mostly men engaged in farming or fishing activities that had been a 'way of life' spanning generations, and male manual workers, including builders, painters, and a second-hand goods dealer.

As a second group, in terms of their route to self-employment, we identified men and women who had made a definite shift in their working careers which took them into self-employment. Some had previously been unemployed and thus accustomed to low incomes. Both men and women had used the Enterprise Allowance (Business Start-Up) to try to get new businesses going after a spell of unemployment. Some of those who made a career change had previously been well-paid employees, who had been attracted by the possibility of high profitability and new interests in deciding to try running a business. Others faced a change in circumstances, when self-employment seemed the best option, for example when one parent or a child faced major illness.

A move to self-employment could mean a move to a completely new occupation – for example, a male construction worker joined a friend's fishing business. Others started to work for themselves in an occupation previously conducted for an employer. Some men felt they had had little choice in the move to self-employment; the route from redundancy to taxi-driving was a path familiar to several. Those men who said that redundancy had actually been an opportunity to try something they had toyed with in the past tended to be in the 30–40 years age bracket, setting up one-person businesses in the service sector – a pattern noted in previous studies (Leece, 1990; Johnson and Roger, 1983).

The third group identified we called the 'developers': they became self-employed by developing some long-term interest or enthusiasm into a form of paid work. In some cases their work was also connected to a chosen life-style. This group, in which there were several women bread-winners, included a potter, musicians, an entertainer, craft workers and 'newcomers' to small-scale farming. Some of these families had the security of being able to depend on a cushion of support from their own parents and siblings while they pursued their interest. This was by no means true of all, however, and for some families in this group, life had been a continual financial struggle. What linked the families trying to 'develop' their chosen activity was their enthusiasm and dedication to their work.

Two-parent families differ from lone parents in that there seems at least some possibility of sharing work and family responsibilities. The pattern found was one of extreme heterogeneity, however. In some families, a conceptual distinction between work and personal life seemed inappropriate. Domestic partners, children, relatives and even friends were drawn into a 'way of life' or 'a family concern', as found among farming and fishing families, and families running hotels. In other families the self-employed workers fitted their activities into the traditional terminology of 'having a job'. It was common for there to be some participation by the domestic partner who was not officially the main self-employed breadwinner. Such participation might appear relatively small-scale, but could be vital and we go on to look at the divisions of responsibility for the work undertaken in the two-parent families. Our work complements that of Wheelock (Wheelock, 1992; Wheelock and Baines, 1994) who has looked closely at small businesses set up in Wearside during the 1980s.

LABOUR MARKET PARTICIPATION – SPOUSES AND PARTNERS

As with the general self-employed population, most of the main breadwinners in the two-parent families were sole traders. Those who were in partnership with others usually had spouses or other relatives as business partners. Spouse partnerships were generally in those businesses which had substantial capital investment or stock, such as the larger farms and a restaurant. Spouse partnerships tended also to be favoured by Asian families. Establishing a formal business partnership between spouses in a family where self-employed work is undertaken may be a sensible arrangement for tax purposes and financial security, but may not always indicate active participation in that work by both spouses. Another arrangement which may be advantageous for tax purposes is for one spouse to be described formally as an employee of the self-employed person. About a fifth of the self-employed main breadwinners formally employed their spouses; in only one case was the man the 'employee'. These business partnerships or 'employee' arrangements may mean that women are making substantial contributions to the self-employed work. In such situations the low profit levels generated are the result of the work effort of two people, who might in other circumstances be bringing in two separate wages, although some of the women involved might be unable or not want to take paid work.

There is sometimes no opportunity for spouses to join the self-employed work, for example when husbands are subcontracted construction workers. Women may then be able to supplement low earnings from self-employment only through their own separate work. For those unable to find a suitable job, and those who wanted to delay taking on the role of dual earner, Family Credit may substitute for a second wage. Only occasionally, among the couples we studied, did women have independent paid work of their own if husbands were self-employed. We have attempted to develop a typology of gender/work relations, and look first at the female earner couples.

Female-Earner Couples

All the female-earner couples were primarily *dual*-earner couples. In some cases the woman had habitually worked, either full- or part-time, and had only taken over the role of the main earner because her husband had become unemployed or ill. In other cases, both spouses worked together but there were specific reasons to call the woman the business owner, for example when she had formal qualifications, or when the man had

Figure 12.2   Work and Participation in Self-Employed Enterprises by Members of Nine Female-Earner Couples

Both members of couple substantially involved in business		Woman's enterprise,with little, or no contribution from spouse
Business in woman's name mainly for technical reasons	Man joined woman's business	
Shop Educational business	Craft retailer Food retailer	Childminders (3) Hairdresser Shop

outstanding debts from a previous enterprise. Figure 12.2 is a matrix which represents spouses' participation in the businesses registered in the women's names.

It seemed likely that several of these families which currently had a woman as the main self-employed breadwinner were unlikely to remain within the 'female earner' group for very long. Indeed, by the time of the research interview two of the husbands had already found full-time work again and it seemed unlikely that their families would qualify for low-income benefits for much longer. Women who have skills or interests such as childminding or hairdressing, which can be run from home with little capital investment, may be able to turn these activities into sufficient self-employed work to keep families out of unemployment for short periods with the help of in-work benefits. Women's work which may seem of secondary importance, or more of a home interest or hobby, when their husbands are working can be of crucial importance in maintaining living standards through spells of husbands' unemployment.

Male-Earner Couples

Women's participation in work among the self-employed male-earner families fell into four main patterns, according to whether they were classified as formal business partners/employees or not, and whether they did or did not participate in the main work. Figure 12.3 is a matrix which represents women's participation in the various forms of self-employed work done by the men.

This simplified picture cannot capture entirely the variety of people's circumstances but does provide some useful pointers to how work was being shared and recognized. Being formally employed by a spouse or his formal business partner did usually represent actual involvement and not just ascribed participation in order to maximize tax-free allowances. The women involved often did book-keeping and secretarial tasks but some had definite separate spheres of work. Thus the male dairy farmer tended the animals, did the milking and maintained the premises while his wife was concerned with the dairy produce and marketing.

Although such women often worked as many hours as their husbands, and their contribution was vital, formal profit sharing or amounts shown as their wages on business accounts had often been worked out by accountants to ensure the most favourable treatment for tax and National Insurance purposes. It was not unusual for there to be some uncertainty as to whether the woman was formally a partner or an employee – this was an accounting convention that was irrelevant to how life went on. Most

Figure 12.3   Work and Participation in Self-Employed Enterprises by
Spouses of 48 Self-Employed Men

	The self-employed enterprises belonging to men with:	
	substantial contribution from spouse	no substantial contribution from spouse
Spouse formally employed in business, or a formal business partner	farmers (4) hotelier restaurant owner smallholder craftsman entertainer fisherman shopkeepers (2) scrap dealer sales consultant minister artist cleaning contractor	insurance agent carpet dealer farmer consultant food wholesaler
Spouse neither formally employed, nor a business partner	fish processor builder instrument repairer ice-cream vendor food wholesaler	taxi drivers (5) fishermen (3) subcontracted construction workers (3) shopkeepers (2) musicians (2) farmers (2) roofer motor mechanic therapist consultant

Source: Eardley and Corden (1996a), p. 139.

wages recorded in accounts were notional 'paper' transactions and nobody suggested that any actual payments were made to women for their work. The only woman who reported having any personal control of a portion of profit was a farmer's wife who managed the letting of a holiday caravan and retained control of the modest profit.

Women whose work in the business was *not* formally recognized also had no direct income from the enterprise in their own right, although the men acknowledged the support and help from their partners. In this group were women who did their husband's business accounts, as well as women who were essential in preparing equipment or dealing with clients. It was the ice-cream salesman's wife who scalded all the containers and utensils every night, and laundered the cloths and uniforms, for example – vital tasks acknowledged by both partners. What was clear was that the capacity for second earnings among the self-employed couples could be substantially reduced by the need for partners to contribute to the business. Men often relied on women being at home during the daytime to answer the telephone or deal with deliveries and purchases. While partners of men who are employees sometimes use their evenings to boost family income with part-time jobs, leaving men in charge of children, this was often not a realistic option for the partners of the self-employed men. The men sometimes had to work at night themselves, for example agents who called on clients after office hours. The women's role might also extend into the evening, as described for the ice-cream business. The work that these women did, both during the day and at night, was invisible in the formal economy.

As would be expected, women's involvement in the subcontracted and quasi-self-employed work was less than in the 'businesses'. Among the women who were making no substantial contributions to spouse's self-employment, few had any paid work outside the business. Where they did, it was usually part-time and sometimes a few hours only – for example, a few hours' shop work in the evenings. Responsibility for their children was often cited as a primary reason for not having their own paid job, while some also pointed to a lack of suitable jobs, or jobs that would pay more than they received in Family Credit. Such attitudes may be partly a rationalization of decisions among women whose supportive role in their husband's business gives them little opportunity for paid work of their own. This may be particularly true where men are out of the house for long periods, but their work simultaneously requires the woman's presence at home. Overall, it seemed that women's opportunities to seek paid work outside the home were often limited by traditional gender divisions of labour, which, while accepted by many of the women involved, were being reinforced by the demands of the type of work conducted by self-employed husbands or the nature of the business enterprise. In this respect, our findings differed from those of Wheelock (1992) and Wheelock and Baines (1994) whose study of small businesses suggested greater sharing in the domestic division of labour within small-business families. Their findings emphasized the flexibility in the familial economic unit that was achieved by linking and sharing productive and domestic work. The difference in findings may be associated with the different kinds of occupations represented among the families we studied, including the construction workers, the taxi drivers, and the sea fishermen, where there was less opportunity for women to participate and men had to work long periods away from home.

Although the structure of work seemed to be reinforcing traditional gender divisions in some couples, and women had little in the way of separate earnings of their own, they were by no means powerless in financial decision making within the household. The final part of the chapter considers how far the financial structures of small-scale self-employment may affect the control or allocation of resources in families.

FINANCIAL BUDGETING AND CONTROL IN TWO-PARENT FAMILIES

The problems that may arise for couples trying to manage household budgeting on a low income depend to some extent on how overall family resources are allocated and who controls the sharing out of resources (see, for example, Pahl, 1980, 1989; Brannen and Wilson, 1987).

How far people separated business and household monies reflected to some extent the scale and nature of work. Those running trading or service businesses usually thought it was important to keep separate bank accounts for the business whereas earnings from subcontracted labour were more likely to pass through the same bank accounts as household expenditure, either in single or joint names. Drawings taken from business accounts for household expenditure were usually transferred to personal accounts, but such transactions were less clear cut when part of the takings came in cash. The picture became even more blurred when earnings, expenses and household money were all handled in cash, for example in the families of some of the taxi drivers.

It could be hard to juggle the different monies – people with no overdraft facility could find themselves running a business deficit out of household income. Breadwinners often stressed the importance of keeping drawings to a minimum, and this could be a strain on household budgets. Family Credit and Child Benefit were often the main sources of ready cash for regular household expenditure and played an important role in maintaining living standards.

As to which partner made the household financial decisions, the general view was that this was a joint process. In both male-earner and female-earner couples, men sometimes took responsibility for handling larger bills while women had day-to-day responsibility for housekeeping – a pattern common in low-income households. There was a variety of systems of allocation of money for this purpose. Couples where the men worked in traditional manual trades, particularly subcontracted work where earnings were received in a form close to wages, tended to use modified versions of the 'whole wage' system, an allocative system in Pahl's (1980) well-known typology. The men passed their earnings to their partners, commonly explaining this in terms of their own inability to manage money, and expecting to receive back some portion of their earnings for their personal spending money.

The picture in businesses where women were more involved was different. It was often the women who dealt with the book-keeping and paid business bills. This strengthened their decision-making power as well as responsibility for household budgeting, since they had detailed knowledge of the business finances. In these households, both partners tended to have access to monies – more of a 'pooled system'. In some of these families the women had at least as much, if not more, control over how money was allocated. For some of the parents in these families, success in managing on low incomes was directly due to the executive power exercised by the women, and the men acknowledged the women's skill and contribution in this respect.

The extra power brought extra responsibilities, however, and this could be burdensome for some of the women, some of whom also talked about the areas of potential conflict. For the musician, buying a new instrument had seemed a sensible investment, but to his partner it meant diverting money that could be used for household budgeting. In several interviews the optimistic tone taken by men describing their hopes and plans for their work struck a different chord from the anxiety and doubt expressed by women about the risks being taken and their difficulties in making ends meet.

CONCLUSIONS

This chapter has presented some observations on gender divisions of work and power in households from the perspective of families where the main earner is self-employed, a group which, until recently, has received relatively little research attention. The rapid growth in self-employment since the 1970s has included an increase in the number of self-employed people in the lowest earning groups, among whom families with children are over-represented. We have explored work done by men and women in one group of low-income self-employed families, those using Family Credit to boost low earnings.

We have argued that survey data on the involvement of men and women in self-employment presents only a partial picture of the working lives of people engaged in the more marginal and lower income forms of independent work. Qualitative evidence suggests first that certain forms of self-employment notionally carried out by men is often in practice heavily dependent on participation by their spouses. This has the effect of reinforcing gender divisions of labour, since women's opportunities for labour market participation in their own right can be more limited than in couples where the man is in employed work, irrespective of other factors such as the demands of childcare. In a sense these small businesses are joint enterprises, but to see them in this way may not always be accurate. Women's participation often bears no direct relationship to how it is described for tax purposes, and whatever the formal relationship it appears to be unusual for women to draw any kind of individual income from what they commonly describe as 'their husband's business'.

Paradoxically, however, the responsibility for keeping business records can place women in a better position than in some employee families to exercise power in negotiations over both business and household expenditure (especially since at this level the two are often intertwined). For some families supported by self-employment, financial oversight by the woman is clearly a key factor in business survival and in the success families have in maintaining their living standards under pressure.

It might be expected that where women have a self-employed business themselves they would be in an even stronger position in negotiations over family finances. Indeed considerable emphasis has been placed in labour market research on the rapid growth of female self-employment among women as an indicator of their growing financial autonomy. However, our evidence suggests, at least at the lower income level, a more ambiguous picture. For example, a woman may be recorded as the owner of a business for a range of reasons which can include a record of debt or bankruptcy on the part of the spouse. Rather than increasing their negotiating power, this can lay them open to further financial liability. It also appears that some forms of women's self-employment are developed as stop-gap measures to tide the family over during a period of male unemployment or sickness. Often these couples are likely to continue as dual-earners if the man returns to work, but it is not clear that there has necessarily been any significant shift in the gendered perception of the man as the main breadwinner.

REFERENCES

Arber, S. and Gilbert, N. (1992) *Women and Working Lives: Division and Change.* London: Macmillan.

Blackwell, J. (1994) 'Changing Work Patterns and their Implications for Social Security' in S. Baldwin and J. Falkingham (eds) *Social Security and Social Change: New Challenges to the Beveridge Model.* Hemel Hempstead: Harvester Wheatsheaf.

Boden, R. and Corden, A. (1994) *Measuring Low Incomes: Self-Employment and Family Credit.* London: HMSO.

Bögenhold, D. and Staber, U. (1991) 'The Decline and Rise of Self-Employment'. *Work, Employment and Society*, 5, 2, 223–39.

Bradshaw, J. and Millar, J. (1991) *Lone Parent Families in the UK*. Department of Social Security Research Report No. 6. London: HMSO.

Brannen, J. and Wilson, G. (eds) (1987) *Give and Take in Families: Studies in Resource Distribution.* London: Allen and Unwin.

Campbell, M. and Daly, M. (1992) 'Self-Employment into the l990s'. *Employment Gazette*, June, 269–92.

Casey, B. and Creigh, S. (1988) 'Self-Employment in Britain: its Definition in the Labour Force Survey, in Tax and in Social Security Law'. *Work, Employment and Society*, 2, 3, 381–91.

Cragg, A. and Dawson, T. (1981) *Qualitative Work Among Households*. Research Paper No. 21. London: Department of Employment.

Curran, J. (1990) 'Rethinking Economic Structure: Exploring the Role of the Small Firm and Self-Employment in the British Economy'. *Work, Employment and Society*, May, 125–46.

Curran, J. and Burrows, R. (1989) 'National Profiles of the Self-Employed'. *Employment Gazette*, July, 376–85.

Dale, A. (1986) 'Social Class and the Self-Employed'. *Sociology*, 20, 3, 430–34.

Daly, M. (1991) 'The 1980s – a Decade of Growth in Enterprise: Self-Employment Data from the Labour Force Survey'. *Employment Gazette*, March, 109–34.

Department of Employment (1993) *Labour Force Survey Historical Supplement – April* (1993). London: Department of Employment.

Department of Employment (1996) *Labour Force Survey Quarterly Bulletin, No. 16 June*. London: Department of Employment.

Department of Social Security (1992) *Social Security Statistics 1991*. London: HMSO.

Department of Social Security (1996) *Social Security Statistics 1996*. London: The Stationery Office.

Dex, S. and McCulloch, A. (1995) *Flexible Employment in Britain: a Statistical Analysis*. Manchester: Equal Opportunities Commission.

Eardley, T. and Bradbury, B. (1997) *Self-Employment and Social Security*. Social Policy Research Centre Reports and Proceedings No. 132. Sydney: Social Policy Research Centre, University of New South Wales.

Eardley, T. and Corden, A. (1996a) *Low Income Self-Employment: Work, Benefits and Living Standards*. Aldershot: Avebury.

Eardley, T. and Corden, A. (1996b) *Self-Employed Earnings and Income Distribution: Problems of Measurement*. Social Policy Reports No. 5. York: Social Policy Research Unit, University of York.

Goffee, R. and Scase, R. (1985) *Women in Charge: the Experiences of Female Entrepreneurs*. London: Allen and Unwin.

Hakim, C. (1988) 'Self-Employment in Britain: Recent Trends and Current Issues'. *Work, Employment and Society*, 2, 4, 421–50.

Hulen, M., Kenny, W., Robinson, J. and Vaughan, M. (1993) *Independent Contractors: Compliance and Classification Issues*. A White Paper prepared for the American Tax Policy Institute. Washington DC: American Tax Folicy Institute.

Jenkins, S. (1995) 'Accounting for Income Inequality Trends: Decomposition Analyses for the UK, 1971–1986'. *Economica*, 62, 29–63.

Leece, D. (1990) 'Redundancy, Unemployment and Self-Employment'. *International Journal of Manpower*, 4, 4, 35–40.

Leighton, P. (1983) 'Employment and Self-Employment: Some Problems of Law and Practice'. *Employment Gazette*, May, 197–203.

Johnson, P. and Rodger, J. (1983) 'From Redundancy to Self-Employment'. *Employment Gazette*, June, 260–64.

McCarthy, J. (1993) 'Employee or Self-Employed?' *Legal Action*, May, 16, 15–17.

Marsh, A., Heady, P. and Matheson, A. (1981) *Labour Mobility in the Construction Industry*. London: HMSO.

Meager, N., Court, G. and Moralee, J. (1994) *Self-employment and the Distribution of Income*. Brighton: Institute of Manpower Studies.

Pahl, J. (1980) 'Patterns of Money Management within Marriage'. *Journal of Social Policy*, 9, 3, 313–35.

Pahl, J. (1989) *Money and Marriage*. London: Macmillan.

Prescott-Clarke, P. (1990) *Employment and Handicap*. London: Social and Community Planning Research.

Rainbird, H. (1991) 'The Self-Employed: Small Entrepreneurs or Disguised Wage Labourers?' in A. Pollert (ed.), *Farewell to Flexibility*? Oxford: Blackwell.

Rees, H. and Shah, A. (1986) 'An Empirical Analysis of Self-Employment in the UK'. *Journal of Applied Econometrics*, 1, 95–108.

Rubery, J., Earnshaw, J. and Burchell, B. (1993) *New Forms and Patterns of Employment: the Role of Self-Employment in Britain*. Baden-Baden: Nomos Verlagsgesellschaft.

Steinmetz, G. and Wright, E.O. (1989) 'The Fall and Rise of the Petty Bourgeoisie: Changing Patterns of Self-Employment in the Post-war United States'. *American Journal of Sociology*, 94, 5.

Twigg, J. and Atkin, K. (1991) *Evaluating Support to Informal Carers (Part 2): Final Report*. Social Policy Research Unit Working Paper, DHSS 809. York: University of York.

VandenHeuvel, A. and Wooden, M. (1995) *Self-Employed Contractors in Australia: What are the Facts*?, Working Paper No. 136, National Institute of Labour Studies. Adelaide: Flinders University of South Australia.

Wheelock, J. (1992) 'The Flexibility of Small Business Family Work Strategies' in K. Caley, E. Chell, F. Chittenden and C. Mason (eds) *Small Enterprise Development: Policy and Practice in Action*. London: Paul Chapman Publishing.

Wheelock, J. and Baines, S. (1994) 'Dependency or Self-Reliance? The Contradictory Case of Work in the Small Business Family'. Paper presented to the Social Policy Association, University of Liverpool, July.

Index

In this index, italics are used for page references to tables/figures and for journal titles. The bibliographic references at the end of each chapter have not been indexed, except in the case of individual authors whose work is discussed in the text.